8.5.77

How South Africa came to have the most advanced industrial economy in Africa is of interest to economist and non-economist alike. This comprehensive yet succint account will be of great use at a time when there is general discussion of the problems confronting developing nations and when the eyes of the world are so firmly focussed upon Southern Africa.

Political scientists, industrialists, historians, investors, sociologists, and all other people interested in present-day South Africa need a book of this nature. The fact that this is the fourth edition shows how popular it has been. It has been kept up to date and since its original publication two new chapters have been added dealing with the great boom of the Sixties and the more difficult times in the Seventies, the text has been revised, more recent material added and the book has been metricated.

University students will find it essential: a select bibliography and twenty-five statistical tables provide material for intensive study. After a brief historical introduction chapters follow on the national income and population, agriculture, African migatory labour, mining, industry, labour and finance. The concluding chapter reviews the forces which have promoted the rapid expansion of the past, and discusses the conditions essential to the maintenance of a high growth rate in the future.

Although the emphasis throughout is on the economic aspects, the author considers, where relevant, the impact of political forces on the economy.

PROFESSOR D. HOBART HOUGHTON

The author was Professor of Economics at Rhodes University until the end of 1966 and then Director of the Institute of Social and Economic Research at Rhodes University until 1974 when he retired to his home in the Hogsback mountains.

He is a member of the Economic Advisory Council to the Prime Minister and has also been a member of the Human Sciences Research Council. He was President of the Economic Society of South Africa in 1960 and 1961 and was for several years a Vice-President of the South African Institute of Race Relations. He was a member of the (Franzsen) Commission of Enquiry into Fiscal and Monetary Policy in South Africa. In 1974 the University of Witwatersrand conferred upon him the degree of LLD *honoris causa.*

He has written a number of books and articles on economics and Oxford University Press has recently published three volumes of *Source Material on the South African Economy 1860–1970* edited by D. Hobart Houghton and Jenifer Dagut, which will be a valuable adjunct to this book.

THE SOUTH AFRICAN ECONOMY

The South African Economy

D. HOBART HOUGHTON

CAPE TOWN
OXFORD UNIVERSITY PRESS
LONDON   NEW YORK

RRR

Oxford University Press

OXFORD   LONDON   GLASGOW   NEW YORK

TORONTO   MELBOURNE   WELLINGTON   CAPE TOWN

DELHI   BOMBAY   CALCUTTA   MADRAS   KARACHI   DACCA

KUALA LUMPUR   SINGAPORE   JAKARTA   HONG KONG   TOKYO

NAIROBI   DAR ES SALAAM   LUSAKA   ADDIS ABABA

IBADAN   ZARIA   ACCRA   BEIRUT

First published 1964
Second impression 1965
Second edition 1967
Second impression 1969
Third edition 1973
Fourth edition 1976

ISBN 0 19 570080 5 (boards)
ISBN 0 19 570081 3 (limp)

Printed by Citadel Press, Polaris Road, Lansdowne, Cape
Published by Oxford University Press
11 Buitencingle Street, Cape Town, South Africa

Preface to the First Edition

This book is intended mainly for university students who wish to study the economy of the Republic of South Africa as it is today. The sub-title might have been 'A Study of Growth and Growing Pains'. It was designed as an introduction, not only for economists, but also for historians, political scientists, sociologists and workers in related fields. Technical language has therefore been avoided, and many points of theoretical interest have not been explored. Nevertheless, it is hoped that economists who wish to go deeper may find useful pointers in the footnotes and bibliography.

It is primarily for South African readers, but as South Africa is the most modern and highly industrialized economy in the continent of Africa, it may attract readers in other parts of the world who are concerned with problems of development or have special interests in this country. For their benefit certain explanations are given of things obvious to all local inhabitants. Many parts of this book are purely factual, but when matters of policy arise one sometimes enters a highly controversial area where personal bias may easily obtrude. I have not attempted to avoid these basic issues, but have tried to treat them objectively and dispassionately. Few people can wholly subdue their prejudices, but I have done my best.

There is little here that is original, and I have drawn heavily upon the writings of many persons, to all of whom I express my deep obligation. I hope that acknowledgement in footnotes will be taken as an expression of appreciation and gratitude for the debt I owe them. In this same category I would wish to include my senior students in recent years at Rhodes University, who have acted as guinea-pigs, and with whom many opinions have been thrashed out in seminars.

To Dr. J. E. Butler, Mr. F. J. Grover, Dr. Guy B. Johnson, Dr. C. B. Strauss and Dr. L. M. Thompson, all of whom have read portions of the manuscript and made valuable suggestions, and to Mr. M. Park and Mr. A. Hammond-Tooke, who helped to compile the statistical tables and graphs, and Mr. R. T. Bell, who assisted in the collection of certain data, I give my very sincere thanks.

I should also like to thank others to whom I am under a slightly different kind of obligation. The Librarian and Staff of the university library, and the Director and staff of the Institute of Social and Economic Research at Rhodes University, and in particular Mrs. H. S. Mostert, who typed the manuscript and saw it through the press; the United States-South Africa Leader Exchange Program, Inc., which gave me time to revise the manuscript during my visit to America; the Director and staff of the African Program of Boston University, who gave my office accommodation, access to libraries, and clerical assistance, and to Dr. W. O. Brown personally, who put his excellent private library at my disposal: all these provided the 'necessary infrastructure' without which this book could not have been produced, and I appreciate their kind assistance and thank them for it.

The editors of the *South African Journal of Economics*, *Optima*, and *Race Relations Journal* have kindly permitted me to include material previously published in their journals.

To my wife this book owes far more than any formal acknowledgement can convey. I thank her for her encouragement throughout, for her wise judgement and for her long-sustained labours in checking and proof-reading and in compiling the index.

D. HOBART HOUGHTON

Rhodes University
Grahamstown
March 1963

Preface to the Fourth Edition

The first edition appeared in 1964 and covered events up to about 1960. It has proved extremely popular and a fourth edition has now been called for. Since the first edition every effort has been made to keep the book up to date, and it was considerably revised for both the third edition, when metric measurements were introduced and a chapter added on the great boom of the Sixties; and for this edition, where the attempt is made in a new chapter to recount the problems and difficulties in the first half of the Seventies when the economy had to face international monetary disintegration, world recession, and a series of political crises in Southern Africa. Considerable changes have also been made throughout the book and more recent information has been introduced.

In addition to those mentioned in the preface to the first edition, I wish to thank Mr. D. Hindson, Mrs L. C. Vroom, Mr. N. Brown, and the Librarian and staff at the University of Fort Hare and, once again, the Librarian and staff at Rhodes University for their most valuable assistance with these two revisions.

D. HOBART HOUGHTON

Little Timbers
Hogsback
March, 1976

Contents

RRR

Figures

1 Out of Small Beginnings

Although far removed from Europe at the southernmost part of the continent, the Republic of South Africa is today the most industrially developed country in Africa. Human societies, in one form or another, have existed in South Africa for some 50 000 years.[1] The purpose of this book, however, is to describe the twentieth-century economy of the country, and this did not come about through the gradual evolution of indigenous societies. It was, on the contrary, the result of the impact from without of the more economically advanced nations of western Europe. Therefore, it is fitting to take as the starting point of this account the establishment of a settlement by the Dutch in 1652 because this event for the first time forged effective and lasting links between the Cape of Good Hope and the modern world. This was the period of the great expansion of European influence throughout the world, and the Cape settlement occurred in the middle of the century in which the earlier Spanish and Portuguese empires were consolidating, the French were advancing up the St. Lawrence, the Dutch were establishing themselves on the Hudson River at New Amsterdam[2] (now New York), and the British colonies in Virginia and New England were founded. The Cape was thus linked to the international economy in the seventeenth century almost 150 years before Australia and New Zealand, and two and a half centuries before the inland portions of Africa were to be similarly influenced.

Over three hundred years ago, three sailing ships dropped anchor in Table Bay on 6 April 1652, and Jan van Riebeeck, an officer in the service of the Dutch East India Company, stepped ashore with

---

[1] For an account of the archaeological background and early history see the first four chapters of the *Oxford History of South Africa*, vol. 1, edited by Monica Wilson and Leonard Thompson.

[2] The first Dutch settlers arrived in 1624

1

instructions to build a fort and develop a vegetable and fruit farm. No thought of conquest or colonization lay behind this move. Its object was to provide a half-way port of call where Dutch ships on their way to the Far East could revictual, rest their crews, and leave their sick; for the normal run from Holland to Batavia was six months or more. The fort was to protect them from attack by their British and French rivals.

Within five years of its establishment, however, a change was made which shaped the future course of the country's development. Official farming was not proving satisfactory so the Company decided to see whether private enterprise could do any better. Accordingly, in 1657, nine married servants of the Company were released from its employ, and were established as free burghers on small farms. Thus it was that the first white South Africans came to make their permanent abode in the southernmost tip of the continent. Their descendants, reinforced by subsequent immigration from Europe, numbered four and a quarter million in 1975.

When the Dutch arrived at the Cape there were no black African people there. Indeed it was over half a century later that contact was first made between the expanding white settlement and the Bantu-speaking tribes migrating slowly down the east coast. Van Riebeeck found a country sparsely populated by Bushmen and Hottentots (San and Khoikhoi peoples). Some of these people were hunters with bows and poisoned arrows. Others were herders, who owned domesticated cattle and fat-tailed sheep, and some had developed the art of working iron and copper. Bushmen and Hottentots can never have been very numerous because of the extensive character of their economies, and their numbers were decimated by wars and smallpox epidemics. Today there are few pure-bred members of either group for they have interbred with other groups to form what are now known as the Cape coloured people.

Shortage of labour was acute in the early days of the settlement because the Hottentots were averse to working for the white settlers, and the institution of slavery was introduced from the Dutch East Indies to the Cape. In the same year that the nine free burghers were established on their farms, a dozen slaves were sent from Java and Madagascar, and proved so useful that others soon followed. This had important consequences, for the introduction of slaves automatically closed the doors to unskilled European workers, who formed the bulk of the emigrants to America and Canada, and later to Australia and New Zealand. Nevertheless there was a small trickle of European immigrants. The advent in 1689 of 200 Huguenots, who fled from religious persecution in France, brought new skills and stimulated wine farming, but the growth of the white population was slow. By 1740 the total white population of the Cape was only 5 500, of whom 1 500 were officials of the Company and their families.

A new type of society was in the process of developing at the Cape. In Holland there were no Hottentots and slaves, nor were there the vast tracts of rolling veld to beckon the more adventuresome ever on towards the last horizon. The Company was in principle opposed to the expansion of the settlement, and edict followed edict in vain forbidding the colonists to go farther afield, but economic forces were working in a contrary direction. Around Cape Town, Dutch governors and officials maintained an outpost of their native land where cultivated fields, orchards and vineyards indicated intensive farming, and the spacious elegance of the old farm-houses and estates proclaimed a settled and established way of life. Elsewhere there was a frontier on the march.

The new economic environment transformed people who had come from countries with an intensive agricultural system, first into cattle farmers (*veeboere*) and then into semi-nomadic pastoralists (*trekboere*). Except in the immediate neighbourhood of Cape Town, intensive arable farming was unprofitable because of the difficulty of transport, and cattle ranching was a better proposition.[3] More-over, as C. W. de Kiewiet has observed, 'as they came of age, young people sought not work, but land. Because there were slaves in Cape Town and on the wine farms was one reason why more white men trekked into the interior. It was easier to carve out a farm than a career.'[4] Land was abundant and practically free, for the coastal areas were sparsely populated, and fire-arms gave the white farmers mastery over any who would dispute their rights to occupy the land. Thus it was that the very small white population came to be widely dispersed. Turning his back upon the solid houses and settled life at the Cape, the frontiersman took to the ox-wagon and trekked ever farther into the interior in search of grazing-land

[3] For an account of the economic forces favouring pastoral farming in the interior see S. D. Neumark, *Economic Influences on the South African Frontier, 1652–1836*, ch. 4

[4] C. W. de Kiewiet, *A History of South Africa: Social and Economic*, p. 23.

for his increasing herds of stock, and the area of white settlement was pushed northwards and eastwards. The similarity to America was great: but in South Africa the covered wagons rolled east, not west; and whereas America's seaboard was constantly reinforced by waves of new immigrants, the Cape's was not.

At the same time that the white *trekboere* were moving east with their herds of cattle, black African tribesmen were moving south and west, coming down the well-watered eastern coastal belt, and at the time of Van Riebeeck's landing they were established in Natal and the Transkei and had probably even penetrated south of the Kei River.[5] Contact between the advance parties of white and black was made early in the eighteenth century, but it was not until the latter part of that century that the main bodies of rival colonists came into contact. The vanguard of the great mass of Bantu-speaking peoples were the Xhosa. They were semi-nomadic pastoralists, and cattle played an important role, not only in their economy, but in the whole system of their tribal life. Unlike the Hottentots, however, they had also developed the art of cultivation of the land, although it was regarded as of relatively minor importance and was relegated to women. This had important social and economic consequences. It made for somewhat greater permanence of abode, so that they were not true nomads, but only semi-nomadic. It also probably increased political stability because of the added prestige of chiefs, arising from their duties as distributors of the land.

There was a marked resemblance between the economic life of the frontier farmers and the black African tribesmen: both were pastoralists, and had the land-hunger born of increasing herds of cattle. All was well as long as there was new land into which to trek. The Africans moved on, driving weaker folk from their path until they clashed with the white settlers along the line of the Fish River at the end of the eighteenth century. In the conflict which ensued, the superior weapons of the white farmers, aided by the greater tactical mobility which their horses gave them, matched the superior numbers of the Africans, and for half a century a frontier was held along the line of the Fish River.

Meanwhile events in Europe cast their distant shadow over southern Africa. When Napoleon invaded Holland, the British

[5] See Monica Wilson, 'The Early History of the Transkei and Ciskei', *African Studies*, vol. 18 no. 4, 1959.

occupied the Cape in 1795 at the invitation of the *émigré* Dutch government. As a result of the Treaty of Amiens the Cape was handed back to the Dutch in February 1803, but was reoccupied by the British in 1806, and formally ceded to the British under the general European peace settlement of 1814. When the British took over the Cape in 1806 they assumed responsibility for an area of some 80 000 square miles (207 000 square kilometres) with a population of 76 000,[6] of which about 26 000 were white, 30 000 slaves and 20 000 Hottentots.[7] The eastern frontier was on the Fish River, which was somewhat precariously held against the pressure of the African tribesmen, and wars and cattle-raiding were endemic.[8] Thus commenced the triangular struggle of 'Bantu, Boer and Briton',[9] which has dominated South African political development ever since.

Poverty and unemployment were rife in Britain after the Napoleonic wars, and the settlement of British immigrants along the eastern Cape frontier was undertaken to relieve unemployment at home and in the hope that they would form a bulwark against the African tribes. The first settlers arrived in 1820, and they greatly strengthened the position. Altogether some 5 000 settlers arrived. This was a notable acquisition to the small population of the eastern frontier, but within a decade and a half the eastern Cape was faced with the exodus of an almost equal number of the Dutch-speaking farmers. Never very amenable to government from Cape Town, resentful of new laws and attitudes towards Hottentots, slaves and black Africans, and wearied by repeated depredations of their farms and the lack of protection for their wives and children on the frontier, they turned their wagons northwards and trekked into the great interior away from British colonial rule.

In the grand strategy of the conflict between white and black, the Great Trek was a wide encircling movement. Across the Orange River, through the present Orange Free State and Transvaal, over the Drakensberg mountain range, they finally reached the sea in Natal. But this was unacceptable to the British, who would not tolerate foreign lodgement on the coast. Natal was annexed by

---

[6] Population density was thus less than one per square mile.

[7] E. A. Walker, *A History of Southern Africa*, p. 144.

[8] There were wars on the eastern frontier in 1779, 1789, 1799, 1811, 1818, 1834, 1846, 1850 and 1877.

[9] Title of book by W. M. Macmillan, *Bantu, Boer and Briton*.

Britain in 1843, and many of the Voortrekkers trekked back over the Drakensberg. In 1848 British sovereignty was proclaimed over the land between the Orange and the Vaal rivers. However, in 1852 and 1854 the British recognized the independence of the Transvaal and Free State respectively. The involved political history of the next half century with its wars, annexations and abortive attempts at federation cannot be discussed here, but the discovery of precious minerals should be mentioned. Diamonds were discovered in Griqualand West in 1867 and the diamond fields were annexed by Britain in 1871. Gold was discovered in the Transvaal in 1884, and the Witwatersrand was proclaimed as a gold-mining area in 1886. The Jameson Raid of 1895 laid the powder trail which fired the Anglo-Boer War of 1899-1902 in which the Boer republics were defeated. By 1902 British power was supreme in southern Africa: two colonies with responsible government, the Cape (whose frontiers had gradually been pushed forward to join Natal) and Natal; the subjugated Boer republics of the Transvaal and the Orange Free State; the protectorates of Basutoland, Bechuanaland and Swaziland; and the Company-controlled Rhodesia – all were British. In 1906-7 the new Liberal government of Campbell-Bannerman in Britain granted responsible government to the Transvaal and the Orange Free State, and in 1910 the Cape, Natal, the Transvaal and the Orange Free State joined to form the Union of South Africa; the three protectorates and Rhodesia did not join, although a permissive clause envisaged the possibility of their doing so at a later date. By the Statute of Westminster in 1931 the Union was recognized as a sovereign and independent member of the British Commonwealth. Thirty years later, on 31 May 1961, the Union became the Republic of South Africa and withdrew from the Commonwealth.

This book is about the economy that has been developed during this period of turbulent history. No attempt is made to write a detailed economic history,[10] because the emphasis throughout is upon the end product – the national economy as it is today. Some reference must, however, be made to the forces which have transformed the largely subsistence farming of both white and black into a modern

---

[10] This has been well done by others, in particular: M. H. de Kock, *Selected Subjects in the Economic History of South Africa;* C. W. de Kiewiet, *A History of South Africa: Social and Economic,* C. G. W. Schumann, *Structural Changes and Business Cycles in South Africa 1806-1936.*

market-oriented exchange economy with its vast potentialities for
further growth. However briefly it is done, the stages of development
must be traced from Van Riebeeck's garden on the one hand, and
the primitive subsistence economy of semi-nomadic Bushmen,
Hottentots and Bantu-speaking people on the other, to the present
position where South Africa stands as the most economically
advanced and highly industrialized country in the continent of
Africa.

In earlier editions of this book W. W. Rostow's[11] five stages of
economic growth were used as comparative terms of reference.
This is discontinued in the present edition and in its place some
salient features in the 'seamless web of history' will be noted.

The traditional society

In *Analysis of Social Change*[12] Godfrey and Monica Wilson stress
the importance of *scale* for the social and economic structure of any
society. What are often described as primitive economies are those
where economic activities are carried out within small units which are
almost wholly self-sufficient except for a few items which may be
obtained by barter from neighbouring groups. Hence the tremen-
dous significance of a newly made contact with the outside world
which may change the scale of all human relations.

Rostow defines traditional society as

'one whose culture is developed within limited production
functions, based on pre-Newtonian science and technology, and
on pre-Newtonian attitudes towards the physical world. Newton
is here used as a symbol for that watershed in history where men
came widely to believe that the external world was subject to
a few knowable laws, and was systematically capable of productive manipulation.[13]'

This does not imply a wholly static concept of traditional society,
for production could increase through expanded acreage or the introduction of certain limited innovations. Trading nations could rise
or fall, manufacturing might be developed, but in all fields 'the
level of productivity was limited by the inaccessibility of modern
science, its applications, and its frame of mind'. As a result of this

---

[11] W. W. Rostow, *The Stages of Economic Growth (A Non-Communist Manifesto)*.
[12] Godfrey and Monica Wilson, *Analysis of Social Change*.
[13] Rostow, p. 4.

ceiling to the level of obtainable output per head 'the value system of the societies was generally geared to what might be called long-run fatalism: that is, the assumption that the range of possibilities open to one's grandchildren would be just about what it had been for one's grandparents'.[14]

The economy and culture of the Bushmen, Hottentots, and African tribesmen was definitely pre-Newtonian, and all three must be classed in the traditional society stage. Degrees of pre-Newtonianism must, however, be recognized, for the Bushman's stone-age culture was as far behind the iron-working Hottentots and Africans as they in turn were behind seventeenth-century Europe. In view of the great cultural difference between Van Riebeeck and his free burghers and even the most advanced of the native African peoples, one must regard 1652 as a critical point in South Africa's economic development because it forged a permanent link between the Cape and the expanding world economy. This link was in the first instance only with Cape Town and its environs rather than with the whole country, for the early settlement did not carry forward the spirit of scientific inquiry and innovation; in fact particularly for those who penetrated the interior, there was economic retrogression from the highly-developed market-oriented economies of Holland and France to the semi-subsistence farming of the *trekboere*. Indeed the *trekboere* were better at adapting themselves to their environment than at remodelling it to their needs.

Early settlement and slow growth

Southern Africa had little to attract the Dutch in the early days of the settlement except its value as a station on the way to the East. With few natural resources or known mineral wealth and being further from Europe than America and Canada few immigrants arrived. Moreover the adoption of slavery produced a rigidity in the labour structure which impeded economic initiative. The economic policy of the Dutch East India Company was strongly mercantilist and trade was burdened with many restrictions. It was a highly conservative colonial outpost.

Perhaps there might have been a change after the French Revolution. Governor Janssens and Commissioner De Mist were certainly men of the new age – much more so than most of the Bri-

[14] Rostow, p. 5.

tish governors who followed them. These two men were sent out from Holland in 1803 and had been influenced by the ideas of the French Revolution, but their rule was too short to have any impact on the life and attitudes of the Colony. Thus traditionalism was unshaken until after the second British occupation.

British rule made little difference to the basic economic disabilities of the Cape, but it did introduce new ideas, and the advent of the British settlers in 1820 is a clear landmark. These people had lived through the earlier stages of the industrial revolution in Britain. In a sense they were casualties caused by the process of industrialization and the protracted wars with France. Not only were they post-Newtonian, they were post-Adam Smith. Prior to their arrival the population had had little experience of urban life or contact with new ideas. The British government officials were anything but revolutionary, and most of them had spent their lives fighting the ideas and men of the French Revolution, but the reforms they introduced as a matter of course had a shattering effect upon the traditional society of the Cape. The Circuit Court of 1812, prepared to hear cases brought by servants against their masters;[15] Ordinance 50 of 1828, which permitted coloured persons to move freely without passes;[16] emancipation of the slaves in 1834; and perhaps, as much as anything, the appointment of civil magistrates and qualified judges and the attempt to establish the rule of law in the frontier: all these innovations were anathema to the traditional frontier farmer. Those who could not accept the new order turned their wagons to the north, and the Great Trek away from the ideas of the nineteenth century carried the traditional notions far into the interior.

Among those who remained, the new ideas took root. Schools, newspapers, missions, hospitals, local government, representative government, and finally responsible government with a qualified franchise irrespective of race or colour, were the fruits. In other ways, too, the pre-conditions for economic growth were being established. Pioneers such as Andrew Geddes Bain built new roads, harbours

---

[15] Many of the cases were discharged, and the accusations proven false; but other accusations were proved and severe sentences were imposed upon white men for ill-treatment of their servants.

[16] It was very much as a disciple of Adam Smith that the Rev. John Philip wrote to Huskisson, 'All I want is that the Hottentots be allowed to bring their labour to a fair market'.

were improved, banks began to appear[17] and merchants at the ports conducted a growing and lucrative two-way trade, exporting wine, hides, skins, wool and ivory, and importing manufactured goods for the local market. But progress was slow. Apart from the coastal towns, life was almost wholly rural, and farming was the main occupation of the vast bulk of the population as late as the 1860s.

Indeed, for the first two hundred years of its settlement, South Africa had little to attract the European immigrant or investor. The distance from Europe compared unfavourably with that from America; it offered no opportunities of trade with the indigenous population comparable to those found in the highly developed civilizations of India and China; and there were few easily exploitable natural resources suitable for export on a large scale. The quest for mineral wealth, which dated back as far as Van Riebeeck's time, had failed to produce anything significant. Agricultural development was hampered by the difficulty of transport as there were no great navigable rivers. In the absence of railways, only the ox-wagon was available; and the semi-arid Karoo and the Cape coastal and Drakensberg mountain chains proved serious barriers to large-scale transportation. The relative unattractiveness of South Africa is illustrated by the fact that, in 1841, 23 950 people left the British Isles for Canada, 14 552 for Australia and New Zealand, but only 130 for the Cape.[18]

In the middle of the nineteenth century wool became the first large export commodity and offered a means of escape from the bondage of largely subsistence farming. Although it never assumed the position which it held in Australia, wool exports increased significantly between 1846 and 1866.

Wool Exports[19]

1846	R356 000
1856	R1 676 000
1866	R4 164 000

---

[17] The first private bank – the Cape of Good Hope Bank – was opened in 1837. Before this, banking at the Cape had been a government monopoly. By 1862 there were no less than 28 banks in the Cape Colony. See ch. 9.

[18] L. C. A. Knowles, *The Economic Development of the British Overseas Empire*, vol 3, *South Africa*, p. 21.

[19] C. G. W. Schumann, p. 47. Values have been converted from pounds to rands at a rate of R2 = £1.

This certainly helped the struggling colony, but sheep-farming was never likely to attract large capital investment from abroad or large numbers of immigrants.

The small band of original Dutch settlers came in 1652 and were reinforced by the Huguenots some thirty years later, but by 1815 the total white population was only about 35 000. Some 5 000 British settlers came in 1820 and perhaps an equal number between 1840 and 1850, and 12 000 German and British settlers between 1850 and 1862. In Natal about 4 500 people came between 1849 and 1851. But the great nineteenth-century wave of emigration from Europe, which sent hundreds of thousands of people to America, Canada, Australia and New Zealand, passed South Africa by. It was not until the middle of the century that South Africa's white population reached the 200 000 mark, and its growth was mainly due to natural increase, not immigration.[20]

The Mining era

In 1867 an event occurred which altered the whole course of the development in the sub-continent; for the discovery of diamonds in this year, followed by the discovery of the world's greatest gold-bearing reef less than twenty years later, provided South Africa with just those things the lack of which had inhibited its earlier development. As S. H. Frankel has said, it was with prophetic insight that the Colonial Secretary when placing one of the earliest diamonds upon the table of the House of Assembly in Cape Town remarked, 'Gentlemen, this is the rock on which the future success of South Africa will be built.'[21]

Gold and diamonds between them brought about an economic revolution in the sub-continent which, both for the speed with which it was accomplished and for its far-reaching consequences upon the whole character of the country, is without parallel elsewhere in the world except perhaps where a backward country has struck oil. The patriarchal subsistence economy was suddenly drawn into the full stream of world economic development. Southern Africa became one of the major investment areas of the world. Immigrants poured into the country. Kimberley and Johannesburg were magnets

[20] Cape (1854) 140 000; Orange State (1854) 15 000; Transvaal (1872) 30 000; Natal (1856) 8 500. M. H. de Kock, part 2, ch. 3.

[21] S. H. Frankel, *Capital Investment in Africa*, p. 52.

attracting labour not only from abroad, but from every part of southern Africa.

The combined effect of gold and diamonds was to cause an almost insatiable demand for labour, and a huge and heterogeneous labour force came into being. Men from England, Germany, America and Australia, indeed from all parts of the world, came streaming in, and immigration between 1890 and 1913 averaged 24 000 per annum. Miners from Cornwall, Canada and Wales, accustomed to a highly industrialized life, rubbed shoulders with thousands of farmers' sons from the backveld. Tens of thousands of Africans, from every tribe south of the Zambezi and from many farther north, worked shoulder to shoulder with traditional tribal enemies. At one time there were also over 50 000 Chinese indentured labourers.

Skilled labour was scarce, and high wages were necessary to attract workers from abroad; so that, from the start, mining operations were based upon the employment of a relatively small number of skilled and a large number of unskilled workers. The latter were recruited mainly from African tribes in the sub-continent; and they were paid wages which, though high in relation to prevailing farm rates or earnings in subsistence agriculture, were low in comparison with the skilled rate. This structure fitted conveniently into the traditional pattern of society, and the notion that white men should undertake the administrative, supervisory and skilled occupations, while black should supply the unskilled labour, became fixed in the mining industry and has influenced subsequent industrial development.

Urban centres sprang up in the very centre of the sub-continent, Kimberley attracted a population of 50 000, and by 1907 there were over 160 000 workers employed in the Witwatersrand gold mines. Railways were pushed forward from the ports to Kimberley and then Johannesburg, for the new sources of wealth were able both to finance their construction and to provide an economic justification for the enterprise. In 1861 there were only about 3 kilometres of railway in South Africa; by 1891 there were 4 067; and by 1909 11 095 kilometres in operation. The large urban populations had to be fed; and a major change took place in agriculture to produce for the growing markets. International trade was stimulated, as the earnings from the mines raised personal incomes and the general standard of living. This led to a greater volume of imports

financed by the export of gold and diamonds. The table below
reflects the changes in South Africa's exports from 1820 to 1905.

Exports of South African Produce*

(R millions)

Annual average	Food and drink	Raw materials	Diamonds	Gold	Total
1821–5	0,3	0,1	—	—	0,4
1831–5	0,3	0,2	—	—	0,5
1841–5	0,2	0,3	—	—	0,6
1851–5	0,2	0,7	—	—	1,4
1861–5	0,2	3,8	—	—	4,2
1871–5	0,2	7,8	2,6	—	11,3
1881–4	0,2	8,2	6,5	—	16,0
1891–5	0,2	7,9	7,9	11,3	28,6
1901–5	0,1	8,7	11,6	24,4	48,3

'Food and drink' comprised mainly wine, fruit, maize, sugar and
meat; 'raw materials' mainly wool, hides and skins. (From 1841
the increase is mainly accounted for by wool.) The spectacular
effect of the advent of diamonds from 1871 and gold from 1891
on the value of the exports is seen in the fact that for the period
1901–5 gold and diamonds together accounted for R36 million out
of a total of R48,3 million per annum.

Then, too, other developments arose from mining; but they do
not appear in the table of exports. The gold-mining industry directly
stimulated manufacture of explosives and other mining requisites,
and these industries further accelerated the process of urbanization.
This in turn provided a growing local market for industrial products,
and the manufacture of a variety of consumers' goods came gradually
to be undertaken locally. Nevertheless mining remained a major
contributor to the national product so that, in a sense, the mining
era continues even to the present day.

Manufacturing

Notwithstanding the continued importance of mining, a major
structural change occurred during the inter-war years in the national
economy. Mining had always been the leading sector of the economy
but after World War II its place was taken by manufacturing. The
nature of this change is clear from the table on page 42 which shows
that in 1911–12 the relative contributions to the Gross Domestic

*Adapted from a table in C. G. W. Schumann, p.44.

Product was: mining 27,1 per cent, and manufacturing 6,7 per cent. By 1951–52, however, these percentages had altered to manufacturing 25,0 and mining only 13,0 per cent although the value of mining output had increased two-and-a-half times between these two dates. In 1910 the national economy was narrow-based with gold as its main powerhouse; but gold was a wasting asset and the need to extend modern technology over a wide range of natural resources and make the economy more broadly based was recognized and accepted as basic policy.

Various factors combined to accelerate economic diversification. Of great importance was the Act of Union in 1910, which brought into being a common market of nearly six million people in a country of 1 220 000 square kilometres. Then the 1914–18 war, when imports were severely restricted, gave a boost to the local manufacture of many articles. Although some of these mushroom factories collapsed after the war, many survived; and a sympathetic government granted some measure of tariff protection. In the 1920s other foundations of future industrial expansion were being laid, particularly in the formation of the South African Iron and Steel Industrial Corporation (Iscor) to work South African ores. Agriculture too had almost succeeded in making the adjustment to production for the growing urban centres. There were many growing pains. Farming in white areas was often unscientific, and too little attention was paid to the protection of the soil and the maintenance of fertility, and in the African reserves the traditional subsistence economy continued to deteriorate. Urbanization, however, was increasing apace; and the last great trek was on – the trek from the country to the towns. The trek was not away from the new age, but into it. The casualty rate was high – some 200 000 to 300 000 poor whites[22] – but their sons are today the efficient industrial workers who are carrying manufacturing output to ever-higher levels.

The year 1933 is significant for a number of reasons. Devaluation of the South African pound gave a new impetus to gold-mining, which proved to be a strong leading sector for the remainder of the decade.[23] Iscor came into production and the first pig-iron and steel from South African ores was produced in commercial quantity.

[22] See the Carnegie Corporation report, *The Poor White Problem in South Africa*, vol. 1, pp. vii, viii.
[23] See ch. 5.

Politics ceased, for a time, to bedevil economic development, because the United National Party led by General Hertzog was practically without opposition and Afrikaans-speaking and English-speaking South Africans were able to co-operate harmoniously in the progress of a common homeland. Moreover, the restrictionist 'civilized labour policy' of the 1920s tended to disappear in the face of the vastly increased demand for labour in all sectors of the economy. Employment of whites in industry increased rapidly after the depression, but employment of other groups was yet more rapid.[24] The result was that the movement of Africans out of the low-productivity subsistence farming into the modern sector of the economy was accelerated. The general boom condition of the country attracted foreign capital, and domestic capital formation also increased markedly. The banking and financial sector was strengthened by the inflow of capital and by the new-found confidence of the South African Reserve Bank after it had been able to withstand the whirlwind of the great depression and the difficult sixteen months during which South Africa decided to 'go it alone' on the gold standard. The gross value of farming output increased from R75 million in 1933 to R246 million in 1945.[25] Manufacturing grew both in the size and number of the individual firms and in the variety of products produced. When war broke out in 1939 many goods normally imported were no longer available and local manufacturing expanded to make good the shortage and to participate in the war effort by the manufacturing of explosives and bullet-proof steel plates for armoured cars and other war materials. The end of the war left South African manufacturing industry larger, more diversified and with enhanced technical skill and confidence. Between 1933 and 1945 the number of private manufacturing establishments increased, from 6 543 to 9 316; employment rose from 133 000 to 361 000 and an increased number of Africans were drawn into the modern sector of the economy. The value of net manufacturing output rose from R61 million to R276 million.

Once the war was over South Africa was all set to recommence the drive to economic maturity. The country's international prestige was high and tens of thousands of allied soldiers and sailors, who had called at Cape Town and Durban and had been warmly welcomed and entertained, were the best publicity any country could desire.

[24] See ch. 6.   [25] See *Union Statistics for Fifty Years*, p. 1-23.

Economic prospects were excellent and capital[26] and immigrants[27] came pouring in. The reversal of this immigration policy by the new government in 1948 was, from the viewpoint of expanding the country's white population, a major disaster. Hundreds of thousands of emigrants from war-devastated Europe were thus deflected to other lands, to South Africa's permanent loss. Notwithstanding, the economy continued to expand and was given a further boost by the development of the rich gold fields in the Orange Free State and by devaluation in 1949.[28] The government began to take bold measures to increase the range of manufacturing activity and encourage greater diversity. A war-time commission[29] had stressed the need to stimulate the processing and manufacture of articles from South African raw materials, and the encouragement of import-replacement industries received priority together with a drive to expand exports of manufactured products. Textile manufacture, expansion of metals and engineering industries based upon local iron and steel, and the growth of a liquid fuel and chemicals industry based upon cheap coal were the most significant developments in manufacturing. At the same time the gold-mining industry had been going from strength to strength, and the quality of farming had been greatly improved. Gross capital formation had been maintained since 1949 at between 20 and 30 per cent of gross national product.[30] In spite of a major capital outflow in 1959 and 1960 the net national income continued to rise. All these matters are, however, discussed in later chapters.

SEPARATION OR INTEGRATION

One further topic should receive mention in this introductory chapter, because not only has it been a recurrent theme throughout

---

[26] Net private capital inflow (R-millions):

1946	1947	1948	1949	1950	1951	1952	1953	1954
82	357	173	115	151	176	139	120	177

See *Quarterly Bulletin*, South African Reserve Bank, March 1960, p. 40.

[27] Net immigration of whites (arrivals minus departures):

1946	1947	1948	1949	1950
4 201	29 702	33 169	555	5 953

See *Union Statistics for Fifty Years*, table C-3.

[28] Devaluation was not initiated by South Africa but by Britain. After the experience of 1931, however, South Africa this time devalued immediately to maintain parity with sterling.

[29] *Third Interim Report of the Industrial and Agricultural Requirements Commission*, U.G. 40/1941.

[30] For details see table 6.

South African history, but it is today the central core of most problems of adjustment in the process of economic expansion. It concerns the relationships between the different racial groups that constitute the population, and, therefore, the labour force and consuming public of South Africa. These relationships cover all fields of human intercourse, domestic, social, religious, and political; but it is with the economic relationships that we shall be primarily concerned. It is not, however, possible to treat economic matters in complete isolation, because in a living society each aspect has repercussions on the others.

In many parts of the world the advent of modern western-type society has annihilated the indigenous populations, who have either disappeared or become an insignificant factor in the new society. This is what happened to the Bushmen and Hottentots, and to the indigenous populations of the United States, Canada and Australia. The Indian population of America, when white settlers first arrived, is estimated to have been about 1 000 000. By the 1880s it had been reduced to 200 000, but after settlement on reservations their numbers increased to about 334 000 by 1940, and by 1960 to 524 000.[31] When the first settlers arrived the number of black Africans in the territory now comprising South Africa may well have been also about 1 000 000 (a mere guess, probably on the high side). In 1970 Africans in the Republic numbered 15 000 000, having more than trebled in number since 1911, when the census of that year recorded 4 019 000. The Africans, unlike the Bushmen, the Australian aborigines and the American Indians, have shown remarkable virility and adaptability. In the hundred years war between white and black in South Africa neither succeeded in annihilating the other; indeed each has waxed stronger and has enjoyed a rising standard of living. Each group has become increasingly dependent upon the other, and both are becoming integrated in a common society through an ever-widening range of co-operative activities. In the process the primitive African subsistence economy has largely been destroyed, but the African himself has not. He has increasingly been drawn into a modern industrialized economy with new vistas of advancement opening before him. Africans in South Africa are becoming highly efficient industrial workers, and produc-

---

[31] M. B. Parker, *The United States of America: A History*, p. 425. The 1960 figures are taken from *Statistical Abstract of the United States*, 1962, p. 29.

tive workers in agriculture on farms owned by whites, and are beginning to enter the commercial field as traders and business men. Only in the areas of land reserved exclusively for occupation by Africans (hereafter to be referred to as 'reserves') has progress not taken place. In these reserves the traditional type of farming has been perpetuated and productivity has tended to decline.

The great gulf which exists between the modern sector of the economy and the traditional subsistence sector has created a dualism in the economies of all African countries, and it is generally accepted that the economic development of Africa requires a progressive change from the low-productivity subsistence economy to the much higher productivity exhibited in the modern market-oriented sectors. For tropical Africa as a whole 70 per cent of the cultivated land and 60 per cent of the labour were still being used in subsistence agriculture in 1954[32] In South Africa the whole of the land, except for the reserves or Bantu areas, which represent about 16 per cent of the total, is employed in production for the market; and even here strenuous efforts are being made to modernize land use. Practically the whole of the male labour force is now employed in the modern sector, working in commercial farming, mining, industry and commerce; and a larger proportion of Africans are engaged in the modern sector of the economy in South Africa than anywhere else south of the Sahara. There have been, and still remain, many fields of tension and possible conflict. Almost from the day of Van Riebeeck's landing two sets of conflicting forces have been in continuous operation – the one tending to draw the races together, the other tending to keep them apart. H. M. Robertson, in one of the best studies of the historical aspects of the problem yet made, wrote: 'Economic contact between Bantu and European has two main aspects, the broadly co-operative and the broadly competitive. A directly co-operative aspect emerges when members of each race jointly take part in the production of commodities. This usually takes place in the form of employment of Native workers by Europeans. An indirectly co-operative aspect emerges in the form of trade. An essentially competitive aspect is the struggle for control of natural resources. The results of this struggle may, however, lead to the establishment of new economic relationships of the former

[32] *Enlargement of the Exchange Economy in Tropical Africa*, United Nations, 1954, p. 17.

type – Natives having been worsted in their attempts to retain sufficient land for carrying on their accustomed pastoral and agricultural pursuits may, as a result, be forced to participate more directly in the economic system of the Europeans, and earn their living by accepting employment from Europeans.'[33]

The official policy and desired aim of all governments at the Cape up to 1847 was that of containing white settlement and keeping the races apart. The governors of the Dutch East India Company issued edicts prohibiting the colonists from going farther afield, of which the most emphatic was that of Governor Van Plettenberg in 1774, which stated that anyone trading with the Africans would be punished, and penalties up to the death sentence were stipulated. When the British came, they tried to enforce an inviolable frontier: by a chain of forts along the Fish River to the sea; by a system of treaties with African chiefs; and, at one time, by the establishment of a buffer zone or no man's land. But all efforts to keep the races apart failed because of the mutual desire to trade. Cattle raiding and retaliation were a normal feature of the frontier, and after the war of 1846 the Governor of the Cape annexed the territory between the Fish and the Kei rivers and created the district of British Kaffraria as a military bulwark to protect the frontier. 'So ended the long sustained attempt to maintain territorial segregation along the line of a river, and so began the attempt to rule black and white as inhabitants of one country.'[34] In 1854 Sir George Grey arrived as High Commissioner and Governor of the Cape and almost at once initiated a new frontier policy.

'The plan I propose . . . is to attempt to gain an influence over all tribes included between the present north-eastern boundary of this Colony and Natal, by employing them upon public works, which will tend to open up their country; by establishing institutions for the education of their children, and the relief of their sick; by intoducing among them institutions of a civil character suited to their present conditions; and by these and other means to attempt gradually to win them to civilization and Christianity, and thus to change by degrees our present unconquered and apparently unreclaimable foes

---

[33] H. M. Robertson, '150 Years of Economic Contact between Black and White', *South African Journal of Economics*, vol. 2 no. 4, December 1934 and vol. 3 no. 1, March 1935.

[34] Walker, p. 238.

into friends who may have a common interest with ourselves.'[35]

He thus initiated a policy of gradual political and economic integration of the two races, which remained the basic principle of the Cape even after responsible government had been granted. The essence of the policy was that the degree of civilization, rather than race, was the criterion by which a man should be judged, and it is enshrined in Rhodes's famous dictum 'equal rights for every civilized man south of the Zambezi'. This policy persisted in the Cape up to Union in 1910.

In pursuance of this policy Grey encouraged white settlers in British Kaffraria, but he rejected the idea of large tracts of African reserves, preferring in its place intermixed settlement of white and black, for four reasons: it would prevent a concerted uprising of the Xhosa; it would provide the white settlers with labour on their farms; by such work the Xhosa would acquire habits of industry and learn more progressive methods of farming; and by their propinquity the Xhosa would learn the habits of civilized living from their new neighbours. It was in fact a policy of economic and social integration. When subsequent annexations took place, however, no attempt was made to interplant white settlers, except in small administrative villages, and therefore the Transkei remains today a homogeneous unit with a wholly African rural population.

In the Free State and Transvaal very different ideas prevailed. The Voortrekkers were not prepared to countenance equality between white and black, and sought to preserve 'the proper relations between master and servant'. Yet it was by no means a purely white society, because Africans were drawn into the economy as workers on the farms, and once the Witwatersrand was opened up, huge concentrations of African miners came into being.

In Natal the population was sparse at the time of annexation, because the Zulu wars had decimated and dispersed weaker tribes. With the establishment of stable government under white rule, many Africans returned, but there was adequate land for all, and large native reserves were created. This resulted in complaints from white farmers that they were unable to secure labour on their farms

---

[35] Sir George Grey to Colonial Secretary, December 1854, quoted by A. E. du Toit, *The Cape Frontier* – A Study of Native Policy with Special Reference to the Years 1847–66, *Archives Year Book for South African History, 1954*, vol 1, p. 85.

because the Africans had no need to leave their reserves and seek wage-earning employment. For this reason indentured Indian labourers were brought in to work on the sugar-cane fields. Many stayed after their indenture period was completed, and their descendants form the Indian population of Natal today.

The territorial conquests of the whites disturbed the normal relationship between the factors of production, for the African tribes were forced into circumscribed areas. In the white areas, land, capital and entrepreneurship were relatively abundant, but labour was scarce. In the African areas labour was abundant, but the essential co-operating factors were scarce. Thus there arose strong pressure on both sides for labour to migrate to the white areas. The ambivalent attitudes of the whites is nowhere more clearly seen than in the matter of reserves. The great cultural gulf between themselves and the Africans, and the fear naturally engendered by a century of conflict, made the whites anxious to keep the African tribes as far away as possible. On the other hand, the need for workers on farms, in mines and in industry made it desirable to have them on hand. Thus when tribal reserves were adequate to support their population in the traditional manner, it was necessary to attract African labour by recruitment agencies or to impose money taxes, the payment of which necessitated the African's acceptance of wage-earning employment. When, however, the reserves were inadequate or became so through natural increase accelerated by the introduction of modern medicine, legislation was introduced to restrict the right of entry and to circumscribe African employment opportunities in 'white' areas. This vacillating policy was based upon deeply held but mutually irreconcilable desires.

By the end of the nineteenth century white administration and control had been extended throughout southern Africa. Nevertheless considerable areas remained in African tribal occupation in the Transvaal, Natal and the Cape Colony in 1909. Prior to Union, Africans in the Cape and Natal were free either individually or collectively to purchase land anywhere they wished, but few were affluent enough to avail themselves of the right. In the Transvaal and Orange Free State, with a few minor exceptions, no African was allowed to buy land in freehold. The Land Act of 1913 introduced uniformity by making a schedule of all existing tribal land, mission reserves and some African-owned farms. These were known as 'scheduled areas', and the Act provided that no non-African might acquire land within any scheduled area, and that no African might acquire land outside a scheduled area. Some 9 190 000 hectares were scheduled, but it was recognized that additional land was required. Great difficulty was experienced in securing additional land and it was not until the Native Trust and Land Act of 1936 that the position was improved. This Act released certain areas from the provisions of the 1913 Act and in these 'released areas' of about 5 813 000 hectares Africans might acquire land by purchase.[36] In addition the government has purchased land in these areas through the Native Trust and made it available for African occupation, usually on conditions designed to protect the land from destruction by bad farming.

The position in 1951 was that some 43 per cent of Africans lived in the Bantu areas, some 30 per cent on farms owned by whites, and 27 per cent of Africans in the cities and industrial urban areas of the country.[37] However, the Bantu areas are at present incapable of supporting the population domiciled there, and large numbers migrate temporarily to work in the industrial areas; the remittances they send home account for about half of the money income of the people in the reserves.[38]

The Tomlinson Commission recognized that Africans were subject to severe disabilities in the 'white' areas of the country and expressed the view that the only just solutions were either complete racial integration or complete racial separation. They rejected the former, and proposed a bold policy of development of the reserves to build up a diversified economy capable of supporting Africans in their own homelands, where they would not be subject to the ceiling at present placed upon their development in the 'white' areas. They estimated that a vigorous policy of industrialization would enable the Bantu areas to support a population of about fifteen million by the year 2000, but even so some six million Africans were expected to remain in the 'white' areas, where they would be approximately equal to the estimated white population at that date.[39] The South African government accepted the broad policy of separate develop-

---

[36] See p. 45 of the *Report of the Commission for the Socio-Economic Development of the Bantu Areas within the Union of South Africa*, U.G. 61/1955, better known as the Tomlinson Report, after its chairman. Our references are to the Summary of the Report.

[37] Census 1951.   [38] See ch. 4.

[39] Tomlinson Report (Summary), p. 29.

ment proposed by the Commission and various measures have been taken towards this end.[40]

In 1962 the then Prime Minister, Dr. Verwoerd, announced that the Transkei was to be granted limited self-government, and this was duly implemented in the following year. A legislative assembly was established and a Chief Minister and five other minister were appointed to head departments of Finance, Justice, Agriculture and Forestry, Interior, Roads and Public Works, and Education. Defence and External Affairs remain under the control of the South African Government, but statements were made indicating that full sovereign independence might ultimately be granted. In 1975 it was announced that the Transkei had requested its full independence, and that the South African Government had acceded to this. Accordingly in October 1976, the Transkei will become an independent sovereign state, wholly separate from the Republic of South Africa except perhaps for certain treaty obligations that may be contracted between the two governments such as currency and tariff agreements, and matters of this sort. In 1971 the Bantu Homelands Constitution Act set the stage for the granting of limited independence to other ethnic groups, and a possible total of some eight of these states is envisaged. Some of the economic implications of this policy of separate development of the Bantu areas are discussed in the last chapter of this book. The intervening chapters deal with various aspects of the economy of the Republic as a whole and the development so far achieved.

---

[40] White Paper on the recommendations of the Tomlinson Commission: W.P. F/1956. It should be noted that the government rejected important specific recommendations of the Commission such as the granting of freehold tenure and the encouragement of white capital and entrepreneurship in the Bantu areas. See ch. 11 for further discussion.

2 Resources, Population & National Income

PRODUCTIVE CAPACITY

A country's productive capacity depends both upon the resources it has available and upon the skill with which these are combined and applied. Three broad categories are generally recognized – the natural resources of the country, its human resources or labour potential, and its capital equipment built up as a result of past effort. Each of these will be discussed in subsequent sections, but there are two other things which are more difficult to assess in quantitative terms, but are none the less of major importance. The first is the presence in sufficient numbers of people with drive, initiative and the desire for economic growth, and the second is a socio-political climate in which these people can operate successfully. W. W. Rostow has shown that in most cases fundamental changes in the traditional society were a pre-condition for economic growth, but that a few countries like the United States, Australia, New Zealand and Canada inherited an appropriate modern outlook from Britain, which was already far advanced in the transitional process.[1] Perhaps South Africa may be regarded as a marginal member of this group. Be that as it may, the settlers from Europe brought with them the skills and techniques of a relatively advanced economy; and many of their descendants, refreshed by new immigrants, have maintained a close touch with technological and economic development in the industrially advanced countries. They have thus acquired the industrial know-how which is so often lacking in underdeveloped countries and has proved so difficult to transplant successfully. In contrast with the people of many other countries in Africa where a majority of the population is still engaged in subsistence agriculture, the

[1] Rostow, p. 17.

24

overwhelming majority of South Africans of all races are now involved in a dynamic exchange economy. There were in 1970 over four million Africans employed in mining, industry, trade, transport and commercialized agriculture; and in spite of legal and customary hindrances an increasing number are rising to the ranks of the skilled and semi-skilled. Admittedly the presence of over four million permanently settled white inhabitants in a country in Africa gives rise to social tensions and political problems of great complexity, but from the economic angle their presence has provided enterprise and skills which must undoubtedly rank as the greatest single growth factor in the South African economy. Moreover, these have spilled over to other sectors of the population with the result that, in South Africa, Africans enjoy a higher average standard of living and a higher general education, and have more often acquired first-hand experience of urban industrial life than anywhere else in the African continent.

The whites have not only been the economically dominant group, but they have also been politically dominant. This has in general had a favourable economic consequence in that financial integrity and administrative efficiency have been set to western standards, and legislation and government have on the whole favoured a progressive economic policy. It cannot be denied, however, that since 1911 certain legislation designed to protect the privileged position of the whites has had the effect of restricting economic opportunities for other groups and has prevented optimum resource allocation.[2] To this extent the political and social structure has impeded economic growth, but notwithstanding this the general climate in South Africa for the last fifty years has been more favourable for development than in most underdeveloped countries. Some economists favour the removal of these restrictions and regard equality of opportunity for all races in a common society as an essential condition of continued progress. The contrary view is also widely held, but it should be recognized that the more intelligent people holding this opposite view do so not from a desire to preserve for all time a privileged position for the whites – the objective of so-called *baasskap* – but from the fear that if political control passes into the hands of Africans at their present cultural level the whole foundation of the country's economy may be endangered, and

---

[2] For further discussion of this aspect see ch. 7.

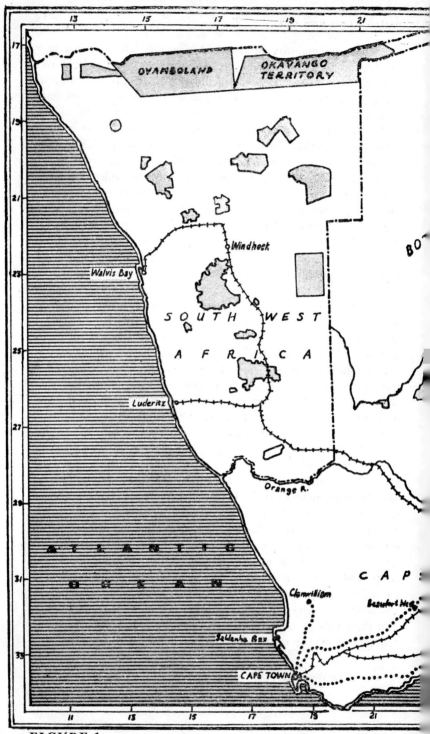

FIGURE 1

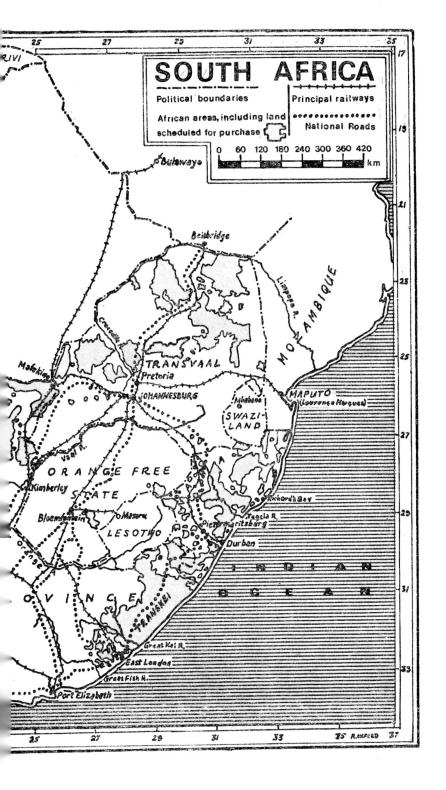

SOUTH AFRICA

Political boundaries   Principal railways

African areas, including land   •••••••••••
scheduled for purchase   National Roads

0   60   120   180   240   300   360   420

km

Bulawayo

Beitbridge

Limpopo R.

MOZAMBIQUE

TRANSVAAL

Pretoria

JOHANNESBURG

Mbabane

SWAZI-
LAND

MAPUTO
(Lourenço Marques)

Mafeking

Vaal R.

ORANGE FREE

Kimberley

STATE

Richards Bay

Bloemfontein

Maseru

LESOTHO

Pietermaritzburg

Tugela R.

Durban

Orange

PROVINCE

TRANSKEI

INDIAN

OCEAN

Great Kei R.

East London

Great Fish R.

Port Elizabeth

R.M.FORD

conditions inimical to further growth may come to prevail.[3] Recent events in the continent of Africa, where Africans have taken over political control, have not tended to allay these fears.

This matter has been mentioned here only to draw attention to the fact that the economic development of any country depends not only upon the available resources but also upon a suitable environment for their effective employment, and that in any study of the South African economy it would be foolish and misleading to ignore political factors. We turn now to the resources of the Republic.

NATURAL RESOURCES

The Republic of South Africa covers an area of 1 222 000 square kilometres[4] lying between 22° and 35° south latitude. It is thus more than twice the area of France or slightly less than one-sixth of the United States. The land rises fairly steeply in the east from sea-level to a high interior plateau of about 2 000 metres, with mountains reaching to over 3 000 metres.

Lying, as it does, outside the tropics, it enjoys an equable climate and is largely spared the health problems associated with tropical diseases and the debilitating effect of a tropical climate upon human energy.

Climate varies from 'mediterranean' in the south-west to near tropical in the north-east; the Transvaal highveld is temperate, with light frost in winter, and moderate rainfall mostly during the summer months. Rainfall is very sparse in the west, becoming more abundant as one moves east. A small area of 41 000 square kilometres in the south has rain all the year round, and the western Cape area of about 130 000 square kilometres is a winter-rainfall zone, but the rest of the country has its main precipitation during the summer months, often in the form of thunderstorms with torrential downpours sometimes accompanied by severe hail. The winter months are normally dry. Added to the seasonal variation in rainfall is the fact that rainfall from year to year is erratic, the highest recorded

[3] For further reference see ch. 12.

[4] Excluding South West Africa (mandated territory) and the former British Protectorates now known as Lesotho, Botswana, and Swaziland. These are, however, closely integrated with the economy of the Republic. If they are included, there is an economic unit of 2 808 000 square kilometres, which is five times the size of France and one-third of the United States.

annual rainfall in most areas being more than twice the lowest. There is also a high evaporation rate, especially during the summer.

It has been estimated that in most parts of the country an annual rainfall of 635 millimetres is the minimum necessary for successful crop cultivation, but in only about one-third of South Africa is this condition fulfilled.[5] Although South Africa's diversity of climate from temperate to subtropical enables the production of a wide range of crops, only about 15 per cent of the land surface is really suitable for arable farming. The possibilities of intensive farming under irrigation are limited by the general topography because, apart from the Orange-Vaal river system, whose fuller exploitation is now being undertaken, most rivers rise on the eastern escarpment and fall rapidly to the sea through broken country in which large-scale irrigation schemes are not feasible. Large areas of the country are well suited for cattle and sheep ranching, but even here the carrying capacity of the pasture is low by international standards, and intensive methods are precluded by environmental factors. Although farming practice has greatly improved in recent years and soil and water conservation is more widespread, there seems no reason to revise the judgement of a government commission in 1941 that 'owing to the physical controls which govern the sub-continent, South Africa must be regarded as a poor crop-raising country. This in turn imposes limitations on animal husbandry for which conditions are however better suited.'[6]

Indigenous forests are few, but various exotics have been successfully introduced: *Eucalyptus* and *Acacia* plantations exceed 400 000 hectares[7] and are a valuable source of hardwoods, while the mountain mist-belt areas of the south and east are very suitable for growing conifers, particularly *Pinus radiata* and *Pinus patula*, and a considerable softwood timber industry is being established producing timber, pulp and pressed boards.

South Africa's long coastline is lacking in natural harbours, but the oceans surrounding it contain some of the richest fishing areas in the southern hemisphere and an important fishing industry has been established. In 1962 South Africa ranked among the six largest

[5] *Third Interim Report of the Industrial and Agricultural Requirements Commission*, U.G. 40/1941, p. 7.

[6] *Third Interim Report of the Industrial and Agricultural Requirements Commission*, U.G. 40/1941, p. 11.

[7] *Statistical Year Book, 1966*, p. J. 17.

fishing nations of the world and the value of the catch was South Africa R15 million and South West Africa R6 million; or a total of R21 million.[8] Fishing fleets of several other nations also frequent South African waters and there is danger that unless due restraint is observed the productivity of these fishing grounds may be seriously impaired.

In mineral deposits South Africa is outstandingly rich. These occur mainly in the Transvaal, the Orange Free State and northern Natal, and are thus centrally placed in relation to the country as a whole. Based initially upon the gold-mining industry, a vast industrial complex has arisen in the southern Transvaal, which has become the site of a large iron, steel and engineering industry, and south of the Vaal there is a growing chemical industry based on coal at Sasol.

It has been estimated that the total value of minerals produced up to December 1960 exceeded R12 000 000 000.[9] The annual value of mineral production in 1964 exceeded R1 000 000 000 and by 1973 it had reached R2 844 000 0000[10] The El Dorado, sought for in vain by Van Riebeeck, was eventually discovered at Kimberley and the Witwatersrand in the latter half of the nineteenth century. The fabulous deposits of diamonds and gold are known the world over. South Africa has been the largest gold producer for three-quarters of a century, and still has great reserves, and the annual output continues to rise. Many base metals occur in abundance – iron ore, coal, limestone, manganese, chrome and many more. Estimated reserves of iron ore are:

high-grade haematite	540 million metric tons
low-grade titanium-free	6 000 million metric tons
titanium-rich	1 800 million metric tons

Coal reserves are estimated to be over 60 000 million metric tons and the pit-head price is probably the lowest in the world.[11] 'The Union thus ranks with the limited number of countries in which the

[8] *Year Book of Fishing Statistics, 1963*, Food & Agriculture Organization.

[9] R11 951 356 038 at December 1959: Department of Mines, *Annual Report Including Reports of the Government Mining Engineer . . . for the Year Ended 31 December 1959*, U.G. 58/1960, p. 37.

[10] *Bulletin of Statistics*, March, 1975 p. 5.2.

[11] *Report of the Commission of Enquiry into Policy Relating to the Protection of Industries*, U.G. 36/1958, p. 40.

POPULATION (millions)

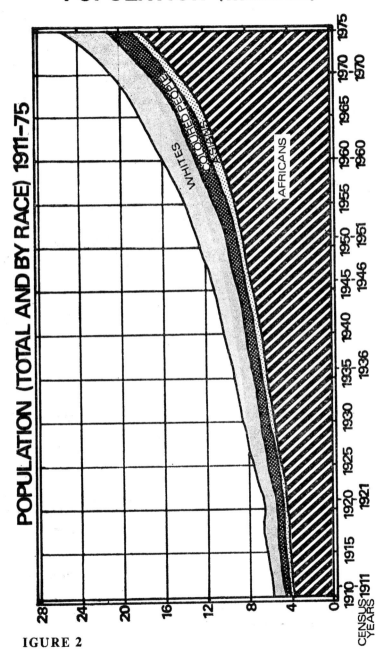

POPULATION (TOTAL AND BY RACE) 1911–75

WHITES

COLOURED PEOPLE

ASIANS

AFRICANS

CENSUS YEARS 1911 1915 1920 1921 1925 1930 1935 1936 1940 1945 1946 1950 1951 1955 1960 1965 1970 1975

28 24 20 16 12 8 4 0

IGURE 2

essential minerals for heavy industry are present in large quantities.'[12] In addition it is a large producer of copper, lead and zinc, and the world's second largest producer of asbestos. Especially important today is perhaps uranium, of which South Africa is a major producer with the world's largest known reserves.[13] No natural oil has yet been discovered, but exploration on a large scale is in progress and there have been some encouraging finds of gas off the south-east coast.

POPULATION

The population of the Republic in 1975 was estimated to have been about 25½ million persons of all races, and at the most recent census (1971) it was recorded as being nearly 21½ million. It is therefore growing at a rate of about one million per annum. During the inter-censal decade the average annual increase was 544 thousand of whom 66 thousand were white, 51 thousand coloured, 14 thousand Asian and 413 thousand African.

	1970 Census[14]	Mid 1975[14] Estimate
Whites	3 751 328	4 200 000
Africans	15 057 952	18 100 000
Coloured people	2 018 453	2 540 000
Asians	620 436	700 000
Total	21 448 169	25 540 000

The 1970 population was exceeded by only three other states in Africa.[15]

The over-all density for the country as a whole was 21 persons per square kilometre, but this low average figure is misleading because in the more arid regions it is very sparse. A population map shows a general tendency for rural population to be greater in the east and south-east coastal regions. This is partly because of higher rainfall and partly because of the presence there of land

---

[12] *Third Interim Report of the Industrial and Agricultural Requirements Commission*, U.G. 40/1941, p. 12.

[13] For details of mineral production in 1973 and 1960 see statistical appendix, table 14, and for growth of mineral output 1911 to 1970 see table 13.

[14] *See also statistical table number 1.*

[15] Nigeria, Egypt and Ethiopia.

reserved for African occupation where population density tends to be high.

The main concentrations of population are, however, associated with industrial development and urbanization. This is particularly true of the Witwatersrand-Pretoria area, where there is a population of over three million, and the Cape Town and Durban metropolitan areas which are approaching the one million mark. In 1970 in the Johannesburg magisterial district alone there were 1 408 000 persons or a population density of 1 753 persons per square kilometre or almost exactly one hundred times the national average.

The population is very heterogeneous in language, culture and race. Four broad groups may be distinguished:

1. White-skinned people originally of European descent. They will be referred to as *whites*.[16]

2. Black-skinned people, who are members of the Bantu-speaking group of African tribes. Officially members of this group are now referred to as *Bantu*, but in this book the more widely used term, *Africans*, will be employed,[17] in the sense that they are Africans both by birth and by descent. This does not imply that whites and Asians in South Africa are not also Africans, and perhaps the description *Black Africans* would be more accurate.[18]

3. Persons of mixed racial origin, who will be referred to as the *coloured people*.

4. Persons of Asian descent, mainly Indians in Natal, who will be referred to as *Asians*.

These four groups are far from being homogeneous within themselves. In language the whites are divided into Afrikaans-speaking and English-speaking, roughly in the ratio of 3 to 2. There are four main groups of Bantu languages represented in the Republic: Ngune, Sotho, Shangaan and Venda, but the first two are the most important. The Ngune group comprising Xhosa, Zulu, Swazi and Ndebele is by far the most numerous and accounts for about 64

[16] They are often referred to as Europeans, but this is misleading because they are no more 'European' than white people in the United States, and many can trace their South African ancestry back to the seventeenth century.

[17] Except where it is desirable to distinguish them from other African races like the Bushmen or Hottentots.

[18] When slogans such as 'Africa for the Africans' are bandied about, all terminology tends to become emotionally charged.

per cent of the total, of which both Xhosa and Zulu each number about four million persons. Next comes the Sotho group, including Tswana, Pedi and Southern Sotho, which together account for about 30 per cent of the total. The balance of 6 per cent is made up of Shangaan, Venda and other small groups. Culturally, too, the Africans vary from simple tribesmen still engaged in traditional subsistence farming to highly sophisticated townsmen permanently domiciled in industrial centres. Over 90 per cent of the coloured people have Afrikaans as their home language, the remainder being English-speaking; but here too there are wide cultural and religious differences, for instance those of Malay descent being Mohammedan and the vast majority of the others Christian. Similarly the Indians are divided between Mohammedans and Hindus. The majority are Tamil-speaking, Hindi is next in importance, and Telegu, Gujarati and Urdu are also spoken.

It is interesting to note that over 90 per cent of each racial group have been born in South Africa. Numerically the largest group of non-natives is found among the African group, where there are estimated to be between half a million and a million immigrants from other African countries at present in the Republic.

The growth of the total population and that of each of the main racial components is shown in figure 2 (p. 31) and statistics are given in table 1 of the statistical appendix. Between 1911 and 1970 the total population increased from slightly less than six million to over twenty-one million, but the general expansion of the economy has been such that, in spite of this considerable increase in population, there has been a marked rise in *per capita* real income, which is now more than double what it was in 1912.

The racial composition of the population has altered gradually during this period.

	1911 %	1960 %	1970 %
Whites	21,4	19,3	17,5
Africans	67,2	68,3	70,2
Coloured people	8,8	9,4	9,4
Asians	2,6	3,0	2,9

It will be observed that the percentage of whites has declined slightly, and that that of the three other groups has risen; but a part or perhaps the whole of the increase in the African proportion may be

explained, not by natural increase, but by more complete enumeration and by immigration. The 1960 census recorded some 583 000
Africans as having been born outside the area of the Republic.

The average annual percentage increase in the population between
censuses is shown below.

	1911–21 (10 years)	1921–36 (15 years)	1936–46 (10 years)	1946–51 (5 years)	1951–60 (9½ years)	1960–70 (10 years)
Whites	1,76	1,86	1,70	2,18	1,69	2,11
Africans	1,57	2,29	1,73	1,79	1,90	3,25
Coloured people	0,37	2,32	1,89	3,51	3,43	2,94
Asians	0,86	1,90	2,65	5,15	2,87	2,65
Total	1,49	2,19	1,76	2,10	2,54	2,99

1973118

Some of these percentages show an erratic characteristic that is
difficult to explain. The increase in whites of 2,18 per cent per annum
in the period 1946–51 and of 2,11 in the last decade may have been
due to a higher rate of immigration in these periods. It has long
been realized that the Asians and coloured people had a high rate of
natural increase arising from a high birth rate and a relatively low
death rate, but even so the figure of 5,15 per cent per annum for
Asians in the period 1946–51 is difficult to credit. The recent increase
in the African rate in the last inter-censal period is difficult to account
for in the absence of reliable statistics of births and deaths. It may
represent a rise in natural increase or it may be explicable in terms
of fuller enumeration and immigration. If it be the former this will
have important economic consequences, because Africans constitute
so large a proportion of the total population. If this increase is
maintained it would seem to indicate that the African group is
entering the phase of high birth rate and lower death rate which is
known as the 'demographic gap' or 'population explosion', often
found at certain stages of economic growth. Up to now in South
Africa, unlike India for example, the increase in real income has not
been seriously threatened by population pressure, but this may come
to be so. Population increase affects the economy in two ways, both
by increasing the number of mouths to feed, and by increasing the
numbers who will be seeking employment.

Another important aspect is the proportion of the population that
is actively engaged in economic production and the apportionment
of these economically active persons between the various sectors of

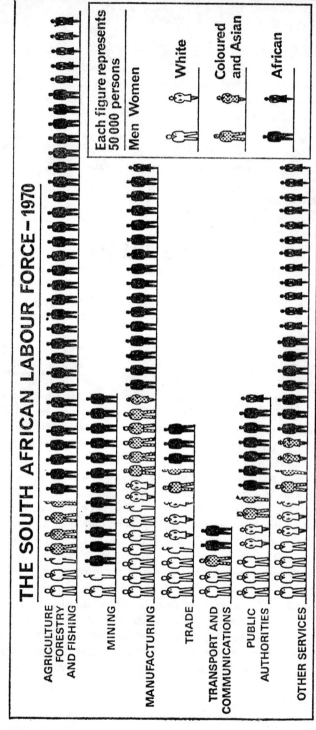

THE SOUTH AFRICAN LABOUR FORCE – 1970

AGRICULTURE FORESTRY AND FISHING

MINING

MANUFACTURING

TRADE

TRANSPORT AND COMMUNICATIONS

PUBLIC AUTHORITIES

OTHER SERVICES

Each figure represents 50 000 persons

Men   Women

White

Coloured and Asian

African

FIGURE 3

the economy. This is shown in detail for the years 1960 and 1951 in table 2 of the appendix, and the 1970 position is shown below.

Economically Active Population 1970
(in thousands)

	All races	Whites	Africans	Coloured people and Asians
Agriculture (a)	2 239	98	2 014	126
Mining	676	63	605	8
Manufacturing (b)	1 519	389	808	321
Commerce (c)	906	418	349	138
Transport (d)	338	163	140	35
Government (e)	641	237	330	73
Other services	932	88	734	111
Unspecified and Unemployed	732	38	624	69
Total economically active	7 986	1 497	5 605	884

(a) Agriculture, forestry and fishing
(b) Manufacturing, construction, electricity and water
(c) Commerce and finance
(d) Transport and communications
(e) Including local authorities
    Source *Bulletin of Statistics*, March, 1975, page 2.1 and page 2.11.

The racial composition of the 1970 labour force by the main sectors of the economy is depicted in figure 3.[20] It will be observed that in all sectors except communications and transport white workers are greatly outnumbered by workers of other groups. In agriculture the ratio was 1 white worker to 21 other workers; in mining 1 to 9 in other services and manufacturing 1 to 4; in public authorities and wholesale and retail trade about 1 to $1\frac{1}{2}$ and in transport and communications they are approximately equal. In the aggregate the Africans constitute 68 per cent, whites 20 per cent and coloured people 12 per cent of the labour force.

CAPITAL

Building up the capital structure of the economy of a poor undeveloped country is a slow and difficult task because, as R. Nurkse has so clearly shown,[21] domestic capital formation is inhibited by poverty, and foreign capital is unlikely to be attracted owing to the inability to find remunerative investment opportunities because of

[20] For detailed figures of the breakdown of the labour force by race in 1960 and 1951 see table 2 in the statistical appendix.

[21] R. Nurkse, *Capital Formation in Underdeveloped Countries.*

the lack of a domestic market. Only the exploitation of something for which a ready world market exists is likely to attract the foreign investor. Prior to 1865 South Africa was a poor country with little to attract capital from abroad. The diamond discoveries of 1865 and the gold discoveries of 1886 altered the situation profoundly, for they provided the attraction to put South Africa suddenly in the forefront of the world's investment markets. Precious minerals rapidly became the leading sector of the whole economy, acting as a magnet to draw funds from abroad. S. H. Frankel has estimated that, in 1881, the capital of seventy-one diamond-mining companies was R16 million; and, between 1887 and 1905, R208 million had been invested in gold mining. [22] He gives the figure of R296 million as the sum invested in the gold-mining industry of the Witwatersrand up to 1932. The prosperity of the gold- and diamond-mining industries spilled over into other sectors. Government revenue rose sharply and the improved financial position of the Cape and the Transvaal made them credit-worthy borrowers in the eyes of the world. Heavy expenditure was incurred on railway construction and a modern transport system was created. Investment in coal mining, explosives and other industries related to gold was a natural consequence. Moreover the large urban concentration of population provided a market for agriculture and manufacturing. Thus, led by diamonds and gold, and assisted by the vast inflow of capital from abroad, South Africa was at last able to break the 'vicious circle of poverty'. S. H. Frankel estimates that by 1936 a total of R1 046 million had been invested in the area now constituting the Republic of South Africa.[23] This represented 43 per cent of the total foreign investment in the continent of Africa. It amounted to approximately R110 per head of the population of South Africa.[24]

Immediately after World War II there was another heavy wave of investment associated with the discovery of the Orange Free State gold fields. Then the capital inflow declined and there was even a reverse movement from 1959 to 1964. In 1965, however, there was a strong revival of private investment in the Republic which continued to the end of the decade.[25] By the end of 1969 the total foreign liabili-

[22] S. H. Frankel, *Capital Investment in Africa*, pp. 81, 95.
[23] S. H. Frankel, *Capital Investment in Africa*, p. 158.
[24] Frankel, p. 170.
[25] See figure 13, p. 185

ties of South Africa were R4 990 million, against foreign assets (including gold) of R2 449 million. Some R3 074 million of the liabilities were to the sterling area, mainly to the United Kingdom, R1 065 million to western Europe and R741 million to the dollar area. South Africa's foreign assets were mainly in the sterling area, and western Europe.[26]

There is no doubt that the large foreign investment greatly accelerated the economic development of the country and enabled a rate of growth which would otherwise have been quite impossible. It is sometimes suggested in anti-colonialist writings that foreign investment in extractive industries for export is of little benefit to a country and is merely exploitation by foreigners. This has not been the case in South Africa. Gold mining led to a rapid increase in national income which in turn provided a stimulus to agriculture and manufacturing and thus stimulated general expansion and a more diversified economy. Moreover, rising income accelerated the rate of domestic saving. Since the last war the rate of domestic fixed capital formation has increased remarkably from R284 million in 1945 to R3 061 million in 1970, or about 24 per cent of the gross domestic product.[27] It would thus appear that South Africa is now becoming a mature economy, increasingly capable of maintaining a high rate of capital formation from within itself.

In terms of real capital equipment a major economic revolution has taken place in South Africa during the century from 1870 to 1970. A hundred years ago it was a poor country with a low standard of living based largely upon subsistence agriculture. Transport was mainly by ox-wagon, roads were poor and both internal and international trade was very limited. In this last century a great change has occurred; railways link the ports with the interior, a system of excellent national roads and air services exist, electricity supply covers the greater part of the country, forward strides have been made in water conservation and distribution, banking and financial institutions have developed including an effective short-term money market. In short the country has acquired the essential infrastructure for a modern industrial economy. Upon this there has been built a large mining industry with issued share capital of over R562 million in 1962, of which 78 per cent was held within South Africa,[28] em-

---

[26] S.A.R.B., *Quarterly Bulletin*, March 1971, pp. 61-3.
[27] See table 5 in statistical appendix.
[28] *Statistical Year Book, 1964*, p. L-3.

ploying nearly 633 000,[29] and a manufacturing industry employing in the private sector alone over 655 000,[30] with a capital investment of over R1 210 million.[31] The Republic of South Africa is today certainly the most favoured country in Africa with respect to its capital equipment.

THE GROWTH OF THE NATIONAL INCOME

In spite of the relatively rapid increase of population from 6 million in 1911 to 21½ million in 1970 and to an estimated 25½ million in 1975, the people of South Africa have enjoyed a rising average *per capita* income because the output of goods and services has grown more rapidly than the population.

The Gross Domestic Product at current prices rose from R226 million in 1912 to our R10 000 million in 1969 and over R25 000 million in 1975. These figures must of course be deflated to offset the decline in the purchasing power of money that has occurred during the period; but, even so, there has been a rapid rise in the real domestic product. It has been estimated[32] that the average annual increase in the *real* national income has been as follows:

1919–29	5,0%
1929–39	5,8
1939–49	5,8
1949–59	5,0
1959–69	6,0

Thus throughout this half century the real growth rate has considerably exceeded population increase, and *per capita* average income has been increasing at between 2 per cent and 3 per cent per annum.

The general upward movement was interrupted three times: in 1920–2 during the short depression following World War I, which was accompanied by serious labour disturbances on the Witwatersrand; in 1928–32 during the great depression; and lastly

[29] Ibid., p. H-23.

[30] Ibid., p. H-25.

[31] *Statistical Year Book, 1966*, p. M-8: land and buildings, R557m.; machinery, R670m.

[32] South Africa Foundation, *South Africa in the Sixties*, p. 17, for all except the last decade which is calculated from data in *Quarterly Bulletins* of the South African Reserve Bank.

GROSS DOMESTIC PRODUCT

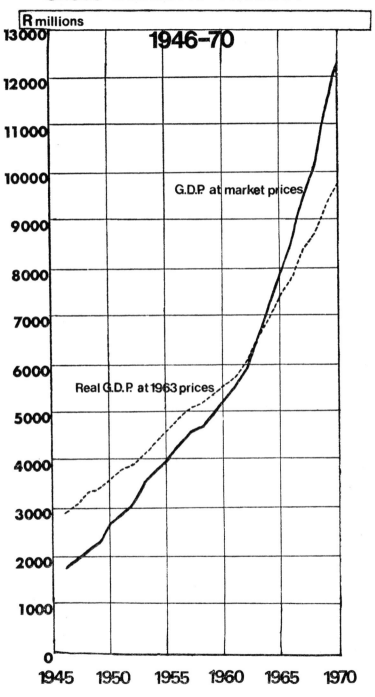

FIGURE 4

in 1951–2 when national income at constant prices showed a slight decline. Apart from these setbacks the movement has been strongly upward. Periods of particularly rapid growth were in the 1930s after the abandonment of the gold standard, and again after devaluation of the pound in 1949. The spectacular increase of the 1960s was not due to a change in the price of gold; but, nevertheless, gold-mining played an important part in the boom, the value of gold output rising from R530 million in 1960 to R847 million in 1969 – an increase of 58 per cent and a powerful stimulus to the economy. This illustrates the importance of gold production in the national economy and shows that throughout the greater part of the last half century gold was undoubtedly the leading sector.

Value of Output of Three Main Sectors
as a Percentage of Gross Domestic Product*

Sector	1911/12	1924/5	1932/3	1938/9	1951/2	1970
Agriculture	17,4	19,9	12,2	12,6	13,8	9,5
Mining	27,1	17,4	24,3	20,7	13,0	11,7
Manufacturing	6,7	12,4	13,6	17,7	25,0	27,1
All other sectors	48,8	50,3	49,9	49,0	49,6	51,7

* *Union Statistics for Fifty Years*, p. S–3 (up to 1951–2); S.A.R.B. *Quarterly Bulletin*, March 1971, p. S–67, for 1970.

The contributions to the national income of the three main sectors – agriculture, mining and manufacturing – have changed most markedly. In 1911–12 mining was in the lead with an output equal to 27,1 per cent of the geographical national income, agriculture came second with 17,4 per cent, and manufacturing third with 6,7 per cent. In 1924–5 agriculture held first place because agricultural prices still remained high, while mining was passing through a difficult period of adjustment to a lower price for gold as a consequence of a return to the gold standard at pre-war parity.

In 1932–3 mining was again in first place and its output was equal to nearly a quarter of the whole national income. The importance of the gold-mining industry as a stabilizing factor in the economy was most marked at this time. Agriculture fell to third place as the prices of farm products had sunk to very low levels. Just before World War II the order was unchanged, but manufacturing continued to grow in relative importance. By 1951–2 manufacturing had moved into first place contributing a quarter of the total national income. The most striking structure change in the economy during the fifty-year period has been the steady increase in importance of

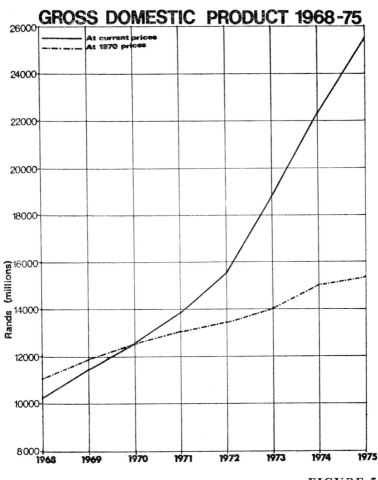

FIGURE 5

manufacturing. This has been particularly marked since the end of World War II.

From 1958 to 1960 the upward trend of the national product was less emphatic, and there was talk of a 'period of consolidation'. The gross national product increased less rapidly. Adverse political events in Africa led to a sudden withdrawal of capital in 1960–1 and a serious balance of payments crisis. Recovery began towards the end of 1961 and boom conditions prevailed up to the end of the decade. The events of these years, during which the net national income rose from R4 060 million in 1960 to R9 987 million in 1970, and to R18 341 million in 1974, are described more fully in chapters 10 and 11. The Gross Domestic Product for the years 1967 to 1974 at both market prices and constant (1970) prices is presented in figure 5 (p. 43) and in table 4 of the statistical appendix.

3 Farming

COMMERCIAL AGRICULTURE

In most countries it is customary to divide farming into two main categories, animal husbandry and arable farming; and to subdivide these into more particularized groups such as cattle farming, sheep farming, and other stock, in the first case, and into major field crops, fruit farming and horticulture in the second. In South Africa, however, there is a more fundamental line of cleavage which cuts across these divisions and is of such importance that there may be said to be two different types of rural economies existing side by side in the same country. One is the esentially market-oriented farming, as practised by white farmers, and the other is the largely subsistence-oriented farming of African peasants in the reserves. The difference between the two is deep-seated and manifests itself in a variety of ways reflecting cultural differences and fundamental attitudes to the exploitation of the natural environment. Productivity on the white farms is generally several times higher than in African farming, both in yields per hectare and in the output per unit of labour. The white farmer employs labour and pays wages, whereas the labour in peasant agriculture is provided by members of the family. On the white farms there is also a much higher proportion of capital employed, and farm units are larger in size than in peasant farming. But more important than these statistical differences is the reasons behind them. The white farmers are scientific and experimental in their approach, while the African is traditional, and even the few progressive individuals are hampered by the communal system of land tenure and other social restraints. This is not to say that all white farmers are scientific and progressive in their approach to farm problems; but, particularly in the last twenty-five years, there has been a great improvement in farming methods and in scientific

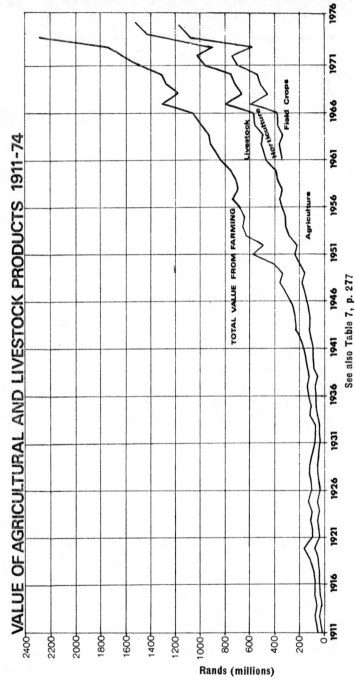

VALUE OF AGRICULTURAL AND LIVESTOCK PRODUCTS 1911-74

See also Table 7, p. 277

FIGURE 6

control over natural factors among the white farming community as a whole. The differences between market-oriented farming and subsistence farming is so great that they cannot conveniently be treated together. Accordingly the first part of this chapter will deal with market-oriented farming, which accounts for 90 per cent of the total agricultural output of the country,[1] and a later section will deal with the structure and problems of subsistence farming in the reserves, where some 95 per cent of the products of arable farming and 60 per cent of the livestock products are consumed at home by the producers.[2]

The gross value of agricultural output increased from R58 million in 1911–12 to R1 336 million in 1969–70,[3] and the number of persons employed as farmers, fishermen and lumbermen was 2 239 000 in 1970.[4] The gross value of output and the contribution from arable farming and livestock respectively is shown in figure 6. The increase in gross value is partly due to the rise in prices, but there has been a marked and relatively steady growth in the *volume* of output. The Department of Agricultural Economics and Marketing has compiled an index of the physical volume of farm output.[5]

Index of Physical Volume of Farm Output
(*base*: 1936–9 = 100)

Year	Livestock and arable	Livestock	Arable
1911	47	53	43
1921	60	68	55
1931	83	97	71
1941	106	110	102
1951	140	133	146
1959	181	162	197

There was therefore almost a fourfold increase in the physical output from farming over this period, and there is reason to believe that this has in many instances been accompanied by a marked improvement in quality. The volume of output of arable farming increased more than that of livestock farming.

[1] Except for a small quantity consumed on the farms, this is all produced for the market.

[2] Tomlinson Report (Summary), p. 85.

[3] *Annual Report of the Secretary for Agricultural Economics and Marketing, 1969/70*, R.P. 23/1971, p. 110.

[4] *Bulletin of Statistics*, June, 1975 p. 2.1.

[5] *Union Statistics for Fifty Years*, tables 1–27, 28.

This increase in physical output has continued in more recent times as the latest indices of physical output clearly reveal.

Index of Volume of Agricultural Production
(*base:* 1958/9–1960/1 = 100)

	All farming	Field crops	Horticulture	Livestock
1960/1	106	110	104	103
1961/2	113	119	113	107
1962/3	115	124	119	105
1963/4	111	105	132	109
1964/5	116	116	137	109
1965/6	119	111	148	115
1966/7	147	178	157	116
1967/8	134	135	172	120
1968/9	138	136	170	127
1969/70	147	157	166	132
1970/71	155	175	177	129
1971/72	164	194	188	129
*1972/73**	138	128	185	131
*1973/74**	179	223	191	134

*preliminary

Source: *Abstract of Agricultural Statistics, 1971,* p. 89 and *Annual Report of Secretary for Agricultural Economics and Marketing,* 1975, p. 102.

If this increase in farming output can be maintained, South Africa will be able to feed its expanding population for the foreseeable future and also to provide a substantial export surplus.

There has been little change in the relative importance of arable and livestock farming by value of output. Below is shown, as quinquennial averages from 1911 to 1974, the percentage contribution of each to the value of the total output from farming.

Percentage of Total Value of Output

Years	Arable	Livestock
1911–15	46	54
1916–20	45	55
1921–5	48	52
1926–30	46	54
1931–5	53	47
1936–40	52	48
1941–5	52	48
1946–50	53	47
1951–5	49	51
1956–60	51	49
1961–5	56	44
1966–70	58	42
1970–74	55	45

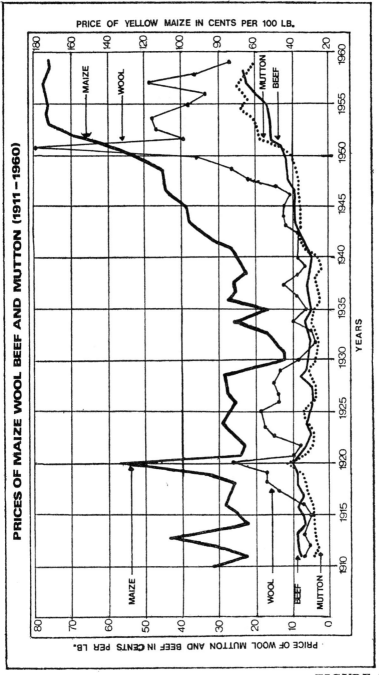

PRICES OF MAIZE WOOL BEEF AND MUTTON (1911–1960)

PRICE OF YELLOW MAIZE IN CENTS PER 100 LB.

PRICE OF WOOL MUTTON AND BEEF IN CENTS PER LB.

YEARS

For later years see Table 12, p. 282

FIGURE 7

50   FARMING

Each branch is seen to account for roughly half the gross farming
income, with a bias towards livestock up to 1930 and a slight bias in
the other direction between 1930 and 1950. The high price of wool
reversed the trend towards arable in the period 1951–5, but since
then the percentage from livestock has declined sharply.

The most important agricultural products are shown below and
a full list is given in table 8 in the appendix.

Value of Output of Principal Products

	1973/74	1969/70
	(Rands millions)	
Maize	552,7	234,6
Stock slaughtered	458,7	246,0
Dairy products	160,8	135,3
Wheat	138,0	88,8
Wool	135,6	83,2
Deciduous fruit	96,8	55,2
Citrus fruit	51,1	33,7
TOTAL PRODUCTS	2 340,9	1 337,1

Source: *Annual Report of the Secretary for Agricultural Economics and Marketing,*
1973/74 R.P. 51/1975 p. 101.

Maize

Maize is the most important single crop, both because of its size
and because it is the traditional staple food of the African people.
Although over the period as a whole there has been a marked
increase in the size of the crop, from 8,6 million bags[6] in 1911 to
the record crop of 123 million bags in 1974–5, maize production
has had a somewhat chequered growth. Climatic conditions have
led to great variation in output in certain seasons, and at certain
times price has fluctuated widely. For example the 1920 crop
sold for R28 million, but in the subsequent year a slightly larger crop
fetched only R14 million, because of a fall in price from R1,38
per 100 pounds in 1920 to 64 cents in 1921.[7] On the other hand the
crop in 1925 was 24 million bags, but in the following year owing
to adverse conditions only 11 million bags were harvested. In 1975
the harvest was almost three times as large as the previous year.
Maize illustrates the extreme instability of a primary agricultural
product and was one of the commodities for which stabilization
schemes were tried as early as the 1920s. These are important as the

[6] A bag = 200 lb up to 1971; thereafter 90 kilograms = 198½ lb.
[7] See figure 7.

forerunners of the present system of controlled marketing. International agricultural prices fluctuated greatly in the 1920s, culminating in the disastrous fall in the great depression. Falling world prices meant ruin to the South African maize farmer, but efforts to support the domestic price gave rise to surpluses which could only be exported at a loss. Indeed the export-quota system, financed by a levy on home consumption, resulted in the situation that the *larger* the crop the *higher* the domestic price of maize, as it had to support the loss on a larger volume of export. During the 1920s and 1930s the disposal of surplus maize was a chronic problem except in years of very poor crops, but during the early 1940s the position changed to one of shortages, as domestic consumption increased more rapidly than output, and in some years maize had to be imported. On one occasion South Africa bartered coal for Argentine maize. During the years 1948 to 1953 annual production was more or less sufficient for local consumption, but since 1953 the problem of surpluses has once more arisen.[8]

Production, consumption, import and export of maize from 1925 to 1970 is shown in table 9 in the appendix. The steady increase in domestic consumption from 10 million to 54 million bags is largely due to the increase of population, but local demand is also increased by greater industrial use and by use as animal feed. In 1970 the total domestic consumption was 54 million bags of which 30 million were used for human consumption, 23 million for animal feed, 700 thousands for industrial use and 800 thousand for seed.[9] South African maize producers also help to maintain life in neighbouring African states as seen from table 10 of exports to Lesotho, Botswana, Swaziland and South West Africa.

Although domestic consumption continues to rise steadily, the difficulties of the Maize Board in establishing a price which will equate supply and demand are great, and climatic variations make for fluctuations in production that nullify attempts at stabilization. In 1953 the Board set up a Special Fund, financed from the profits on export, when these occurred, and by contributions from government and producers. It was to be used to meet the deficits when export had to be undertaken at a loss; but the task of stabilization was not an easy one depending, as it did, upon the size of the local harvest

---

[8] See table 9 in statistical appendix for full detail.
[9] *Report on Maize*, 1970, published by the Maize Board, p. 32.

and the relationship between domestic and international price. The table below indicates the position.

Maize Special Fund: 1965/66-1974/75

Season ending	Production (thousand tonnes)	Export	Profit or loss on export (R 000)	Balance in Special Fund (R 000)
1965/66	4 490	480	915 P	35 659
1966/67	5 056	482	448 L	32 949
1967/68	9 762	3 111	16 911 L	18 347
1968/69	5 316	2 956	34 017 L	2 487
1969/70	5 340	947	3 887 L	756
1970/71	6 133	1 302	404 L	15 634
1971/72	8 600	2 835	16 695 L	11 537
1972/73	9 483	3 917	1 568 L	56 233
1973/74	4 160	327	2 071 P	11 023*
1974/75	11 105	3 320	82 500 P	72 546

*A distress payment was made to the producers of the 1973/74 year of R45 million.

Source: *Report on Maize*, p. 48.

It will be observed that the bountiful harvest of 1967–8 yielded about twice as much as the other years, and the disposal of this large crop involved the country in an export loss over R50 million over the two-year period 1967–9. The even more bountiful harvest of 1974/75 on the other hand yielded a handsome profit of R82 million. While it must be conceded that the foreign exchange earned by these maize exports relieved the country's balance of payments, the economics of maize price stabilization is a matter of some concern.

The output of maize comes from three sources: (*a*) maize grown by white farmers primarily for the market, (*b*) maize grown by servants for their own consumption on white farms in gardens given them by the farmer, (*c*) maize grown in the African reserves for consumption. Little, if any, of the maize produced under (*b*) and (*c*) passes through market channels. In 1957 the relative proportion produced by each type was:

	Total crops %
Produced by white farmers	84,5
Produced by servants on white farms	7,5
Produced by African peasants in the reserves	8,0

Wool and sheep farming

Apart from a relatively small export trade in wine, which has existed since the early days of white settlement, wool was the first major export commodity of South Africa, and since the middle of last century it has played an important role in the national economy. Unlike maize, the greater part of which is locally consumed, wool has always been an export commodity. Only very recently with the growth of wool-processing factories has there been any domestic consumption, and even today this represents only a small fraction of the annual clip. Thus wool has been rigidly tied to the world market price for the commodity, and local price-support policies have only a very limited scope in ironing out the short-term fluctuations.

In 1911 the value of wool sold was only R7½ million compared with over R100 million as the average over the five-year period from 1955 to 1959. The value of the clip has varied greatly from year to year in response both to price variations and climatic conditions. This is illustrated in figures 7 and 8. In 1920 the value of the clip was R45 million; the following year it was reduced to less than a quarter of this figure. Again between 1949 and 1951 it rose from R62 million to R182 million, almost a threefold increase in two years, but the following year, 1952, it was almost halved, dropping to R98 million.[10]

The fluctuations in the price of wool have been at times extremely violent, particularly 1918–23, 1925–32 and 1946–52. The elasticity of supply in response to changes in price is very low and at times appears in the short run to be negative (i.e. a *fall* in price has evoked an *increased* supply). This was very marked when the average price of wool fell between 1925 and 1932 from 8,2 cents per kilogram to 1,7 cents per kilogram. In the table below, price, the number of woolled sheep, and the size of the clip are compared.

Year	Average price* (per kg in cents)	Number of woolled sheep† (thousands	Size of wool clip‡ (1 000 000 kg)
1925	8,2	31 816	73
1926	5,6	35 269	100
1927	5,8	36 006	103
1928	6,4	38 242	118
1929	5,5	40 354	123
1930	3,5	43 927	134
1931	2,4	n.a.	125
1932	1,7	n.a.	132
1933	1,9	n.a.	148
1934	4,2	30 257	107

* *Union Statistics for Fifty Years*, table 1–26.
† Ibid., table I–5.
‡ Ibid., table I–26.

[10] Source: *Union Statistics for Fifty Years*, p. 1–26. See also statistical appendix, table 8.

From the above it is seen that between 1925 and 1933 when the price of wool fell to less than a quarter of what it had been, the size of the wool clip doubled, and a steady increase in the number of woolled sheep was also evident up to 1930. Unfortunately no figures are available for the years 1931, 1932 and 1933 because (as an economy measure) agricultural censuses were suspended during the depression. It seems that when the price of wool fell, sheep farmers, unable to switch to another type of farming, because the Karoo is not suitable for anything except sheep, tried to counter the fall in their incomes by producing more wool. The result was heavy overstocking, which had adverse effects upon grazing and accelerated soil erosion, so that when a drought occurred in 1933–4 Nature reasserted the ecological balance by destroying over a quarter of the sheep population. This is seen in a reduction between 1930 and 1934 in the number of sheep by 13 million, and a smaller clip in 1934 and the years immediately following.

More recently wool has suffered from the competition from man-made fibres and from the peak of 1951 the price has shown a downward trend and, although year to year gross receipts fluctuate with climatic conditions, the general tendency is clearly revealed in figure 8. The average auction price of wool since 1950–1 is given in table 12 in the statistical appendix where the downward trend of prices is seen to contrast with the upward trend of prices of maize, and mutton, produced mainly for home consumption and subject to control board regulation.

The violent fluctuations in the prices of maize and wool illustrate clearly the difficulty experienced by a country which produces agricultural products for the world market. If this production is a significant portion of gross national product, these price fluctuations may have a devastating effect upon the whole economy. South Africa has been fortunate in having the gold-mining industry to act as a stabilizing force in the economy, but nevertheless the instability of agricultural prices has been one of the forces behind the persistent demand for establishing manufacturing industries in South Africa to create a more balanced economy less vulnerable to the movements of the prices of primary products on world markets.

Wool is the major product of sheep farming, but mutton and to a lesser extent skins are also an important source of income to the sheep farmer. Mutton and skins are true joint products, but wool is

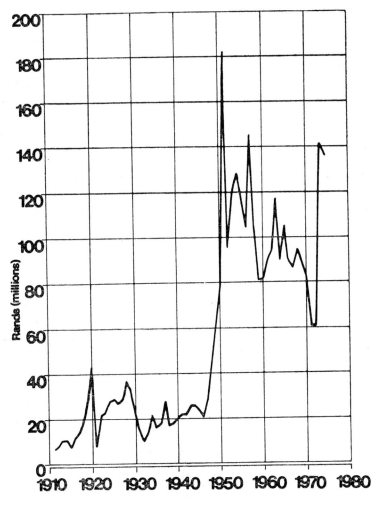

ANNUAL VALUE OF WOOL SOLD 1911-74

FIGURE 8

not. The relationship between wool production and mutton production is a complex one depending to some extent upon the relative
prices of wool and mutton, and to some extent upon ecological
balance, because of the limited carrying capacity of the grazing.
Thus, even if wool prices are high in relation to mutton prices,
sheep will have to be sold for slaughter if farms are stocked to their
full capacity, but in these circumstances there is a tendency for the
number of woolled sheep to increase at the expense of non-woolled
sheep. Some farmers are turning to cross-breeds as a means of
spreading the risk. When the price of wool is high, mutton prices
move in sympathy, but the fluctuation in the price of mutton is not
nearly as great as that of wool because of the ever-present possibility
that consumers will substitute beef or pork for mutton. The tendency
for all meat prices to move together is stronger than the link between
the price of mutton and wool.

The gross value of the product of sheep farming is the total of
the value from wool and from sheep slaughtered, which in 1969–70
amounted to R82 million and R77 million[11] respectively, making a
total from sheep farming of R159 million. In 1970 there were
approximately 40 million sheep in the Republic of which 36 million
were woolled sheep.

Dairy products and beef

Like sheep farming, cattle farming has two major branches – dairy
farming and beef production. Both of these are primarily for the
South African market, although at times both dairy products and
beef have been exported. Thus the marketing situation of the cattle
farmer is more akin to that of the maize farmer than to that of the
producer of wool.

In 1970 the gross value of output of dairy products was R130
million and of slaughtered stock R147 million, making a total for
the products of cattle farming of R277 million. The gross value of
output has risen from R11 million in 1911 to the present figure.
The total number of cattle increased between 1911 and 1957 from
5,8 million to 12 million. The index of physical volume however
increased from 39 to 213 in the case of dairy products and from 39
to 158 in the case of slaughtered stock.[12] These figures illustrate the

---

[11] *Abstract of Agricultural Statistics, 1971*, p. 85.
[12] See *Union Statistics for Fifty Years*, pp. 1–25, 1–4, 1–27.

remarkable advance in animal husbandry that has been achieved. The number of stock had only been doubled between 1911 and 1957, but the physical output of dairy products had increased fivefold and that of slaughtered stock had increased fourfold in the same period. This has been primarily due to selective breeding and improved pasture management.

Other important farm products

Maize, sheep and cattle are the three most important branches of farming, but South African agriculture is diversified and a great variety of other products are also produced in quantity.[13] In the livestock class, poultry and pigs, whose gross values in 1970 were R70 million and R24 million respectively, are the most important. Fruit of all kinds had a gross value of R138 million, and ranged from tropical fruits such as bananas and pineapples and citrus on the one hand to deciduous fruits such as apples, peaches, apricots, pears and grapes on the other. Fruit export, both fresh and canned, is expanding, but competition in international markets is keen. However, South Africa has the advantage of being in the southern hemisphere, and fruit ripens at the time when there is the greatest scarcity in the northern hemisphere. Other important crops are wheat (R90 million), sugar (R82 million) and vegetables, which, if potatoes and dried peas and beans are included, amounted in gross value of output to over R71 million in 1970. Tobacco with an output of R26 million was also significant.[14]

AGRICULTURAL POLICY

The instability of agricultural prices in the 1920s, and the low levels to which they fell during the great depression, together with the very imperfect knowledge of sound husbandry in South African conditions, and the low level of farming practice of both white and African farmers, combined to face South African farming with a really critical situation. Progressive overstocking and burning of the veld, insufficient care in maintaining the humus and water content of the soil, and denudation of the vegetable cover essential to protect the top soil, had given rise to soil erosion on an alarming scale.

---

[13] For list of major products and the gross value of their output in 1970 and 1960 see statistical appendix, table 8.

[14] See table 8.

This was partly due to an ignorance of ecological requirements, and partly due to the plight of the farmers whose income had been drastically reduced by the fall in prices to a level so low that they could not afford to practise sound methods but had to seek profit wherever it could be found even at the expense of the future productivity of the land. Farming in South Africa had indeed degenerated into *Räuberwirtschaft*.

The first aspect of the problem to receive attention was the low level of prices, and assistance to the farming community became a political necessity. Experiments in various *ad hoc* schemes for raising domestic prices were tried in the 1920s, culminating in the Marketing Act of 1937. Large sums of money were spent on subsidies; tariffs on agricultural products were imposed; and grants were made for capital work on farms. Considerable controversy arose both on the general principles underlying the policy and on the detailed methods by which it was being put into effect.[15] That farmers' incomes were deplorably low was not denied, and the 1941 population census revealed the fact that half the owner-occupiers of farms received money incomes of less than R400 per annum, more than half the tenant farmers received less than R200 per annum, and more than half the *bywoners* received less than R100 per annum.[16] The cash wages of farm servants were notoriously low and the general problem of rural poverty stood out clearly. Some means of rehabilitating farming was urgently needed. Criticism, however, was directed firstly at the principle of establishing producer-dominated control boards and granting them monopoly powers over the sale of the product, subject only to what the critics believed were inadequate safeguards of the interests of the consumers. Secondly, they believed that the control-board system must inevitably place the emphasis upon restriction of output and contrived scarcities, rather than upon measures to improve farming methods and so reduce production costs and restore a reasonable profit margin for the

[15] C. S. Richards, 'Subsidies, Quotas, Tariffs and the Excess Cost of Agriculture in South Africa', *S.A.J.E.*, vol. 3 no. 3, September 1935. C. S. Richards, 'The "New Despotism" in Agriculture', *S.A.J.E.*, vol. 4 no. 4, December 1936. Thomas H. Kelley *et al.*, 'Economists' Protest: the Dairy Produce and Maize Marketing Schemes: Memorandum of Objections', *S.A.J.E.*, vol. 6 no. 1, March 1938. P R. Viljoen, 'Planned Agriculture in South Africa', *S.A.J.E.*, vol. 6 no. 3, September 1938. J. M. Tinley, 'Control of Agriculture in South Africa', *S.A.J.E.*, vol. 8 no. 3, September 1940.

[16] Social and Economic Planning Council, Report no. 4, *The Future of Farming in South Africa*, U.G. 10/1945, p. 7.

farmer by increasing his efficiency. Finally, it was asserted that the monopoly price-control powers enjoyed by the boards were tantamount to giving them powers to tax consumers of the product; that this was inequitable; and that assistance to farmers would be better financed from general revenue.[17] C. S. Richards had estimated that in the year 1933 the cost of assistance to agriculture in the forms of subsidies, tariffs, etc., was about R15 million,[18] and the Van Eck Commission believed that in 1939–40 at least an equal sum was transferred to farmers' income from the rest of the community.[19]

The Marketing Act, no. 26 of 1937, set up a National Marketing Council of five members appointed by the Governor-General, and also a Producers' Advisory Committee and a Consumers' Advisory Committee. Commodity control boards could be set up under the Act, subject to ministerial approval. The Act required that a majority of each board should be producers of the product concerned and wide powers were granted to these boards. A control board might act as an agent for the sale of the product and, with the Minister's consent, prohibit the sale of the product through any channel other than itself. Also, with the Minister's consent, it might fix the price of the product and prohibit its sale at any other price. The board had thus a monopoly over the disposal of any product. As a result of criticism of the control boards an amending Act in 1946 (Act no. 50 of 1946) introduced modifications designed to strengthen the Consumers' Advisory Committee and make control boards' accounts subject to the Controller and Auditor-General, but the general principle of producer-dominated control boards has been retained.

The National Marketing Council has the duty of reviewing recommendations of all control boards and in intent it should act to preserve the general economic interest of the country as a whole, but in practice it may not always be strong enough to withstand the powerful sectional interest represented by the control boards.

By 1961 seventeen marketing boards had been established in terms of the Marketing Act, controlling about 70 per cent of all agricultural produce in South Africa.[20] In recent years there appears

---

[17] N. N. Franklin, *Economics in South Africa*, p. 111.

[18] C. S. Richards, 'Subsidies, Quotas, Tariffs and the Excess Cost of Agriculture in South Africa', op. cit.

[19] *Third Interim Report of the Industrial and Agricultural Requirements Commission*, U.G. 40/1941, para. 89.

[20] *Progress and Programme Report of the Republic of South Africa to the Food and Agriculture Organization of the United Nations, 1961*, p. 28.

to have been a slight tendency to relax control of some products. In maize, control over retail prices has been lifted, and in meat the one-channel fixed-price scheme has given place to a scheme of compulsory auction in proclaimed areas.

During the early years of its operation the Marketing Act undoubtedly resulted in stabilizing the prices of controlled commodities at a level appreciably above the world price. The result was large surpluses, which had to be exported at a loss. This aspect came in for strong criticism on the ground that it was fundamentally unsound to subsidize the export of foodstuffs from a country where much malnutrition was known to exist. During the war domestic consumption increased markedly and prices tended to rise. The Marketing Act controls were used to check this price rise, and in general domestic prices were held at a level below the world price. Since 1955 there has, however, been a tendency to return to the earlier position. A 1961 report states:[21]

'The phenomenal increase in agricultural production in the post-war period can, as far as controlled products are concerned, largely be ascribed to the measure of stability in prices maintained under the control system of the Marketing Act. In the case of some commodities substantial surpluses resulted, which, at ruling prices could only be exported at a loss.'

This situation may be expected to revive the old controversy about exporting foodstuffs at a loss. There are close parallels with the agricultural situation in the United States and recent American opinions on the problem of agricultural surpluses may have application to South Africa, in particular the view that the movement of labour out of agriculture into other sectors of the economy should be accelerated.[22]

The other important aspect of agricultural policy has been the increasing emphasis placed both on enlarging our scientific knowledge of farming in South Africa and on the transmission of this knowledge to the practical farmer. In the long run the benefits to be derived from increasing the productive efficiency of farming operations are likely far to exceed any benefits that may derive from mere price stabilization. Early critics of the Marketing Act regretted that

[21] Ibid., p. 28.

[22] See Alan R. Bird, *Surplus: the Riddle of American Agriculture;* and Committee for Economic Development, *An Adaptive Programme for Agriculture* (1962).

insufficient attention was being devoted to the technical and scientific side of farm problems. The Van Eck Commission in 1941[23] reviewed the effects of assistance to farming. While recognizing that in the abnormal circumstances of the early 1930s special temporary assistance to agriculture was necessary, it expressed the view that the form of this assistance did not take sufficient account of the effect of higher prices upon the poorer consumers. 'Moreover, in giving assistance, control is not exercised so as to avoid inefficiency. It often merely keeps inefficient farmers on the land and perpetuates or even accentuates unhealthy farming practices.'[24] The Commission pointed out that bad farming was destroying fertility – and that extensive soil loss was taking place. 'Thus, what should be the most durable of the Union's natural resources is being dissipated extensively and at a cumulative rate.' The Commission, citing the fact that, in 1936, 64 per cent of the total working population were engaged in agriculture, but that they produced only 12½ per cent of the national income, came to the conclusion that movement of workers out of agriculture into more remunerative industries would represent an economic gain to the country as a whole, and be in line with trends throughout the rest of the world.[25]

The need for improvement of farming methods was further stressed in a report issued by the Department of Agriculture and Forestry[26] and in a Report of the Social and Economic Planning Council.[27] The former listed essential elements in improving the quality of farming, among which were the following:

1. Efficient grazing management, for which purpose proper camping of grazing areas is essential so that selective and rotational grazing can be practised.

2. Provision of adequate watering points for stock so that animals would not have to walk long distances for water and in so doing trample grazing unnecessarily.

[23] *Third Interim Report of the Industrial and Agricultural Requirements Commission*, U.G. 40/1941, pp. 32, 33 and 34.

[24] A glaring example was when maize farmers were subsidized on a sliding scale, a larger subsidy per bag being given to the small producer although the statistical evidence proved that the large-scale farmer was more efficient. See Department of Agriculture, *Bulletin* no. 81, table XXXIII.

[25] There had been a strong prejudice in South Africa in favour of 'keeping the people on the land' and restricting as far as possible the 'drift to the towns'.

[26] *The Reconstruction of Agriculture 1944–5*.

[27] Report no. 4: *The Future of Farming in South Africa*, U.G. 10/1945.

3. The making of hay for winter feed in areas where the pasture is suitable.

4. Making of compost and the return to the soil of as many nutrients as possible. The practice of burning cow dung as fuel by Africans is condemned.

5. Crop rotation, including the rotation soil-binding and soil-building crops such as lucerne.

6. Contour farming and strip cropping on sloping ground to assist in conserving both soil and moisture.

7. The planting of trees as shelter belts and to provide timber for domestic purposes.

8. The prime importance of ensuring that good quality seed is planted and that adequate fertilizers are applied to the land.

The report also recommended that certain practices such as up-and-down ploughing, uncontrolled burning of the veld, overstocking and persistent grain monoculture, should be prohibited by law. A later White Paper[28] developed further the concept of and essential requirements for conservation farming. The culmination of growing public opinion in favour of enforcing better methods of farming was the Soil Conservation Act, no. 45 of 1946. The passage of this Act was undoubtedly a triumph over conservatism, because the white farming community had always combined independence of action with a strong sense of their rights of private property. The Act gave legislative sanction to the view that ownership of land could no longer imply the right of the owner to abuse or destroy the land. The Act set up a National Soil Conservation Board charged with the duty, in co-operation with farmers, of improving farming methods, and provided for the proclamation of soil-conservation areas. When an area had been so proclaimed, very considerable powers were granted for the regulation or prohibition of certain practices, going as far as the expropriation (subject to the payment of compensation) of land which was consistently subject to misuse by its owner. The response of the farming community was encouraging and, by 1953, 456 conservation areas had been proclaimed under the Act,[29] comprising 53 000 000 hectares and representing approximately 62

---

[28] *White Paper on Agricultural Policy*, W.P. 10/1946.

[29] *Progress and Programme Report of the Union of South Africa to the Food and Agriculture Organization of the United Nations, 1953,* p. 16.

per cent of the white farming area of the country; by 30 June 1958 this increased to 666 conservation districts covering over 77 000 000 hectares, or about 90 per cent of farm land in the country, excluding the land reserved for Africans.

At the same time the Department of Agriculture intensified its research programmes, special attention being given to discovering the best methods of farming appropriate to each agricultural area. Detailed farm planning is being increased and has been gathering momentum. Conservation farming is, however, essentially a cumulative process. The first stage is the negative one of preventing further destruction of the soil by various anti-soil-erosion measures, including, in extreme cases, the temporary withdrawal of the land from economic use. This should be followed by positive steps to build up productivity. This latter phase must be based upon the progressive accumulation of detailed knowledge of each particular area by the technical experts, and this knowledge must then be transmitted to the general farming community by the extension officers and by mass propaganda in press, radio, etc. 'Since officers and committee members have become more conversant with the technique of farm planning, and the staff position more favourable, and since greater use is being made of aerial photography, it is expected that the annual rate of farm planning will continue to increase.'[30] In 1953 the average maize yield of South Africa was only 636 kilograms per hectare with 2 000 to 3 000 kilograms normally obtained at government research stations. The task was to transfer the higher technical efficiency of these specialized institutions to the general farming community. A similar problem is encountered in the other branches of farming. Great progress has been made; but most South Africans are unaware of the major agricultural revolution that has been taking place since 1945. Whereas the number of sheep increased between 1946 and 1957 by 24 per cent from 30,8 million to 38,2 million, the index of physical volume of wool increased by 46 per cent from 83 to 121. For cattle the increase in productivity is more marked. Cattle numbers in 1957 were slightly *less* than in 1946, yet the index of physical output of dairy products *rose* by 63 per cent from 131 to 213, and of slaughtered stock by 26 per cent from 124 to 158, during this period. Better breeding and sounder pasture management can bring about spectacular increases. The case is cited of a

[30] Department of Agriculture, *Annual Report, 1957–8*, p. 48.

farm of 1 769 hectares in the Aliwal North district where in four years
the carrying capacity was increased from 500 sheep and 15 cattle to
1 500 sheep and 170 cattle. Improvement in field crop yields is also
evident in table 11, where steady increase is shown in yields of
wheat and maize on farms owned by whites.

Between 1946 and 1958 conservation works to the value of R17
million had been completed by farmers with the assistance of
subsidies or loans from the government. In addition work to the
value of R1,5 million had been undertaken by the government
itself, making a total of R18,5 million spent on conservation work
over the twelve-year period.[31] Much still remains to be done, but the
revolution that has taken place since 1946 on the better white farms
is the change from a situation where the productivity of the land
was being destroyed at an alarming rate to one where future productivity is being steadily built up. Unfortunately the same cannot
as yet be said of the African reserves.

THE FARM ECONOMY

Few meaningful generalizations can be made about the farm
economy when individual farms vary in size from some of a few
hectares to others of over 15 000 hectares in extent, and when the
character of the farming may lie anywhere between highly intensive
land use under irrigation and very extensive use of land in vast
sheep and cattle-ranching country, where carrying capacity in the
drier areas is very low.

The total superficial area of the Republic is 122 million hectares
of which 103 million are used for agriculture or forestry. Its distribution between different uses in 1965 was:

	White farm areas (hectares 1 000)	Bantu areas (hectares 1 000)
Cultivated	10 028	2 143
Permanent crops	821	41
Artificial pasture	897	38
Natural pasture	71 342	11 920
Timber	1 071	410
Other	3 636	518
	87 795	15 070

Source: *Abstract of Agricultural Statistics, 1975*, pp. 5 & 6.

[31] Department of Agriculture, *Annual Report, 1957–8*, p. 49.

Number and size of farms

According to the 1964 agricultural census there were in the Republic (excluding areas reserved for Africans) some 101 000 farms covering an area of approximately 91 000 000 hectares. Thus the statistical average size of farms was 901 hectares. This however has little meaning because this average conceals great diversity in size. Moreover, the size of farms is determined among other things by the fertility of the soil and the adequacy of the rainfall, and these vary greatly from one part of the country to another. Three-quarters of the total number of farms were less than 901 hectares in extent, but they constituted only 23 per cent of the total area, while the one-quarter over 901 hectares accounted for 77 per cent of the area.

Of much greater importance than the superficial area of farms is the scale upon which farming operations are conducted. In many branches of farming in South Africa it would seem that large-scale operations are more efficient and more profitable than small-scale ones. This has been demonstrated by some recent field studies in pineapple, milk, tobacco, groundnuts and maize production.

Farming capital

Of the 104 000 farms recorded in 1958, 75 per cent were farmed by the owner, 3 per cent were farmed by managers and the remaining 22 per cent were rented or share-cropped or operated in some other manner.[32] Thus the great majority of the white farms are operated by their owners, and in most cases the owners are themselves working farmers whose physical labour contributes materially to the agricultural output.[33] The tradition of farm ownership in South Africa (as contrasted with countries where tenant farming is the normal practice) places a heavy financial burden upon the would-be farmer, because not only has he to find his working capital for the purchase of stock, machinery and labour, but he also has to find a large sum of fixed capital for the purchase of the land. It is seen from the table below that bonds and long-term loans account for about 88 per cent of the farmers' indebtedness, and short-term loans and bank accommodation for only 12 per cent.

[32] *Report on Agricultural and Pastoral Production and Sugar Cane Plantations 1957–8*, U.G. 70/1960, p. 5.

[33] There is a mistaken notion among many townsmen that the typical white farmer merely directs the labour of others. This s very far from the truth.

Value of Farms, and Farmers' Indebtedness, June 1958

Total value of all farms	R3 087,4 million
Total indebtedness of farmers	R431,0 million

made up as follows:

Farmers' Indebtedness (R millions)

Source	Bonds	Long-term loans without bonds	Short-term loans
Co-operative societies	5,4	4,0	12,2
Other farmers	56,8	14,4	4,0
Other private persons	40,2	12,4	4,8
Government	13,8	6,6	0,8
Land Bank	45,2	5,2	0,6
Insurance companies	53,6	6,2	1,4
Commercial banks	36,0	13,2	21,6
Other financial institutions	38,6	5,0	2,6
Other	15,6	5,6	5,8
Total	305,2	72,6	53,8

Speculation in land is endemic in South Africa. When agricultural prices rise land values tend to soar, and they often reach heights which make it difficult to maintain a profit margin if there is a recession of prices. Thus capital which would have been better employed in operating the farm is often dissipated in land specu-lation.[34] Nevertheless there has been a great expansion of farm equipment in recent years and marked technical advance.

Some idea of the technical progress that has occurred in farming can be gained from a study of changes in farm equipment.

Agricultural Equipment on White Farms*

Year	Motor lorries	Animal-drawn wagons	Tractors (motor)	Stationary engines
1926		84 915	1 302	4 492
1937	8 568	99 302	6 019	10 573
1946	21 256	102 892	20 292	17 008
1950	31 308	72 132	48 422	45 830
1955	52 077	43 770	87 451	53 674
1960	69 376		119 196	83 816
1965	74 631		138 422	
1971	94 649		157 127	

* *Union Statistics for Fifty Years*, table 1–22; and *Statistical Year Book, 1974* p. 9.30.

[34] During the pineapple boom a certain piece of land was sold for R600 in 1934 and R25 000 in 1954 (see C. B. Strauss, *Pineapples in the Eastern Cape: A Study of the Farm Economy and Marketing Patterns*, Institute of Social and Economic Research, Rhodes University, Occasional Paper no. 5, p. 39).

The growth in power-driven equipment since 1945 is quite remarkable: motor lorries have increased more than four times, while
animal-drawn vehicles have been more than halved; motor tractors
have increased over sevenfold, and stationary engines fivefold. Some
critics aver that the process of mechanization has sometimes gone
too far and too fast, and that some farmers have more specialized
mechanical equipment than can be employed to its optimum on a
single farm.

The figures below show the total value of investment in agriculture
for recent years.

	Land and fixed improvements	Machinery, implements, motor vehicles and tractors (R millions)	Livestock inventory	Total
1965	5 224,0	534,4	1 013,6	6 772,0
1966	5 266,1	551,4	1 051,7	6 869,2
1967	6 445,1	591,9	1 138,2	8 175,8
1968	6 993,4	630,9	1 189,5	8 813,8
1969	7 204,0	675,5	1 177,2	9 056,7
1970	6 993,4	728,8	1 188,3	8 910,5
1971	7 288,3	804,2	1 272,2	9 364,7
1972	7 614,7	864,3	1 338,9	9 817,9

Source: *Abstract of Agricultural Statistics, 1975*, p. 88.

Agricultural co-operative societies

Because of the financial, technical and marketing problems of the
lone farmer, co-operative movements have developed over a wide
range of farming activities. The rate of this development is seen if we
compare the position in 1922, when the co-operative movement first
really came into being, with the position in 1960 and 1973.[35]

	1922	1960	1973
Number of co-operative societies	81	319	531
Membership	14 282	285 101	429 055
Turnover	R4 949 000	R1 179 362 000	R1 913 899 000

It is difficult to determine with precision the number of farmers who
are members of co-operative societies. There are about 400 000

[35] For 1960 figures see *Progress and Programme Report of the Republic of
South Africa to the Food and Agriculture Organization of the United Nations, 1961*,
p. 61; and for 1969 see *Annual Report of the Secretary for Agricultural Economics
and Marketing 1969/70*, R.P. 23/1971, p. 106 and for *1973/74* – R.P. 51/1975
p. 96.

68

FARMING

white farmers, but 434 619 members of co-operatives, the reason
being that many farmers are members of two or more co-operative
societies. It is, however, reliably estimated that at least 80 per cent of
all white farmers belong to the co-operative movement. In the purchase of farm equipment, in the provision of technical services and in
marketing, many co-operatives have rendered excellent service to
farmers, but the management and financial control of certain co-
operatives have sometimes been a matter of concern. The Co-operative Societies Act, no. 29 of 1939, however, gives the Minister of
Agricultural Economics and Marketing and the Registrar of Co-
operative Societies power to exercise control over certain aspects of
co-operative societies. The Registrar has under him an inspectorate
with power to investigate the activities of co-operatives and to submit
reports.

THE AGRICULTURAL LABOUR FORCE

Labour employed in agriculture consists of three main groups:
(a) labour performed by the farmer and by members of his family,
(b) labour performed by hired workers in regular employment, and
(c) casual or seasonal labour. In addition to these three, there are
those employed as domestic servants on farms. Although these latter
are not strictly farm labourers, they are part of the farm economy,
and sometimes it is not easy to decide whether they are rightly
regarded as domestic servants or as farm labourers – for example a
woman who is a housemaid in the farmer's house but also assists the
farmer's wife in the dairy. The 1957–8 agricultural census gives the
following numbers in each category.[36] (See table on the next
page.)

There were in June of 1958 a total of 1 846 000 workers in agriculture,
of whom 145 000 were listed as domestic servants. Of the remaining
1 700 000, 751 000 were seasonal or casual workers, and the balance
of 949 000 were permanently employed. If domestic servants on farms
are included with the agricultural workers proper, the agricultural
sector provided employment for nearly 1 850 000 persons (excluding
African peasant farmers in the reserves), or nearly 40 per cent of the
total economically active population of South Africa.

[36] *Report on Agricultural and Pastoral Production and Sugar Cane Plantations
1957–8*, U.G. 70/1960, pp. 53–9.

Labour Employed in Agriculture (*excluding African reserves*) *1957–8*
(*in thousands*)

	Total	Whites		Africans		Coloured people and Asians	
		M	F	M	F	M	F
Family labour (owners, tenants and their families)	132,6	93,2	33,3			4,4	1,6
Regular employees	816,3	13,0	—	621,9	81,2	94,4	5,4
Domestic servants	145,5	—	—	11,5	111,8	1,0	21,1
Total full-time (including domestic servants)	1 094,4	106,2	33,3	633,4	193,0	99,8	28,1
Casual or seasonal workers*	751,2	1,1	—	364,6	271,8	84,7	28,7
Total regular and casual (excluding domestic servants)	1 700,1	107,3	33,3	986,5	352,0	183,5	35,7
Total all categories	1 845,6	107,3	33,3	998,0	464,8	184,5	56,8

*Number actually at work during June 1958.

Figures of employment in agriculture in *Abstract of Agricultural Statistics, 1971*, show a reduction in the agricultural labour force,

Number of Farm Employees and Domestic Servants on Farms at June 1964 (*thousands*)

Total all races	Whites		Coloured people and Asians		Africans	
	M	F	M	F	M	F
888,1	12,1	0,4	102,9	28,1	565,4	179,2

but these figures exclude working proprietors and casual workers. The 1960 Population Census occupational distribution gave a total of 1 689 000 distributed as follows:

	Total (1 000)	Whites (1 000)	Coloured people (1 000)	Asians (1 000)	Africans (1 000)
Farming	1 635	114	111	11	1 400
Agricultural services	8	1	2	—	5
Forestry and fishing	46	4	7	—	34
TOTAL	1 689	119	120	11	1 439

Ten years later, the 1970 census gave a total of 2 239 190 engaged in Farming, Forestry and Fishing:

Total	Whites	Coloured	Asian	African
(1 000)	(1 000)	(1 000)	(1 000)	(1 000)
2 239	99	119	7	2 014

The great divergence in the figures quoted illustrates how difficult it is to give a precise figure for those engaged in agriculture. It depends upon whether working proprietors are included, on how domestic servants on farms are treated and on whether part-time workers are counted and, if so, at what time of the year the count is taken. It would probably be mistaken to argue that because the 1970 census showed 550 000 more persons occupied in Farming, Forestry and Fishing that the labour force had expanded by this number since 1960. It is more likely to be due to a different method of counting. Nevertheless, be it 1,6 million or 2,2 million, it is a large number.

This illustrates the extent to which South Africans, in spite of the great mining and manufacturing industries, are still largely dependent upon farming activities for a livelihood. Although farming contributed only about eight per cent of the net national income, South Africa is still basically an agricultural country in the matter of employment of its people. (See also figure 3, page 38.) One would expect migration from farming areas to the towns and cities to redress this imbalance, and in the case of whites this has taken place steadily during the last half-century but in the case of African farm workers there are severe restrictions upon movement which tend to keep an excessive number upon the farms, thereby depressing farm wages. This policy contrasts strikingly with the attempt in the United States to accelerate movement out of agriculture.[37]

SUBSISTENCE FARMING IN THE RESERVES

A failure in adaptation

Before contact with the western world, the black African tribesman was primarily a semi-nomadic pastoralist, and ownership of cattle played a major role in the social and economic life of the community. Cattle were the sources of meat and milk, which were the principal diet. Cattle were used in sacrifices to the ancestors, and in this way were a means of warding off evil. A man's prestige and social status depended upon the number of cattle he possessed, and when a man

---

[37] Committee for Economic Development, *An Adaptive Programme for Agriculture* (1962).

wished to marry, cattle were given to the bride's father as *ikhasi*.[38]
Thus ownership of cattle had a significance much deeper than purely
economic and, indeed, the emphasis tended to be placed more upon
the number of cattle than upon their quality. Crop production was
of relatively minor significance and tended to be relegated to women.
Hoe cultivation was practised, but no attempt was made to maintain
soil fertility or grow crops in rotation because when a field lost its
fertility it was abandoned in favour of virgin soil. Thus the whole
tribal economy depended upon an abundance of land for its successful operation. When increasing population began to press upon the
land, the tribe moved on to new pastures or expanded its area by
driving weaker tribes away or annihilating them. Moreover, tribal
wars and disease checked population growth, and recurrent droughts
and stock diseases prevented the accumulation of an excessive
number of stock. Thus a system which was most extravagant in the
use of land was enabled to survive.

Contact with the whites prevented further migration and reduced
the area for African occupation. Moreover, white administration
stopped inter-tribal warfare, and the extension of medical services
reduced the number of deaths, so that population increase was
accelerated. Similarly, compulsory dipping and veterinary services
reduced stock losses.

Thus the general effect of contact with the whites was to accelerate
the rate of increase of both men and beasts and to reduce the room
necessary to rear them. The natural consequence was general overpopulation, which today has become desperate, for not only is the
present pressure on the land too great, but overstocking and bad
farming are progressively reducing the future carrying capacity of the
land. An African peasant epitomized the situation in the Xhosa
phrase 'men and beasts beget, but land does not beget'.[39]

The Native Economic Commission,[40] composed largely of practical
farmers well qualified to assess the position, reported on conditions
in 1932 in no uncertain terms:

[38] Cattle paid to the bride's father by the bridegroom at marriage. The practice
is known as *ukulobolo*. For an excellent account of the importance of cattle in
tribal life see Monica Hunter, *Reaction to Conquest*, pp. 65–71; and for some
economic consequences of the use of cattle as 'money' see H. M. Robertson, '150
Years of Economic Contact between Black and White', op. cit.

[39] *Keiskammahoek Rural Survey*, vol. 2, *The Economy of a Native Reserve*,
by D. Hobart Houghton and Edith M. Walton, p. 2.

[40] *Report of the Native Economic Commission*, U.G. 22/1932, paras. 72 and 73.

'The worst effects of overstocking may be seen in some parts of the Ciskeian area, notably Middledrift, Herschel, and Glen Grey. In Middledrift there are large areas where the surface soil has been entirely eroded and no grass whatever grows. In adjoining parts the grass is being speedily supplanted by *Helichrysum* and similar weeds. In Herschel and Glen Grey the vegetation of the mountain sides has almost disappeared, the rainstorms send torrents down the slopes which wash away periodically large parts of very valuable and fertile soil. These two areas with fertile valleys containing great depth of soil show some of the worst donga-erosion in the Union. The difference between these and other areas is one of degree only. In Geluks Location actual desert conditions have in twenty years been created where once good grazing existed.

'Unless precautionary measures are taken against overstocking, the condition in the Transkei and Native areas in the rest of the Union will be tomorrow what that of the Ciskei is today. The same causes are at work there, and they will inevitably produce the same effects in the near future – denudation, donga-erosion, deleterious plant succession, destruction of woods, drying up of springs, robbing the soil of its reproductive properties, *in short the creation of desert conditions*.'

Contrary, perhaps, to the expectations of economists, pressure upon the land did not give rise to attempts to economize the use of land by the adoption of more intensive methods of farming. Instead, relief was found through the large-scale migration of workers to industrial centres like the Witwatersrand. For over half a century labour has been the main export of the reserves. Some went with their families to form a permanent African urban class, but the majority go to work leaving their families behind in the reserves, and return home to them only at infrequent intervals for shorter or longer periods. This migratory labour system is the subject of the next chapter. The absence at any one time of about half the able-bodied male population has led to further decline in the agricultural productivity of the reserves.

Declining productivity, persistent overstocking, soil denudation, and the general poverty of the people, relieved only by the increased number of migrant workers leaving the reserves, have been matters of grave concern for over four decades. In 1930 W. M. Macmillan's study[41] in the Herschel district was perhaps the first to attract public

[41] W. M. Macmillan, *Complex South Africa*.

attention to what was taking place. Two years later the Native Economic Commission[42] carried out a nation-wide examination of the reserves and presented a most disturbing picture which fully confirmed the findings in Herschel. In 1946 the Social and Economic Planning Council published a report on the position in the reserves.[43] This represented an important change in emphasis in that it clearly recognized that no purely agricultural solution would be adequate. The Councils' report stressed the need for improved farming practice, but urged that this should go hand in hand with a diversification of the general economy of the reserves as an integral part of the development of the Union as a whole. The Tomlinson Commission Report, 1955, confirmed to the full the close connexion between general economic development and agricultural rehabilitation, and it stressed the fact that industrial and commercial employment to relieve the pressure of population upon the land was an essential pre-condition for agricultural reform.

This brief list of the major investigations into the state of African agriculture may easily give a false impression. There is today a tendency to denigrate the efforts of those who have gone before, and to speak as if the awareness of the need to modernize African farming methods is only a recent event. This is wholly untrue, because for over a century far-sighted administrators (from Sir George Grey onwards) and many missionaries were acutely conscious of the inadequacy of tribal farming practice. In the Ciskei there were experiments in surveyed allotments and freehold tenure. Many missionaries combined instruction in agriculture and basic crafts with the spread of the Gospel. In the latter half of the nineteenth century Lovedale,[44] for example, operated a farm, and practical farm work was compulsory for all male students. It also provided industrial training in carpentry, wagon-making, blacksmithing, shoemaking, and in printing and bookbinding. Girls were taught to cook and make clothes, and, of course, it was the Lovedale hospital that pioneered the training of African nurses for the whole sub-continent. At a later stage the government of the Cape of Good Hope established agricultural schools, which were afterwards taken over and extended

[42] U.G. 22/1932.

[43] *The Native Reserves and Their Place in the Economy of the Union of South Africa,* U.G. 32/1946.

[44] A famous missionary institution in the eastern Cape Province established by the Church of Scotland in 1814.

by the Union Government, and agricultural demonstrators were trained and sent to work in the tribal villages. In 1945 there were over 400 of these at work. In spite of deep thought and heroic effort agricultural conditions continued to deteriorate. Failure to effect a significant change in agricultural methods should not be attributed to lack of zeal on the part of a noble band of dedicated workers, but must be explained in other ways.

The explanation would appear to be that the African peasants have failed to adapt their farming practice to modern requirements. General conservatism, the system of land tenure, and certain social customs, like *ukulobolo*, combine to perpetuate obsolete methods of farming in spite of the visual evidence of modern methods applied at agricultural schools in the reserves and by adjacent white far-mers.

Traditionally land among Africans was held by the chief in trust for the tribe and the concept of private property in land was unknown. Thus every tribesman had the right to graze his stock upon the tribal commonage and, upon marriage, to apply to the chief for a piece of arable land for his wife (or wives) to cultivate. Thus land was given automatically and at no cost to himself, to every man, regardless of his (or his wife's) capacity as a farmer. With increasing pressure upon the limited area of land, overstocking of the common grazing became widespread, and it also became increasingly difficult to provide each family with a field. Nevertheless these rights were so firmly entrenched in tribal custom that the administration hesitated for many years before attempting to bring about a change, and attempts at stock limitation and culling of inferior animals was fiercely opposed. Those responsible for culling of stock have sometimes been threatened, fences have been cut, and fence patrols murdered.

The result of persistent overstocking is an extremely low yield from stock farming, whether for market or domestic consumption. Most cattle are perpetually undernourished. They receive little supplemen-tary feeding even in winter, and have to rely upon what they can get from the severely overgrazed veld. Even as draught animals, African cattle are far from satisfactory, being frequently too weak to plough when the spring rains come. In addition to acting as draught animals, the same cattle are expected to produce milk and meat. With the communal grazing, breeding for specialized purposes is impossible.

Less than half the cattle are cows and heifers. Milk production in winter is practically negligible, and in summer is very small and almost entirely for immediate family consumption. Indeed, except for wool production the whole economy is directed to subsistence rather than markets, but even with this as its objective it is most inefficient. Peasants are most reluctant to sell or slaughter their cattle, except for purposes of ritual. Instead of slaughtering them in their prime when they would give a good yield of meat they are kept until they die of old age or succumb in the next drought. Moreover the savings of the people are invested in yet more cattle. In a detailed study of a reserve[45] it was found that between 1945 and 1950 stock losses amounted to R80 000, or R29 per family.

The money earned by the sweat and toil of labourers in mines and factories is continuously being poured into the bottomless pit created by their cattle complex. It would seem more rational to devote their earnings to increased consumption, when most of the people are at a bare subsistence level, or to investment so as to raise the productive capacity of the reserve, where capital outlay upon fencing, irrigation, ploughing implements, tractors and fertilizers would increase the yield from arable farming.

The quality of African-owned sheep is even poorer than that of the cattle, for the rams are very inferior. It has been estimated that on the average four to five African-owned sheep yield approximately the same quantity of wool as one white-owned sheep, and the wool is usually much inferior. At the East London wool sales it fetches a price equal to only between half and two-thirds of the average price paid for wool from white farmers.

In 1957 the stock in the reserves was: cattle 3 771 000, sheep 3 722 000, goats 2 890 000, horses, donkeys and mules 412 000. The numbers in 1963 were: cattle 4 100 000, sheep 3 200 000, goats 2 984 000.[46] In many areas the stock is 50 per cent in excess of the estimated optimum carrying-capacity of the land, and if stock numbers could be effectively reduced the yield could be substantially increased.

A similar situation prevails in arable farming because land scarcity has led to individual holdings of 2 hectares or less, and in many cases to families who have no arable land whatever. Small

---

[45] Hobart Houghton and Walton, p. 166.
[46] See *Union Statistics for Fifty Years*, pp. 1–4, 5, 7, 9, for 1957; and *Abstract of Agricultural Statistics, 1971* for 1963 figures.

holdings may be as much as a woman with a hoe could cultivate, but if productivity is to be increased modern farming methods must be adopted and these require land holdings sufficiently large to permit of crop rotation and the use of simple machinery. A comparison between yields per hectare of maize from white farmers and from peasants in the reserves (shown in table 11) indicates clearly the relative inefficiency of primitive agriculture. Whereas the yield from the former rose fairly steadily from 551 kilograms in 1946 to 1 186 kilograms in 1970, that from the African peasants remained about 230 kilograms (see table 11).

Rehabilitation proposals

The Tomlinson Commission, after an exhaustive examination of farming in the reserves, listed the characteristics of African farming as being:[47]

1. wrong use of land,
2. inefficient methods of cultivation,
3. inefficient animal-husbandry practices,
4. increasing soil erosion,
5. diminishing soil fertility,
6. low yields from crops and livestock,
7. extremely low incomes from farming,
8. a qualitatively deficient diet,
9. a low standard of health,
10. a generally low standard of living.

Moreover the Commission considered that as long as 50 per cent of the adult males were away working to supplement the family income, no rehabilitation of the reserves was possible. It therefore put forward a bold programme of reform. The population was to be divided into two broad classes, one of which would in future be wholly engaged in farming, and the other would be wholly dependent upon non-agricultural employment. Instead of the present practice, where every man was alternately both part-time peasant farmer and part-time industrial wage-earner, each group was to be encouraged to specialize. Those who were to be full-time farmers should be given holdings sufficiently large to enable them adequately to support their families

[47] Tomlinson Report (Summary), p. 112.

upon the land, and freehold tenure was recommended for their arable holdings.[48]

The Commission was fully aware that in order to provide adequate land holdings for those families destined to become full-time farmers, large numbers at present on the land would have to be displaced. For the Bantu areas as a whole the Commission estimated that approximately 300 000 families (numbering 1 800 000 persons),[49] or 50 per cent of the existing population, would have to be removed. Much of the Commission's report was devoted to the task of providing alternative employment for these persons, and a vigorous policy of industrialization of the Bantu areas, supported and financed in part by government and in part by private white entrepreneurs (with adequate safeguards for African interests) was envisaged. Effective expansion of secondary and tertiary occupations would, it was believed, ultimately provide alternative sources of income for those moving out of subsistence agriculture, and the establishment of urban centres in the Bantu areas was strongly urged. The Commission envisaged four types – rural settlements (intended as a transitional stage between rural life and urban), villages, towns, and ultimately large cities.[50] The Commission stressed the fact that villages and towns are dynamic institutions and that they can only evolve when they rest upon a sound economic foundation. It realized, however, that migratory labour to the mines and industries outside the Bantu areas would continue for some time to come, both because of the dependence of these industries upon migratory labour and because of the difficulty of establishing employment opportunities in the Bantu areas. Throughout the report the Commission wrote with a strong sense of urgency.

Since 1955 the Department of Bantu Administration and Development has been pursuing a policy much on the general lines recommended by the Tomlinson Report. In particular the basic division of the population into full-time farmers and full-time non-agricultural workers appears to have been accepted as the ultimate objective. Plans are going ahead for the creation of 'full economic land units', but no compulsion is being exercised and present land holders are

[48] For details of the proposals for resettlement see Tomlinson Report (Summary), p. 118.

[49] Ibid. p. 145. The average number of persons in a family is taken as six.

[50] Tomlinson Report (Summary), p. 145.

not being dispossessed. On political, social and humanitarian grounds this is highly desirable, but it means that effective land reform will be a slow business, perhaps spreading over more than one generation. Details of rehabilitation planning are very complex and difficult to explain in general terms, for soil fertility, estimated grazing capacity, population density and topography determine the precise definition of 'full economic units' in each particular area. Basically the idea is that ultimately every family remaining on the land will be in possession of a 'full economic unit'. A 'full economic unit' is defined (following the Tomlinson Commission) as arable and grazing which together are estimated to yield a family income of R120, *under the existing methods of farming and at 1955 prices.* With improved farming the family income should be doubled or even trebled. A senior officer in 1960 stated that he believed a realistic figure for an efficient farmer would be between R500 and R600 per annum.[51] Today with general inflation it would be very much higher.

When a location has been proclaimed a 'betterment area', a rehabilitation scheme is drawn up. An area is set aside for human habitation, and the scattered homesteads are concentrated in a village. The land most suitable for cultivation is then set aside for arable purposes, and the remaining pasturage is camped and fenced so that rotational grazing can be practised. Stock limitation is strictly enforced, water supplies and dams are provided in each camp, and anti-soil-erosion measures adopted. The available arable and grazing land is then reallocated to those inhabitants who previously had had land rights. Those who previously had neither land nor cattle, and who are generally referred to as 'squatters', get nothing in the redistribution except a hut site and garden, or they are encouraged to move to one of the new non-agricultural settlements.

By 1958 planning was well advanced in the King William's Town district. There 'full economic units' were usually somewhere between 5 hectares of arable plus grazing for 14 cattle units and 8 hectares of arable plus grazing for 10 cattle units. The proportions in which arable and grazing land were combined varied with the potential of the area, but in all cases the combined holding was designed to yield R120 per annum under then existing farming practice. The

---

[51] *Economic Development in a Plural Society*, ed. D. Hobart Houghton, p. 88, footnote 35.

average combined holding of arable and grazing worked out at about 35 hectares per family.

Even when the 'squatters' have been removed it will not be possible to give all families 'full economic units'. Indeed, at present, owing to the desire not to dispossess any present landholder, only a small minority get the full unit. For example, in a total of twenty-five locations, 687 full economic units had been planned, but on 1 October 1961 there were only 148 full units in operation. Lesser holdings are given to the majority, and 1 hectare plus two cattle units (which is about one-sixth of a full unit) is given to many families. Nevertheless, the attempt is being made to plan these lesser units so that they can ultimately be combined to form full economic units. It is hoped that, as urban centres develop where there are adequate employment opportunities, those families whose holdings are too small will be induced to leave the land and to become permanent urban dwellers. As this comes about, a larger number of full economic units can be created for the permanent farmers.

It should be noted that the government is not at present implementing the Commission's recommendation to grant freehold title to the arable holdings. This is, perhaps, wise at this stage, because the whole land tenure situation is in transition. Even the 'full economic units' may be shown by experience to be less than the optimum size for efficient peasant farming. To grant freehold tenure precipitately might well crystallize a situation which subsequent experience might show to be uneconomic. Nevertheless, freehold tenure, subject of course to the general soil-conservation legislation, should be the ultimate objective.

Tact and understanding are being shown by many agricultural officers. All plans are discussed at each stage with the inhabitants, and suggestions are welcomed and incorporated in the final plan. For instance in one location a central village had been suggested. The people, however, objected that the location in fact consisted of two different groups who did not wish to be together. One was Christian with long-standing affiliations with a near-by mission, the other was pagan. The original plan was modified to provide for two villages as desired, without upsetting the ecological requirements of the resettlement scheme.

The whole task is so vast and so intricate – to plan the resettlement of 3 600 000 people and to remove at least half of them from the land, to reallocate the use of 15 000 000 hectares of land, and to attempt to do it all by persuasion and not by force – that it calls for the energy of Alexander the Great, the wisdom of Solomon and the patience of Job. At times one is appalled by the whole conception, and it seems to be totalitarian interference with the rights of individuals on a gigantic scale; but a hundred years of failure to rehabilitate tribal agriculture proves that far-reaching changes are essential. Surely by carefully planned and sympathetically executed resettlement schemes the essential change can be brought about without the misery and hardship of, for example, the enclosure movement in Britain, or the liquidation of the Kulaks in Soviet Russia.

The task seems likely to be more difficult than the Tomlinson Commission estimated. They believed that it would be possible to accommodate 50 per cent of the present population as full-time farmers, but the King William's Town experience indicates that this may have been over-optimistic. In 1955 the African areas in the King William's Town district were 115 000 hectares with a population of 68 000. There were estimated to be about 11 400 families, but detailed planning indicates that ultimately there can never be more than 3 400 full economic units. Thus the land could be expected to give support to only a little more than one-third of the existing population, and almost two-thirds of the population *and all natural increase in the future* would have to find employment in secondary and tertiary activities. No amount of agricultural reform or improvement will alone solve the problem of poverty in the African areas. Illustrative of this is the fact that a single factory, the Good Hope Textile Mills, is likely in the near future to support a large number of families than the whole agricultural potential of the district can ever hope to support.

Initially the response of the African peasants was one of hostility and mistrust in most areas. The opposition appeared to come from two very different groups – the ultra-conservative peasant and the intelligentsia. It is a great misfortune that agricultural rehabilitation has come to be associated in the minds of the intelligentsia with the wider policy of separate development to which many are resolutely opposed. Leaders who should be whole-heartedly behind the rehabilitation schemes oppose them because of this political association. Where the schemes have been tactfully presented and official leadership has been sympathetic and patient, many of the rehabilitation programmes have made good progress. In these cases there appears to be growing support from the more progressive farmers, and indeed it is difficult to see how it could be otherwise because the benefits of better agricultural practice are obvious to all genuine farmers.

The difficult and intractable task of transforming a subsistence economy into a more productive type of agriculture is one which confronts practically the whole continent of Africa. Here in the Republic disparity between the traditional and the modern market-oriented farming is most clearly demonstrated.[52] The steady increases in productivity on farms owned by whites contrast vividly with the retrogression in African areas. Certain extenuating circumstances are pleaded. One, which is *not* valid, is that the reserves are inferior land. The contrary is true, because for the most part they lie in the high-rainfall areas of South Africa, and under good management they could be highly productive. Of greater validity is the argument that the unequal distribution of land established by the 1913 Land Act, together with restrictions on movement into the industrial areas, has given rise to severe overpopulation in the reserves. This statement is certainly true, but the deduction often made from this by Africans and others, that the solution is to take land from the whites and give it to Africans, demands careful scrutiny. Under present conditions this would mean taking land from people who, by and large, are using it efficiently and are conserving its productivity, and giving it to those who would use it inefficiently and eventually destroy it. Such a step would be a disaster for all South Africans irrespective of the colour of their skins. What is really needed is to train a limited number of Africans to become good farmers and to give them adequate land-holdings and access to the necessary capital equipment, and to remove the others from the land. It is not possible in a modern community to provide everyone, regardless of his aptitude, with cattle and a field. This change, however, will necessitate a major social revolution for the Africans in the reserves. The success, or failure, of the present programme of rehabilitation of the African areas will be determined by the ability to find alternative non-agricultural employment for those inevitably displaced from the land.

The policy in recent years has been to establish non-agricultural villages or settlement camps for those for whom no agricultural land is available, and the problem has been aggravated by the influx of

---

[52] See also a detailed study conducted in Rhodesia, M. Yudelman, *Africans on the Land.*

large numbers of additional Africans removed from the urban
centres. The mistake has often been made of bringing in the people
there before necessary housing and other amenities have been
provided and conditions at places such as Limehill, Ilinge, Dimbaza,
Chalumna and Mosgat have evoked much criticism in the daily
press and in more substantial studies. Even if living conditions in
such places are improved the question of their economic viability
remains. In most cases there are no employment opportunities in
the neighbourhood, and the only alternative is for the able-bodied
men to go as migrant workers to the large industrial cities, leaving
their wives and families behind. Attempts being made to establish
industries nearer to the African areas are discussed under industrial
location in chapter 6, but progress has been slow and employment
opportunities lag far behind the urgent needs of the people in these
areas.

4 Men of Two Worlds: African Migratory Labour

Reference was made in the last chapter to the fact that low productivity in the African tribal areas forces large numbers of men to migrate to the industrial centres to earn money with which to supplement their families' incomes in the reserves. These migratory workers circulate continuously between the subsistence economy of their tribal areas and the mines and industries which form the core of the modern exchange economy of the nation. The migratory labour system thus has an important impact both upon agriculture in the reserves and upon the mining and manufacturing industries in which workers find wage-paid employment. This chapter comes between that on agriculture and those on mining and manufacturing, to emphasize the ambivalent character of the migratory system.

Although much has been written about migrant labour in South Africa, and certain aspects of it have received detailed consideration, the magnitude of the phenomenon as a whole and the full implications of it as it affects the national economy were seldom viewed in their entirety.[1] The migratory labour system can be seen as both a symptom and a cause of most of the economic, social and political problems which beset our community: and this perpetual mass movement of people is a dramatic illustration of our failure over the past century to create a unified and coherent economy.

The nature of the phenomenon

Migration of workers has occurred in many countries, and it is a sign that there exists some difference, real or imagined, between the

---

[1] The most notable exception was the *Report of the Native Laws Commission, 1946–8*, U.G. 28/1948. See especially pp. 33–47. More recent studies conducted by some church and other organizations have drawn public attention to this matter and an excellent review of the whole subject appears in Francis Wilson's book, *Migrant Labour in South Africa*.

economic opportunities in different regions. It is a symptom of imbalance in the rate of economic development. Workers tend to move from areas where the market value of their labour is low to areas where it is higher. The cause of the higher marginal revenue productivity of labour in certain areas may be the presence there of natural resources, or of greater applications of capital or more advanced entrepreneurship – or it may be a combination of all three of these. The movement of the workers tends to bring about a more efficient distribution of labour, and movement is likely to continue until the original imbalance has been rectified, and an optimum combination of factors of production achieved. Although initially it may be only the younger or more enterprising who migrate, they settle in the new area and make their homes there, and thus a permanent shift of population occurs. So it was in the industrial revolution in Britain, and other countries have experienced a similar flow to the towns as they in turn have become industrialized.

The process of adjustment need not necessarily be brought about solely by the movement of workers, for sometimes there is a reverse movement of capital and enterprise attracted to the less developed areas by the prospect of cheaper labour there, as appears to be taking place in certain southern states in the U.S.A. and in southern Italy. Since 1960 the government in South Africa has offered inducements to industrialists to locate their factories nearer to the main sources of African labour and to bring about greater dispersal of manufacturing activity at present located in four main areas – the southern Transvaal, Durban, Cape Town and Port Elizabeth. But, however it comes about, the movements generally tend to bring about a balance or a state of equilibrium, which once achieved removes the tendency to further migration.

What is generally known as migratory labour in South Africa is, however, a very different phenomenon. It, too, is a movement of workers from areas of low productivity to those where the employment opportunities appear to be better, but the majority of the workers who migrate do not make their permanent homes in the industrial areas. They merely work there for a period, and then return to their tribal homes in the reserves. In this case there is not a permanent shift of population. When one man has completed his period of work he returns home, and his place is taken by another migrant. There is thus no tendency towards equilibrium, and the migrations continue in perpetuity. Mass migrations have been going on for almost a century, and their magnitude has increased with the growth of the industrial centres and the increasing poverty and pressure of population in the reserves. No relief has come in the other direction, for the African areas have as yet attracted little industry of their own. Capital and entrepreneurship come mainly from the whites, and the fact that the African areas are African *reserves*, with severe limitations upon white ownership of land and rights of domicile, has tended to keep them in their undeveloped state.

Moreover the existence of a market is a *sine qua non* for economic expansion; but prior to the contact with the world economy, the indigenous African communities in southern Africa were subsistence economies. In a subsistence economy, where each household produces everything for itself, there is no possibility of specialization. The real impact of the world economy upon southern Africa came only with the discovery of diamonds and gold. Kimberley and the Witwatersrand acted as a magnet attracting international capital for the exploitation of the mineral deposits, and drawing labour from far and wide. The economic impact came from abroad and was not an indigenous and gradual evolution from a subsistence economy to one of specialization and market exchange. Moreover, it was highly concentrated in particular areas, and there has arisen a most remarkable disparity in the rate of economic growth between different parts of the country.

The problems resulting from this economic disparity have been intensified by the great cultural disparity between the whites and the black Africans. It is true that with contact the disparity tends to be reduced, but the impact of western culture upon individuals exhibits great diversity. At first it is tempting to divide the Africans in to two broad classes: the westernized, detribalized, urban dwellers, who have broken from the tribal economy and have been drawn into the orbit of the modern world; and those who still belong essentially to tribal way of life. No such clear-cut division is, however, possible, because there are almost infinite gradations between the two extremes. At the one end of the scale are those with several generations of civilized contacts behind them, who have come to accept not only the externals of civilized living, but to apprehend and embody within themselves its intellectual foundations and inner spiritual values. At the other end of the scale there are those who still remain largely within the narrow confines of their small-scale primitive culture: but these are now becoming few. The vast majority have assimilated western culture to a greater or lesser extent, or have rejected in varying degree their tribal beliefs and practices. Some there are who have accepted many of the conventions of civilized living and at the same time retained much of their tribal heritage, so that their world has in it both Christianity and tribal superstition, modern medicine and magic.[2] Others have rejected or lost their tribal morality and traditional beliefs, but have not been able effectively to replace them.

It must also be realized that there are hundreds of thousands of men who alternate throughout their lives between two worlds, and a single individual may be firmly established both in his tribal world and in the modern industrial world. Such are the migrant workers who spend the whole of their working lives circulating between a primitive tribal society, in which they were born and reared, and the industrial centres where they earn the major part of their livelihood. At home they are primitive agriculturists or pastoralists conforming to the traditional economic pattern and dwelling in the social environment of their tribe: in the cities, with their wage labour, modern factories, many-storied buildings and electric trains, they are part of the world economy; so that in their lifetime they are constantly alternating between the traditional tribal context and membership of an industrial proletariat. These are the 'men of two worlds'.

Migrant labour has usually been studied from a partial viewpoint – either from the rural end or from the urban end. When looked at from the rural end, it appears as the continuous exodus of temporary migrants, which, being highly selective of the young adult males, gives rise to problems of declining productivity in the reserves. From the urban end it appears as a continuous influx of temporary unskilled workers, giving rise to problems of training, lack of continuity of employment, high labour turnover and the general instability and low productivity of the labour force. From the administrative viewpoint there is a continuous problem of handling these mass migrations, which has led to an intricate system of passes, reference books and all the machinery of labour bureaux and influx control. Few attempts have been made to see the phenomenon as a whole, and in consequence governmental policy has often been at cross purposes with itself.

---

[2] Monica Hunter, *Reaction to Conquest*, pp. 455–6, speaks of the use of magic in town to secure a job and avert unemployment.

In an attempt to present a wider account let us take a fictitious individual,[3] John Mvalo, and sketch in outline his life history. John, conceived during one of his father's visits home from the mines, was born in 1906 at Chatha near Keiskammahoek. Before John's birth his father had returned to the mines, and the first time he saw his son was in 1908, when the boy was two years old. Thenceforward his father was a mysterious figure in the boy's life, returning at intervals for six months or so at a time. When his father was away the family often went to live with an uncle or grandparents.[4] The child was surrounded mainly by women and children and old men.[5] When he was six years old his mother took him with her to the trading store where for the first time he saw a white man. His parents were pagan and he never went to school; but he learned to manage cattle, to fight with sticks, to shoot birds and to snare hares. From the older boys he heard much about life in town, and in 1922 when he was 16 years old his father, who was at home at the time, said he could go to work in East London. He travelled there with a friend from Chatha, who had worked in East London before. They both lived with his mother's sister, who had a shack in the West Bank location. He was there for two years, during which time he had six different jobs. He never stayed long in any one job, and had periods of unemployment between each – gardener, golf caddie, dock labourer (but the work was too heavy), messenger and casual labourer. He then got into some trouble with the police and returned home to Chatha. His father, who was at home, said it was time for him to become a man. So he attended the initiation school and was circumcised in July 1924. After this was over he went to work on the mines from September 1924 to July 1925 and then came home for six months. He made five further trips to work on the mines with visits home between each. When in 1931 he returned home from his sixth visit to the mines, he had some money saved, and his father helped him with cattle for *ikhasi*,[6] so he was able to marry. He stayed at Chatha for two years, seeing the birth

---

[3] Although a fictitious person, John Mvalo is based upon a study of some 340 employment histories collected in the *Keiskammahoek Rural Survey* (1950–1) and the *Border Regional Survey* (1955–60).

[4] This constant change in the composition of households was noted in the *Keiskammahoek Rural Survey*, vol. 2, by Hobart Houghton and Walton, p. 53.

[5] It was found in Keiskammahoek that to each square mile of land (259 hectares) in the reserves there were some 53 children and aged persons to 28 adult workers, of whom only 9 were men: Hobart Houghton and Walton, p. 139.

[6] Cattle paid as bride price.

of his eldest child, but money was needed for the support of his family, and the trader would give no further credit, so he went off to work again. This time he went to Cape Town and worked in a dairy delivering milk. Several of his friends were there, as there was a regular connexion between his village and this particular firm. He stayed there three years before returning home, but he sent money back to his wife regularly. He made several further visits to Cape Town, where he often worked for the same dairy; but he once had a job as a domestic servant, and once as a cleaner at the post office. His next job was at the Iscor steel works in Pretoria. This was in 1942, when the war brought him good wages. Then he had a job at the Drill Hall, in Johannesburg, in 1945. He came home in 1947. He was now over 40 years old. His wife had borne him four sons (one of whom had died in infancy) and two daughters. Although he was still pagan, he insisted that his children went to school because he wished them to learn to read and write. He had now eight head of cattle and ten sheep. His eldest son was 15 years old and would soon be able to go out to work, so John thought he would stay at home. In 1948, however, there was a serious drought in the Ciskei, six of his cattle died and the mealie crop failed completely. He set off to work again – this time to Port Elizabeth, where he found employment in a newspaper office, moving rolls of paper. He worked there for four years with two short visits home, but in 1953 he returned home to settle there permanently. He was then 47 years old, and his eldest son of 21 years was doing his second stint on the gold mines.

Of his working life from the age of 16 to 47 (thirty-one years) 36 per cent of his time was spent at home and 64 per cent in employment away. He had had thirty-four different jobs, and the average length of a job had been forty-seven weeks.[7] He began work as a youth in East London, and found it difficult to hold down a job for long. After circumcision he went to work on the mines, but when he had become more accustomed to town ways and was a settled married man, he turned to the more lucrative employment in trade and industry. All these features in his life history are typical of many. No period in prison has been included in John's history,

---

[7] These figures are based upon the averages of 193 employment histories, see D. Hobart Houghton (ed.), *Economic Development in a Plural Society*, p. 317. The Tomlinson Commission found the proportion of the working life spent in employment away from home to be 62 per cent: see Summary, p. 96.

and in this respect he is perhaps not truly representative, for many Africans experience it.[8]

THE ROLE OF THE MIGRANT WORKER IN THE NATIONAL ECONOMY

It is not easy to determine how many migrant workers there are, because in spite of all the machinery of registration and control, there are no official statistics of internal migration, and the periodic censuses merely give a person's location on the night of the census. According to estimates made by the Tomlinson Commission, there were 503 000 males temporarily absent from the Bantu areas at the time of the 1951 census.[9] They represented about 40 per cent of the males between the ages of 15 and 65. But as the Commission rightly points out, practically every able-bodied African man in the reserves goes out to work in industrial areas. The total pool of migrant workers from the Bantu areas of the Republic is therefore in the neighbourhood of 1 140 000. In addition there were estimated to be some 420 000 migrant workers from adjacent countries working in the Republic in 1951,[10] and, assuming the same ratio between the numbers employed at any time and the pool from which they are drawn, they must represent a further 1 000 000 men. Thus John Mvalo is representative of some 2 140 000 of his fellow migrant workers. Over two million men spend their lives circulating between industrial employment and their tribal subsistence economy.

How are these migrant workers employed? In the first place they are all in some small measure peasant farmers, but the amount of productive work in farming performed by them in the reserves would seem to be very small. Most of the agricultural labour is done by women and children.[11]

At the industrial end the gold-mining industry is the vortex of the migratory system.

'They come on foot, on horseback, on bicycles, by dug-out canoe, by lake and river steamers, in lorries, by train and some even by air. They come from as far afield as 2 000 miles. They come from all

---

[8] Convictions of African males in 1955 were 210 029. *Statistical Year Book, 1965*, p. G–3.

[9] Tomlinson Report (Summary), p. 53.

[10] Tomlinson Report (Summary), p. 40.

[11] Hobart Houghton and Walton, pp. 136–49.

points of the compass – from the peaceful hills of the Transkei, from the lion country of the Bechuanaland bush, down the broad reaches of the Zambesi, from the tropical shores of Lake Nyasa and the mountain fastnesses of Basutoland. They come, too, in their thousands from the hills and valleys of Portuguese East Africa, from the rocky uplands of Sekukuniland, the tangled swamp country of the Okavango delta and the green fields of Swaziland. From these far corners of southern Africa men from more than 100 different tribes are attracted every year to the Witwatersrand by the magnet of the mining industry.'[12]

It is probably the most fantastic labour set-up of any industry in the world. Imagine an industry located in Paris drawing some 340 000 workers from as far afield as England, Scotland, Norway, Poland, Germany, Italy and Spain, and returning them to their homes once every year or eighteen months, and you have a European equivalent. The mining industry as a whole employs 500 000 non-white workers and the vast majority of these are migrants.

Manufacturing industry and commerce also employ a large number of migrant workers, but there is an almost total blank in our information as to how many of the 800 000 Africans employed in industry, commerce and other urban employment are migrants and how many are urbanized. There is urgent need for more information on this vital point, but some satisfactory definition of a migrant is an essential prerequisite. In East London[13] a random sample of the total African male population showed that:

(a) 30,4 per cent were unmarried or widowed;
(b) 24,4 per cent were married and had their wives in East London;
(c) 45,2 per cent were married, but their wives were living elsewhere.

If it is assumed that all in category (c) were migrant workers and that two-thirds in category (a) were also migrants, then migrant workers would constitute about 65 per cent of the adult African males in East London. However, when the criterion selected to distinguish the migrant was whether or not the man sent money away to relatives

---

[12] *Mining Survey*, Transvaal and O.F.S. Chamber of Mines, June 1951.
[13] Hobart Houghton (ed.), p. 239

elsewhere, it was found that 80 per cent of the males in East London claimed to be sending money away. There may be no real discrepancy here, because many cases were found where both husband and wife were working in East London but their children had been left at home in the reserves with relatives. It serves to show, however, how difficult it is to define the migrant worker. East London is near the Transkei and may not be representative. Perhaps the proportion of urbanized Africans may be higher in other industrial areas. A large textile factory in Uitenhage found in 1962 that 100 per cent of its employees lived with their wives and families in the town.

The third main field of employment of the migrant workers is in farming in white areas. Practice differs widely in different parts of the country. In many parts the African farm worker lives with his family upon the farm, and has lived there often for generations. In other parts the white farmers rely extensively upon migrant male labourers, who come to work on contract. The Tomlinson Commission estimated that there were some 210 000 extra-Republican Africans employed in agriculture.[14] They would presumably all be migrant workers. There is, however, no information about the number of Africans from the Republic who are migrant workers on white farms. This number is not likely to be very large.

In summary then it can be said that migrant labourers account for about 400 000 of the workers in mines, over 200 000 of the agricultural workers, and a large, but unknown, proportion of the workers in industry, commerce and transport.

SOME CONSEQUENCES OF THE MIGRANT LABOUR SYSTEM

Quantitative waste

The first and obvious consequence is the extremely inefficient and wasteful character of the system. The Tomlinson Commission attempted to estimate the loss of manpower involved in travel, in periods of rest or unemployment, and in the relatively unproductive time spent in the reserves.[15]

'Thus out of a total annual potential of 1 140 000 man-years (1 year's labour rendered by 1 man) available in the Bantu areas (or somewhat less, if 2 to 3 weeks' leave per year is allowed for), only

[14] Tomlinson Report (Summary), p. 41.
[15] Tomlinson Report (Summary), p. 96.

480 000 man-years are economically used, and of this latter total, only 433 000 man-years are applied in paid employment in the non-Bantu areas. *This means that there are always on the average 600 000 man-years of labour available which are not economically applied.*'

Of course it is possible to criticize the details of this estimate; but, nevertheless, the fact remains that it is probably of the right order of magnitude. Moreover, it applies only to African migrants from within the Republic, and if the extra-Republic migrants are included, the waste involved in the system would come to almost one million man-years per annum.

Then there is the cost of transporting these 923 000 migrants[16] to and from their homes. Even on the assumption that their homes are on the average only 500 kilometres from where they work and that their average stint is eighteen months, this would amount to about 310 000 man-kilometres per annum in addition to their normal daily journey to work.

Inability to acquire skills

Perhaps even more important than the waste of man-hours and the cost of transport is the effect of the system upon the quality of that labour which actually finds its way to the mines, factories and farms. There are many aspects to this matter of quality, but the first to be noted is that from its very nature the migrant system tends to inhibit the acquisition of skills and tends to condemn the workers to being in perpetuity merely undifferentiated units of unskilled labour. The intermittent character of their employment means that just when they are becoming proficient at a particular job and of real value to their employer they leave to return home. Next time they go out to work they may find a different job in a different industry – probably in a different town. They learn their new job, and then leave it to repeat the process of going home and finding a new job. They tend to become jacks of all trades and masters of none. Moreover, if they feel themselves to be merely birds of passage, they have little incentive to excel, to acquire skill or to make a permanent career for themselves with a particular firm. They merely 'take their wages and are gone'.

[16] 503 000 from Bantu areas of the Republic, and 420 000 migrants from abroad, see Tomlinson Report (Summary) p. 96.

There are however exceptions, and within the unpropitious framework of the migratory system one sometimes finds surprising continuity of employment with a single firm. Certain definite attachments develop between a group (probably of kinsmen) in a village in the reserves and a particular firm in an urban centre. A group of men take it in turn to work for this firm. Each man will go back to this firm after his spell at home, and sometimes a man has been working intermittently for the same firm for fifteen or twenty years. The more intelligent employers encourage this, condone the absences, and make provision for steady promotion. In these cases great loyalty to the firm develops in the migrant workers. But the stricter enforcement of urban influx control is imperilling these arrangements, for a man who has worked in, say, Cape Town for several years for the same firm suddenly finds he is no longer permitted to enter the area because there is a labour surplus. This aspect of influx control has aroused great opposition among both migrant workers and their employers. Employers affirm that it prevents them from getting the type of labour they require and forces them to take wholly unsuitable labour from the bureau.[17] One employer said: 'They say I must get "a boy" from the bureau, but I don't want "a boy"; I want Sam Kopo who has worked for my firm for eight years; but they say he is redundant.'

Labour turnover

This leads on to the whole question of labour turnover in industry. The Tomlinson Commission stated.[18]

'Large firms in Johannesburg (apart from the mines) are credited with having a labour turnover of 117 per cent per year, or a replacement period of 10 months. The shortness of this period may be due, however, to the fact that the results were obtained 12 or 15 years ago, when the turnover of labour was more rapid than at present and war-time conditions were more conducive to change.'

But two later surveys confirm what are presumably R. H. Smith's findings.[19] One in East London gives an average labour turnover

[17] For a fuller discussion of this see Hobart Houghton (ed.), p. 302.

[18] Tomlinson Report (Summary), p. 95.

[19] R. H. Smith, in *Native Urban Employment*, a study of Johannesburg employment records by Industrial Research Section, University of Witwatersrand, 1948.

of 119 per cent per annum in 1956[20] and the other in Cape Town gives the even higher figure of 138 per cent per annum.[21]

The investigation in East London revealed great differences between the labour turnover of one firm and another, and between the length of continuous service of one employee and another. Firms engaged in construction (where from the nature of the work a higher labour turnover than in manufacturing was to be expected) varied from 96 to 600 per cent per annum. In manufacturing the turnover of male African employees varied from 48 per cent per annum in the firm with the most stable labour to 204 per cent per annum.[22] Viewed from the angle of length of service of employees, the disparities were even greater. Interest was aroused in this matter by the fact that in spite of a high average turnover of African labour, many of the better firms stated that they found their African labour remarkably stable. The investigation revealed that over one-third of all African adult males had been in their existing jobs for three years or more – a remarkable stable element in the labour force. At the other end of the scale 10 per cent of adult males were unemployed at the time of the survey, and a further 16 per cent had been in their present job for less than three months.[23] These two groups together account for over a quarter of the whole, and instances were found of individuals having as many as eight different jobs in a single year with periods of unemployment in between. It is the instability of this group of workers which brings up the over-all average labour turnover.

One might have expected the stable group to consist of the permanently urbanized workers with their homes in town, and the unstable group to be the migrant workers. This however was not the case: stable and unstable workers were found in both the urbanized and the migrant groups. The inability to hold down a steady job seems to be largely a matter of the individual's character, and many in the unstable groups appear to be virtually unemployable. The unstable groups consisted largely of young unmarried men, both urban and migrant; whereas the stable group was composed of

[20] Hobart Houghton (ed.), pp. 314, 315.

[21] Sheila T. van der Horst, 'A Note on Native Labour Turnover and the Structure of the Labour Force in the Cape Peninsula', *S.A.J.E.*, vol. 25 no. 4, December 1957.

[22] Hobart Houghton (ed.), pp. 313, 314.

[23] Hobart Houghton (ed.), p. 315.

older married men, and both urban and migrant workers were represented in approximately the proportions in which they appear in the total labour force. It would seem therefore that labour instability and high turnover cannot be *directly* attributed to the migratory system.

There is, however, ground for believing that the migratory system is *indirectly* the cause of much labour instability among both the urban and the migrant workers. This operates in three ways. Firstly the very existence of the migratory system and its survival for nearly a century have set a certain pattern of intermittent employment. The tradition of steady regular labour, with only a limited annual holiday, has not arisen even among many permanently settled in town. The young urban worker sees his fellow-workers from the country go home for periodic holidays, and decides to do likewise. The reasons advanced by urban workers for leaving a job reflects this attitude, and 'tired of working', 'wanted a rest' were commonly given.

The second way in which the migratory system indirectly causes labour instability is that it is a powerful factor in the disruption of social and family life. The presence of large numbers of unattached males in the urban areas makes for prostitution, crime and general social disintegration, and the prolonged absence of hundreds of thousands of fathers from the reserves leads to a lack of discipline in the home. All these factors make for unstable labour, particularly among the younger workers.

The migratory system also has an indirect influence upon labour stability and productivity through its effect upon management, but this merits a subsection to itself.

Effect of the migratory system upon labour management

With certain outstanding exceptions the general management of African factory labour is slipshod and inefficient in the extreme. This is a direct consequence of the migratory system, because the majority of employers have come to regard the African worker as not worth taking trouble over. They come and go, and when one leaves there is another to take his place. The better employers, who select their labour with care, give adequate supervision and training and seek to make the best of the human material with which they are dealing, generally report themselves to be wholly satisfied with the quality of their labour, and their labour turnover is low. The majority of employers on the other hand report adversely upon their workers and experience high labour turnover. One such employer, who complained bitterly about this and the general inefficiency, was asked whether he had not tried some method of selection. He replied that selection was useless, because 'the workers come and go, and it is just the luck of the draw'. He recruits all and sundry, and sacks those who do not work satisfactorily. His complaint was that even the good ones did not stay long! Such an employer soon acquires a bad reputation, and he attracts only the least efficient workers who cannot find employment elsewhere. Bad management draws bad labour. The general instability caused by the migrant system has led the majority of the employers to accept unstable and inefficient African labour as inevitable and in the nature of things. That this is not the case is clearly demonstrated in the experience of better firms. The largest employer of African labour in East London has an excellent reputation for careful selection, sound training, adequate supervision and sympathetic understanding of its African workers. It draws the best type of worker, has a low turnover and has a large number seeking employment with the firm. Those Africans employed by this firm are regarded as fortunate by their fellows. Such a firm has an excellent effect upon the quality of labour, and benefits not only itself but the labour force generally, because it helps to rehabilitate the workers. Many of its workers are habitual migrants, and the stricter enforcement of influx control by the urban authorities hits it hard. Unfortunately there are relatively few such firms, and the bad employers are lowering the efficiency of the labour forces and magnifying the instability inherent in the migratory system, and in some measure creating conditions in which delinquency will thrive.

Must the migratory system continue?

When the desire for the products of modern industry was first awakened in the tribal African people and when Kimberley and the Witwatersrand provided an insatiable market for their labour, it was perhaps natural that the young men should go forth. The primary motive was economic, but there were other incentives, as I. Schapera has pointed out,[24] such as the desire for adventure, boredom with tribal life and the desire to escape from its ties. The migratory system acted as a cushion to the full force of the economic impact of the

[24] I. Schapera, *Migrant Labour and Tribal Life.*

western world upon a primitive subsistence economy. But as the Fagan Commission so aptly pointed out, 'a cushion' is not the only appropriate figure of speech. 'The idea has also been expressed to us in the form of another simile: that of a bridge. But a bridge is intended to be crossed, not to serve as a permanent abode.'[25] It was a natural initial phase, but one would have expected that in time it would have given place to a more permanent shift of population. It is astonishing that a system which is manifestly so inefficient and wasteful and so destructive of human values should have persisted for almost a century. What then are the reasons for its growth and survival?

From the rural areas the forces impelling migration are becoming increasingly urgent. The pressure of population upon the primitive means of subsistence is getting greater with natural increase and declining agricultural productivity, and the tribal African's wants are expanding and becoming more diversified as his contact with the modern world is strengthened. It is estimated that about 45–50 per cent of the cash income of the reserves is derived from the earnings of migrant workers.[26] J. L. Sadie sums up the situation in these words:[27]

'As the population of the Reserves increased and their primitive agriculture could no longer feed them all, some of them could migrate on a temporary or permanent basis, to the neighbouring "White" parts of the country where ample opportunities for earning a livelihood already existed. The necessity for creating new sources of income on their own initiative did not arise. The position boils down to the economic domination of a lower by a higher form of industrial civilization.'

The last sentence contains a clue to many problems of the reserves, for had it not been for the adjacent exchange economy of the whites the population in the reserves would either have been kept in check by mortality or there would have been an economic revolution away from the low-productivity subsistence economy towards more productive employment of the available resources. Indeed the possibility of escape by migration has probably inhibited develop-

[25] *Report of the Native Laws Commission, 1946–8* (Fagan), U.G. 28/1948, p. 43.

[26] The Tomlinson Commission gave a percentage of 46,5, see p. 99 of the Summary Report; and the Keiskammahoek Survey gave 49,9 per cent of cash income as derived from migrant labour, Hobart Houghton and Walton, p. 47.

[27] J. L. Sadie, 'The Native Reserves of the Union – Industrial Areas of the Future', *Finance and Trade Review*, vol. 1 no. 5, July 1954.

ment. A Xhosa peasant, when asked why he did not grow some cash crop, replied that the black people grew mealies to eat, but if they needed money they went out to earn it in the towns.[28] Any successful plan for the agricultural rehabilitation of the reserves will have to substitute cash-crop production for the subsistence (or sub-subsistence) concept of farming.

From the urban end the forces perpetuating migrant labour are no less insistent. The mining, industry, transport, commerce and agriculture of the so-called 'white' areas are all based upon large number of unskilled workers, the majority of which must be recruited through the migrant system – for the immediate future at all events.

A certain amount of family movement has taken place, and many of the urban workers now live permanently in town with their families. But this process has not been sufficient to reduce the flow of temporary migrants. There are strong resistances to the permanent settlement of the African people in urban areas – resistance from the whites and from the Africans themselves.

From the white side there has been a fairly consistent policy of discouraging permanent urban settlement of Africans. Initially when the life of the gold mines was problematical there may have been some wisdom in this, but later, when it became clear that the Witwatersrand was to be a permanent large industrial area, the migratory system was firmly established. The notion had taken root that the towns are reserved for whites and that Africans come only as temporary workers.

On the African side too there were resistances to family migration.[29] This was partly due to the fact that the migratory system and lack of town planning had made their quarters into slums in which living conditions more closely resembled the worst type of mining camp than a settled urban community. African men often say that the towns are good places in which to earn money, but bad places in which to rear a family.

There is also a strong conservative element in the reserves, which clings tenaciously to the tribal practices and is averse to urban life.[30]

---

[28] Hobart Houghton and Walton, p. 154.

[29] D. K. Chisiza, *Africa – What Lies Ahead*, p. 37, makes the point that to feel at home in an urban area an African should take his *whole* family with him. 'Unfortunately it includes parents, uncles, aunts, brothers, sisters, nephews and cousins', and this is not easy to arrange.

[30] For a detailed study of this see P. Mayer, *Townsmen or Tribesmen*.

Perhaps the strongest desire is that of cattle owning, for cattle have traditionally played an important role in tribal life; but it is not possible to keep cattle in an urban community. Although there are some Africans who would welcome permanent urban residence, if living conditions there were improved and if they could acquire security of tenure and were made to feel that they had a permanent place in the city, others would undoubtedly be reluctant to surrender their holding in the reserve and forsake the traditional way of life. Perhaps the migratory system reinforces this by insulating the family group from the full impact of modern life.

H. R. Burrows commented upon this in a memorandum he submitted to the Fagan Commission.[31]

'Though the traditional structure of African family and tribal life is disintegrating because of its inadequacy when brought into close contact with the developing exchange economy with its implicit wage system, its breakdown is being protracted by the system of segregation and migrant labour. The social disadvantages of sudden disruption have been avoided at the cost of delaying specialization. As a result, there is today no self-supporting peasant economy, no permanent agricultural labour force, and no stable urban population.'

In view of the conditions in both towns and reserves, the migratory system cannot be said to give the best of both worlds – it would seem to be the worst of both worlds that the Africans get – yet it does enable the conservative elements to go on having their two worlds and to postpone the final abandonment of their traditional past. Tightening influx control is restricting the ease of movement and is forcing some to opt for permanent urban life. This result was probably not foreseen by those who devised the legislation. Men are afraid to go back to the reserves lest they be prevented from returning to their jobs in town. Others, who have acquired urban skills, find themselves excluded from the industrial areas, and in the absence of any suitable employment in the reserves these men are unemployed and a source of disaffection in the African areas.

Migratory labour cannot suddenly be abolished because the very survival of both white and black depend upon it, but it should be recognized for what it is – an evil canker at the heart of our whole society, wasteful of labour, destructive ambition, a wrecker of homes and a symptom of our fundamental failure to create a

[31] *Report of the Native Laws Commission, 1946–8* (Fagan), U.G. 28/1948, p. 23.

coherent and progressive economic society. But a realistic view should be taken and it must be recognized that for the forseeable future some migrant labour is likely to remain. This is particularly true of the mining industry, for the complete removal of the families of the 500 000 mine workers to town would pose great economic and social problems. Moreover, the mining industry employs mostly the younger unmarried men, it facilitates their movements to and fro, and it houses and feeds them. Indeed it provides something of a bridge for the young African workers between their rural environment and urban life. It is the older man, often employed in secondary or tertiary activities, and trying unaided to make his own way backwards and forwards, who feels the full weight of the influx-control legislation. Every effort should be made to establish settled urban communities with security of tenure for those workers in secondary industry and their families both in the older industrial centres and in any new towns that may arise as a result of the policy of decentralization of industry. Similarly in the reserves the aim should be to encourage stability and full-time employment in farming – on a cash and not on a subsistence basis – or in new industries to be developed there. Meanwhile, the rural towns that are being established to house those necessarily displaced by the agricultural reforms should be carefully watched. They are in danger of being merely dormitories for the families of migrant workers, and adverse social conditions can easily arise, especially if the earning of the migrants are not adequate to provide for the *full* support of the families who will no longer be able to augment their incomes by subsistence farming. Finally, the new industries suggested for the periphery of the reserves must be so planned and sited as not to perpetuate the migrant system.

Unless these things are done, there is the danger that although the evils of the migratory system may be removed from those who are to become full-time farmers, the full burden will fall upon those who are displaced from the land, for whom perpetual migrancy will become the normal way of life, unmitigated by ownership of cattle and possession of land in the reserves.

Even when these reforms have taken effect, there will be some residue of migrant labour, and every effort should be made to lessen the evils of the system by rationalizing influx control legislation so as to facilitate the movement of the industrious worker. If the system must continue let it be as efficient and as humane as possible.

The aim of this chapter is not to review the South African economy as a whole, but merely to focus attention upon a particular institution. This institution is, however, a symptom of deep underlying weaknesses in the whole national structure. Perhaps the most insidious effect of the migrant system as a whole is that it perpetuates poverty, and prevents the raising of the consumption standards of the mass of our population. As long as this wasteful system continues and the low productivity of the mass of our workers is unchanged, it will not be possible for the 25 000 000 people of South Africa to be an effective market, nor can they enjoy the vastly greater output which it is within their capacity to produce.

Two million men perpetually on the move – men of two worlds, lacking the feeling of belonging anywhere – perhaps only the eye of the artist sees things in their wholeness, and *Cry, the Beloved Country*[32] and *Blanket Boy's Moon*[33] say more than the economist or sociologist can ever hope to say.

[32] Alan Paton, *Cry, the Beloved Country*.
[33] P. Lanham and A. S. Mopeli-Paulus, *Blanket Boy's Moon*.

5

Mining

Mining is today an activity of supreme importance in the South African economy, and it has held this position for almost one hundred years.[1] In 1974, the value of output from all types of mining was R3 928 million, and over 600 000 persons were engaged in it. Of these totals gold mining alone yielded R2 619 million and employed 370 000 workers, while all other types of mining produced R1 309 million, and employed 239 000 workers.[2] The total paid out in wages by all types of mining was R572 million in 1973.[3]

It is a large industry by any standards, and the Transvaal and Orange Free State concentration probably represents the greatest value of mining output found anywhere in the world in an area of similar size. In the South African economy it is truly a colossus. For sixty years South Africa has been the world's greatest producer of gold, accounting today for about 70 per cent of the total output in the world, excluding the U.S.S.R. Of diamonds, chrome and asbestos, South Africa is the second largest producer; and, although its production of iron is as yet small by comparison with some of the largest producers, its reserves of iron ore are exceeded by only Brazil and India, and coal reserves by only four other countries.

The mining industry is expanding rapidly at the present time. In table 13 of the statistical appendix it is seen that from 1965 to 1974 total output of mining increased in value from R1 153 million to R3 928 million an increase of over 200 per cent in the decade. Further large increases in gold output are considered unlikely, but the prospects for rapid growth in the output of other minerals is excellent.

---

[1] The value of annual output (gold: other mining: total) from 1911 is given in table 13, and the quantity and value of major minerals produced in 1973 is given in table 14.

[2] *Bulletin of Statistics*, June, 1975, p. 5.3

[3] *Bulletin of Statistics*, June, 1975. p. 2.3.

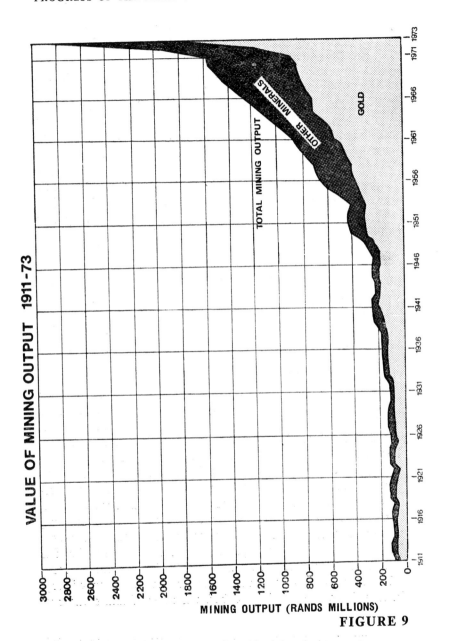

VALUE OF MINING OUTPUT 1911-73

MINING OUTPUT (RANDS MILLIONS)

FIGURE 9

The development of mining falls into a number of more or less clearly defined phases. The first was the diamond period. Although gold had been discovered at various places in the 1850s the first mineral discovery of real commercial value was that of diamonds. The first diamond was picked up near Hopetown in 1867 and by 1870 a diamond-mining rush to Griqualand West was well under way. The spectacular finds there attracted prospectors, diggers and speculators from many parts of the world. Unlike alluvial diamonds, these were found in the Kimberlite or 'blue ground' of ancient volcanic pipes. Mining was at first undertaken by a large number of small producers using spade-and-bucket techniques, but these soon proved inadequate. Improved techniques, consolidation into large mining companies with adequate capital resources, and above all the recognition that here was no flash-in-the-pan diamond rush, but the foundation of an industry with a long life ahead of it, these were the lessons learned at Kimberley. Thus it was that Kimberley paved the way for later developments on the Witwatersrand. The diamond industry has had its ups and downs, but after one hundred years of continuous operation it is still a flourishing industry with unfathomed reserves of diamondiferous rock, even though it has already yielded precious stones to a value of almost R1 200 million.

The next important phase in development began with the proclamation of the Witwatersrand gold field in 1886. Since then, right up to the present day, gold mining has dominated the economic life of southern Africa. Gold initiated the rapid economic expansion which transformed the economy from subsistence farming to one in which industry has come to play an ever-increasing role. At first, the full import of the Witwatersrand was not appreciated, but as the extent and depth of the gold-bearing deposits came to be more accurately assessed, the best brains in the country were devoted to overcoming the enormous technical difficulties of their exploitation. Difficulties of water disposal, of heat, of dust, of ventilation, of faulting of the rock formation, of gold recovery, and of the supply of power for such a vast industry, were progressively solved by the application of the most modern scientific techniques to each problem as it arose.[4]

The reorganization of mining through the formation of large financial houses, each of which had a number of mines under its

[4] Perhaps the most important single development was the application in 1890 of the Macarthur-Forest cyanide process of gold recovery.

control, enabled considerable economies of scale to be achieved. While the Transvaal Chamber of Mines concerned itself with problems of the industry as a whole, the 'group system', as it is commonly called, provided each mine with the best technical and scientific advice available, and has been particularly valuable in steering mines through the long and expensive period of development before production actually began. Efficiency and economy were the foundations on which this industry was built. Mining at ever-deeper levels might have been expected to raise working costs, but so efficient became the organization that average working costs between 1897 and 1937 actually fell from R2,95 to R1,90 per ton.

The next phase in mining development arose from the need for power; and coal mining was developed on the rich and extensive deposits of the Transvaal and Natal. Initially coal mining was an offshoot of the gold-mining industry, but it has increasingly become a major economic activity, supplying fuel also to the railways and electric power stations and in ever-increasing quantities to a variety of chemical and other manufacturing industries. Mining of other minerals, mainly for export, was also extended; and copper, manganese and chrome assumed significance.

An entirely new phase in the development of mining was initiated during the 1930s as a result of the development of iron and steel production from local ores. Prior to this, all minerals, except coal, were produced almost wholly for the export market, but the growing activity of the Iron and Steel Industrial Corporation stimulated a domestic demand for iron ore, limestone and coal, in approximately equal quantities. The huge deposits of these minerals in close juxtaposition, and their low cost of mining, are the foundations upon which a rapidly expanding iron, steel and engineering industry is in process of being built. More will be said about this in the next chapter: here it is the expansion of mining stimulated by this domestic industry which commands attention.

In the 1920s grave fears were being expressed that the gold-mining industry was nearing the zenith of its production, and its early decline and extinction were regarded as inevitable.[5] During the following two decades, however, a fortunate series of events altered

[5] Even as late as 1930 the Government Mining Engineer estimated that the peak would be reached in 1932, after which decline would be fairly rapid. The estimated value of gold output for 1940 was R51 million. In fact it was R236 million.

the outlook, and future prospects have greatly improved. First, there was the general devaluation of currencies throughout the world, led by the devaluation of sterling in 1931. South Africa clung to the old gold parity for sixteen unhappy months, but after 1933 the gold mines benefited from a rise in the price of their product of nearly 100 per cent during the following few years.[6] This created a substantial margin between working costs and revenue and initiated a period of rapid expansion for the gold-mining industry. The value of gold output rose from R94 million in 1932 to R236 million in 1940.

This enhanced profitability led to renewed efforts to discover new mining areas, and a spectacular advance was made in two dimensions. In the first, new areas of gold-bearing deposits were discovered and the Witwatersrand reef was found to be much more extensive than was originally believed, stretching away both to the east and to the west. But there were also major advances in the scientific and technical fields, which have greatly prolonged the life of the mining industry. Water from the dolomite formations, which had hindered development in these areas in the past and had long baffled mining engineers, was at last brought under control, enabling the gold reef below to be mined. Technical advance in a wide field of applied science also permitted mining to take place at ever-deeper levels. In the 1920s it was believed that no mine could operate at a depth greater than 2 100 metres. When the Village Deep exceeded this in 1928, 2 500 metres was regarded as the limit. Today, mining is being successfully conducted at depths down to and below 3 000 metres, and plans are in hand for pushing the depth as far as 3 800 metres. All this has greatly increased the potential ore and thus extended the life of the mines. The gold-mining industry today is a miracle of applied science and efficient organization. Each shift, some 200 000 miners are brought flown to the underground labyrinth, some to a depth of 3 000 metres below surface. While below, they are supplied with downcast air at the rate of 34 000 000 c.f.m., and each shift they are brought to the surface to be replaced by other workers. Collectively they mine over 8 000 000 metric tons of rocks per annum,

[6] Average price of gold per oz.:

1925–32	R	8,495
1933		12,473
1935		14,206
1939		15,433
1940–5		16,8

Source: Department of Mines, *Annual Report, Including Reports of the Government Mining Engineer, 31 December 1959,* U.G. 58/1960, p. 39.

all of which has to be brought to the surface, crushed, and have the gold extracted from it.

In addition to the extensions, both horizontal and vertical, of the Witwatersrand a vast new gold field was discovered in the Orange Free State, and mining began there in 1946. Notwithstanding these new discoveries, the gold-mining industry was in severe difficulty in the mid 1940s because the margin between working costs and revenue was closing rapidly and profits were being eroded by inflationary pressure. Even the new Free State mines were endangered by the increasing cost of bringing a mine into production. The industry was, however, again relieved by devaluation in 1949,[7] and further assisted by the discovery that many mines could produce uranium oxide as a by-product of gold mining.

Although some of the old mines are closing down, new mines are being opened up and from 1951 to 1970 each year has shown an annual increase in gold production, and each succeeding year has established an all-time record for the value of gold produced. Table 13 shows the value of mineral production since 1911 for gold and for other minerals. The value of gold output increased from R294 million in 1952 to R2 620 million in 1974.

Equally spectacular, and perhaps in the long run of greater significance, is the expansion of base-mineral output. As seen in table 13, the value of 'other minerals' increased since the war from R46 million in 1945 to R1 309 million in 1974 – a more than twenty-eight fold increase in twenty-nine years.

In 1974 the six most important mineral products in terms of the value of output were.[8]

	R (millions)
gold	2 620
copper	223
coal	200
diamonds	143
manganese	78
asbestos	54

It should be noted that information regarding platinum and atomic minerals is not available for publication.

By 1974 the total value of mineral output had reached R3 928 million of which gold accounted for R2 620 million.[9]

[7] The price of gold rose from R17,25 to R24,82.
[8]. Department of Mines *Annual Report, 1974*, p. 10.
[9] Department of Mines *Annual Report, 1974*, p. 10.

THE IMPORTANCE OF THE GOLD-MINING INDUSTRY

Ever since 1886 the gold-mining industry has been the great driving force in South Africa's economic expansion, and the analysis of its expenditure from revenue in 1974 shows that even now its importance in the nation's economy is very great. The table below, kindly supplied by the Chamber of Mines, shows how its total working revenue of over two-and-a-half thousand million rands in 1974 was allocated.

ANALYSIS OF EXPENDITURE FROM REVENUE OF PRODUCING GOLD MINES, MEMBERS OF THE CHAMBER

	Year 1974
Total gold working revenue	R2 552 593 348
Gold Working Costs:	
Labour Charges	491 242 206
Stores and Materials, Electric Light and Power,	
Compressed Air and Water Charges	408 723 989
Other Charges	84 748 839
Total Working Costs:	R 984 715 034
Gold Working Profit	R1 526 878 314
Profit from Uranium, Acid and Pyrite	1 426 000
Sundry Revenue	54 396 221
Total Profit:	R1 623 700 535
Taxation and State share of Profit	812 630 958
Net Profit available for appropriation to cover capital expenditure and dividends	R 811 069 577

Source: Chamber of Mines of South Africa.

To list only the most important aspects of its influence is no easy matter, but the following cannot be neglected: (1) Income generation, and its contribution to the national product. (2) Employer of labour. (3) Attraction of capital, skill and entrepreneurship from abroad. (4) Source of government revenue. (5) Provider of foreign exchange. (6) Stabilizing factor in the economy. (7) A brake upon inflation. (8) Leader in technical advance and good management. (9) Direct stimulus to certain industries. (10) Indirect stimulus to general industrial advance. (11) Educative influence on tribal Africans. (12) Provider of a modern transport system. They will be discussed in turn.

(1) Income generation and its contribution to the national product

For over three-quarters of a century the gold-mining industry has been a major contributor to the national product of southern Africa. The value of gold output in 1910 was R64 million, in 1974 it was R2 620 million. Moreover, because of the sums which the industry pays out in wages and in the purchase of supplies it puts a large income into the hands of South African consumers. It has been argued that in this gold mining is in no way different from any other economic undertaking,[10] but its particular value lies in the fact that unlike many branches of manufacturing, gold mining, except during periods of expansion, has a relatively low propensity to import. A second important feature to be noted is that as a result of the migratory-labour system, a very large part of the wages paid to the African labour force generates income in the poorest and most backward parts of the country. The African homelands in the Republic are largely dependent upon the income earned in gold mining by migrants from these areas. Without this source of income hundreds of thousands of families would be in dire straits. The same is true also of many countries outside the Republic, and the South African gold mines are indirectly a major support for the economies of Lesotho, Botswana, Swaziland, Malawi and Moçambique. Estimates of income derived from the South African gold mines which accrued to these territories are.[11]

	1954		1965		1975	
South Africa	R(000)	R(000)	R(000)	R(000)	R(000)	R(000)
Transkei	1 958		4 153		⎰ 14 083	
Ciskei	368		852		⎱	
Natal	258		414		656	
Other South African	468		985		1 665	
		3 052		6 404		16 404
Foreign countries						
Lesotho	1 090		2 571		15 491	
Botswana	914		1 693		5 205	
Swaziland	364		550		1 645	
Moçambique	3 232		4 717		33 026	
Other	380		630		322	
Malawi	842		3 781		22 443	
		6 822		13 942		78 132
		9 874		20 346		94 536

[10] *Economic Aspects of the Gold Mining Industry*, Report no. 11 of Social and Economic Planning Council, U.G. 32/1948, p. 10.

[11] *Mining Survey*, vol. 5 no. 1, March 1954, p. 16, for 1954; and information kindly supplied by Chamber of Mines for 1975.

(2) Major employer of labour

In the early days the mining industry offered almost the only employment alternative to agriculture: since then secondary and tertiary activities have developed greatly and employment in manufacturing is now larger than in mining. Nevertheless the number employed in the gold mines has remained large. Numbers employed in gold mining were:

	1910	1959	1962	1965	1969	1975
Whites	24 757	48 600	49 000	44 000	40 000	37 000
Others	195 551	380 473	382 000	369 000	364 000	330 000
(mainly Blacks)						
	220 308	429 073	431 000	413 000	404 000	370 000

The whites have their homes mainly in the vicinity of the mines, but the Blacks, except for a relatively small number, are migratory workers whose families remain at home in the tribal areas.

African mine workers were drawn from the following areas.[12]

	African workers on gold mines			
	1951	1962	1965	1975
From the Republic	122 000	150 000	137 000	103 000
From Lesotho, Botswana & Swaziland	56 000	75 000	80 000	98 000
From Moçambique (south of latitude 22°S)	122 000	85 000	85 000	90 000
From other African states (north of latitude 22°S)		72 000	67 000	31 000
	300 000	382 000	369 000	323 000

(3) Attraction of capital, skill and enterpreneurship from abroad

'For nearly fifty years the gold mining industry has been the power house of modern enterprise in the Union, and the main attraction for capital from the money markets of Europe . . . Nearly one-half of the private listed capital from abroad has been directly invested in the Rand gold mines.'[13] Thus wrote S. H. Frankel in 1938, and since then there has been a further vast inflow to assist in the development of the Free State fields. It has been estimated[14] that between 1886 and

---

[12] Figures kindly supplied by Chamber of Mines; 1951 figures from *Mining Survey*, vol. 3 no. 3, June 1951, p. 5.

[13] S. H. Frankel, *Capital Investment in Africa*, p. 75.

[14] W. J. Busschau, 'Mining's Part in the Growth of Union', *Mining Survey* vol. 11 no 2, 1960, p. 3.

1960 the gold-mining industry raised R1 220 million in 'new money' and appropriated out of profits an additional R470 million for capital purposes. Much of the 'new capital' came from abroad, and it is clear that had South Africa been obliged to depend solely upon domestic savings, development would have been much slower. Moreover, the inflow of foreign capital to the gold-mining industry has enabled much of the domestic saving to be channelled into other industries. Attention has often been drawn to the power of gold to attract foreign *capital*, but there is another aspect which has been no less significant. This is the way in which gold mining has attracted *men* from abroad with drive, energy, vision, and the courage to take chances; and on the Witwatersrand they found an opening for their talents. The great difficulty confronting a simple agricultural community is to find the leadership to bring it forward. Other countries in Africa are desperately seeking technical aid from more advanced countries, but these men freely and in large numbers responded to South Africa's lure of gold. Some may have been mere adventurers, but others were not; and as a group they brought new vitality, enterprise and progressive notions; and these qualities have been perpetuated in the modern generation of South African industrial leadership. Whether this enterprise would have arisen without this injection from abroad is doubtful.

(4) Source of government revenue

The gold-mining industry has always been a major source of revenue to the State. It was this industry that first put the Transvaal into a sound financial position; and, ever since Union, the South African government has relied heavily upon it as a major source of revenue. For many years the gold-mining industry has been subjected to special taxation which is not applied to other sectors of the economy. In addition the government participates in the profits of many mines in terms of the mines' lease. In 1910 the gold-mining industry paid R2,8 million in taxation, in 1974 it was estimated to have paid the state R812 million in taxation and its share of profit.[15] Moreover the stability of the industry during a general recession, to which further reference is made below, makes it invaluable in sustaining government revenue when sums derived from other taxation may tend to decline.

[15] Information supplied by Chamber of Mines.

(5) Provider of foreign exchange

Gold has kept South Africa from the serious balance-of-payments difficulties experienced by so many other countries. Since its first discovery it has been a major provider of foreign exchange, and until recently has often accounted for more than half the country's total exports.

Year	Total export (R millions)	Gold (R millions)	Gold as percentage of total exports %
1946	359	203	56
1950	730	294	40
1955	1 106	365	33
1960	1 409	530	38
1970	2 240	837	37
1974	5 783	2 552	44

'The possession of an export article, particularly one with the attributes of gold, which all the world wants, is a great advantage to a young country. Gold as the final means of settling international indebtedness can enter through doors which import controls close against other commodities. And hence, from the establishment of Union, South Africa could pay, without undue difficulty, for the capital goods it urgently needed to expand its total national production.'[16] So wrote W. J. Busschau in 1960.

Indeed gold has been able to finance the imports without which industrial expansion would have been impossible, and even today it is gold, and the other export products, which provide the essential foreign materials which our manufacturing industries are as yet unable to earn by their own exports. More is said on this matter in the next chapter.

(6) Stabilizing factor in the economy

Gold mining has exerted a remarkable stabilizing effect in the South African economy because of the peculiar relationship between its cost structure and the price of its end product. Under the International Gold Standard the use of gold as the basis of international money meant that the price of gold was fixed and that there was an infinitely elastic demand for the product at the prevailing price. During periods of general economic prosperity there was a tendency for costs to rise, and since in gold mining these could not be passed

---

[16] Busschau, p. 2.

on to the consumer, the profit margins contracted. During periods of general recession, on the other hand, mining costs tended to fall and the profit margin in gold mining increased C. G. W. Schumann has shown that dividends were maintained and in contrast to the general employment index, employment in gold mining expanded during the great depression.

'Summing up, we may say that the total effect of the gold-mining industry on the general business cycle in South Africa, through the demand for labour and the distribution of the total mining income, has been distinctly stabilizing. In this respect South Africa is in a unique and very fortunate position.'[17]

Recent changes in the international role of gold in monetary affairs, the introduction of Special Drawing Rights from the International Monetary Fund, and the emergence of a two-tier price for gold, the Fund's decision to auction some of its gold, and recent violent fluctuations in the price of gold, have all combined to reduce the stabilizing effect of this industry upon the South African economy but the role of gold in international trade is still important and its use as a metal in industry and the arts is likely to sustain its demand for the forseeable future.

(7) A brake upon inflation

As a result of the relationship between costs and the fixed price of gold noted above, the gold-mining industry is particularly sensitive to anything making for rising costs. Thus inflationary pressure are likely to have a serious effect upon the profitability and output of one of the country's major industries. The knowledge of this fact has had a salutary effect upon successive governments, and any tendency to take the easy path of inflation has been checked by the realization of its effect upon South Africa's major export. It may well be that the presence of the gold-mining industry has saved South Africa from the progressive currency decline that has frustrated the efforts towards economic growth in many South American countries.

(8) Leader in technical advance and good management

Only by the exercise of strict economy, careful costing, sound labour management, and the constant application of advanced

---

[17] C. G. W. Schumann, p. 333.

techniques and modern scientific development, has the gold-mining industry grown and prospered as it has done. In this, gold mining has set a standard for all industry in South Africa. Many of the great mining houses have branched out into new ventures in other fields of industry and they have carried with them the standards of industrial efficiency that were developed in gold mines.

(9) Direct stimulus to certain industries
Several important industries owed their origin or growth to the demand from the gold-mining industry — explosives, engineering, cable manufacturing, footwear and many more. It also provided an important market for many agricultural products.

(10) Indirect stimulus to general industrial advance
Indirectly the gold-mining industry has been a major force in the expansion of manufacturing industry in several ways. First, by being the initiator of the great urban concentration of population on the Witwatersrand, which has become the chief market for almost all manufactured products, it has indirectly created a domestic market without which manufacturing of consumers' goods would have been impossible. Secondly, in the words of the Social and Economic Planning Council's report:

'Many agricultural products and a large number of secondary industries receive protection from the State in the form of tariffs, subsidies, controlled marketing, differential railways rates, etc., and this cost must ultimately be borne by those economic activities which receive no protection, of which gold mining is one of the most important.'[18]

(11) Educative influence on tribal Africans
One of the greatest tasks in the economic development of Africa is to replace subsistence agriculture by one which is more productive, and in order to bring this about it is essential to change the outlook of the African himself and orient him towards modern society. In this process the gold-mining industry has been a powerful influence; and it has affected the lives and cultural boundaries of millions of African peasants. It has tended to break down traditional tribal

---

[18] *Economic Aspects of the Gold Mining Industry*, Report no. 11 of the Social and Economic Planning Council, U.G. 32/1948, p. 12.

isolation, for workers from some forty different tribes live and work shoulder to shoulder in the mines; and a new laguage – *Fanakalo*[19] – has grown up there to assist intercommunication. In the mines millions of Africans have had their introduction to the world of modern industry, with its concepts of punctuality, large-scale organization and modern machinery, and its routine of regular labour. They have also incidentally been subjected to modern ideas of diet, health, hygiene,[20] housing, transport and to all the allures of modern manufactured products of all varieties. In short the traditional African tribesman who has once worked in the mines, like Plato's caveman who has seen the light, can never be quite the same simple tribesman again.

(12) Provider of a modern transport system

Finally, diamonds and, later, gold have been important in providing both the *raison d'être* and the means for financing railways from the ports to the interior, as has been mentioned in an earlier chapter.

The future of the gold mines

All attempts made in the past to forecast the life of the gold-mining industry have subsequently proved to have been gross underestimates. There are four major unknowns – the price of gold, costs of production, scientific and technical advance, and the discovery of new mines. No one can know how much gold there is in a mine until the mine has been fully developed. How much ore is payable depends upon the future costs. Scientific advance in the past has greatly increased the possible depth of mining and thus extended the life of the mines, and the industry is today spending about R4 million a year on mining research. Although some of the older mines are now closing down, new mines are opening up to replace them, and gold output has increased annually to a peak in 1970: thereafter it has tended to level off or to decline, although the *value* of the output has risen with the increased price of gold. The index of the physical output of gold with 1963–64 = 100 is as follows:

---

[19] *Fanakalo* is a patois of mixed origin which arose in the Witwatersrand and is now being used and taught by the mines as a general medium of communication.

[20] Over 1 000 000 Red Cross certificates have been issued to Africans who have received training in first aid on the mines

1964	103,9	1969	111,2
1965	109,0	1970	114,9
1960	109,9	1971	112,0
1967	108,2	1972	104,2
1968	110,9	1973	98,1

Gold should remain an important sector of the South African economy for the next two decades at the very least. Much, however, depends upon the government's ability to halt the creeping inflation that has continued since the 1940s and on the world price of gold. In 1962, it was estimated that for an increase of 25 cents per ton in mining costs the country loses 11,5 million ounces of gold; for the next 25 cents, 8,9 million ounces; and for the next 25 cents, a further 7 million ounces. On this basis the country lost, for all time, gold worth between R450 million and R500 million on account of a rise of 45 cents per ton in the costs of production between 1961 and 1964.[21]

DEVELOPMENT OF OTHER MINING

Although gold has been the core of the mining industry of South Africa since 1886, other branches of mining make substantial contributions to the gross national output, as indicated in tables 13 and 14. Moreover the marked increase in the value of mineral output, other than gold, from R44 million in 1945 to R1 055 million in 1973, shows that great development is taking place in these other branches of mining. Much of this is associated with the growth of manufacturing industry in South Africa, particularly the iron, steel and engineering industries and the chemicals industry. These will be discussed further in the next chapter. Three mineral products are the foundation of these industries and their production figures since 1926 indicate the importance of these developments.

Year	Iron ore	Coal	Lime and limestone
	(thousand metric tons)		
1926	47	12 977	1 515
1936	365	14 873	2 440
1946	919	23 652	5 350
1956	2 069	33 673	5 542
1966	7 702	48 075	10 656
1969	8 788	52 295	13 917
1970	9 192	54 612	15 076
1971	10 496	58 666	16 035
1972	11 223	58 440	15 115
1973	10 955	62 352	16 825

Sources: *Union Statistics for Fifty Years*, pp. K-10, K-15, K-12; *Bulletins of Statistics*, March 1970 and 1975.

[21] Statement by Mr. H. C. Koch (President of Chamber of Mines) in 1965.

The tendency for gold-mining output to level off, might have most serious consequences for the continued growth of the national economy because of the important role mining has played in economic growth. Fortunately, however, other mining activity has expanded rapidly, and the graph of the total value of mineral output has continued to climb. Moreover, both iron ore and coal are finding important export markets and are joining the group of mineral exports which have always been large earners of foreign exchange.

Two new ports are being developed primarily for the export of mineral products, Richard's Bay, on the east coast north of Durban, and Saldanha Bay, on the west coast north of Cape Town; and new railways from the interior are being built to each. When these have been completed large exports of coal, iron ore and, perhaps other minerals or semi-processed material can confidently be expected.

In a short book such as this no exhaustive account of mineral resources is possible, but they should at least be named. Table 14 gives recent production figures and the value of output for some of these, but there are many more. In addition to gold, the precious minerals group includes silver, diamonds and other gemstones, and the platinum group of metals. Base minerals already mentioned are iron ore, coal and limestone; but there are others: antimony, asbestos, chrome, copper, fluorspar, lead, manganese, nickel, phosphate, salt, sulphur, tin, vanadium, zinc. Many of these minerals are required by the iron and steel industry, and as this expands, especially in the production of stainless steel, the local demand for these will also grow. There is in addition uranium, but discussion of atomic materials is prescribed, and exploration and production figures are not available to the public. It is, however, well known that considerable uranium oxide is produced at low cost as a by-product in some of the gold mines.

Potential for development is great, and the growing export market for coal, iron, steel, and certain chemical products indicates that, given a favourable international situation, the possibility of future expansion is almost without limit.

It is interesting to note in passing that ownership of shares in mining companies is increasingly coming to be in the hands of South African nationals and that the proportion of dividends paid outside the country is declining. In 1935 only 40,5 per cent of total dividends of R36 million were paid within the country. By 1968 74,6 per cent of total dividends of R233 million were paid within South Africa.[22] Thus not only has there been the remarkable increase of mining activity, but also ownership of the industry is increasingly in South African hands.

[22] *Statistical Year Book*, 1970, p. L-5.

Manufacturing

THE GROWTH OF MANUFACTURING INDUSTRIES

The mineral discoveries and their exploitation transformed the South African economy during the last forty years of the nineteenth century, increased the national income and greatly accelerated the tempo of economic growth. Industries immediately related to mining, such as the manufacture of explosives, certain branches of engineering and the production of miners' boots, soon came to be established, but little general expansion in manufacturing occurred. South African experience has been that in the early stages of the economic development of a predominantly rural society, manufacturing is unlikely to expand rapidly or to become the leading sector of the economy. As long as population is widely dispersed and transport facilities meagre and expensive, large-scale factory production is impossible owing to lack of markets.[1] Small local industries, such as brick-making, hand-sawn timber production, hand-made furniture and small-scale mills for grinding wheat and maize, had sprung up at an early date throughout the country, and the mining developments caused a boom in wagon building during the 1860s, but it was short-lived, because railway expansion soon rendered the ox-wagon obsolete. Moreover, in the predominantly rural economy of nineteenth-century South Africa many things now factory-produced were home-made: bread and biscuits were baked at home, ham and bacon were home-cured, soap and candles were often made of animal fat rendered down by the housewife, many articles of clothing and rough footwear were also home-made, and the washing of clothes was essentially a domestic chore. Likewise the African peasants used gourds, home-made clay

---

[1] The hope current in some underdeveloped and subsistence-oriented countries that the establishment of manufacturing industries will rapidly modernize the country is contrary to South African experience, where it was the growth of a modern sector of the economy which stimulated manufacturing.

119

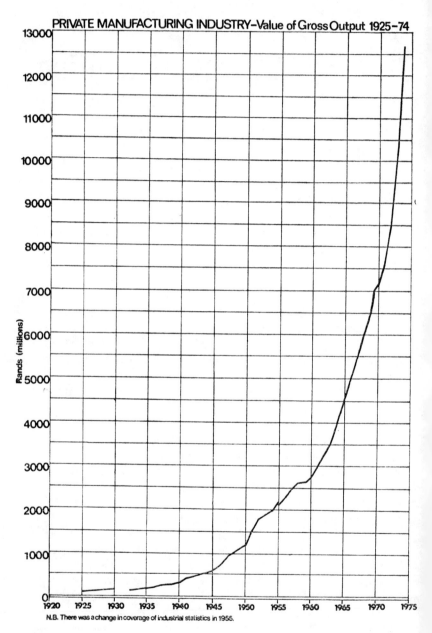

PRIVATE MANUFACTURING INDUSTRY–Value of Gross Output 1925–74

N.B. There was a change in coverage of industrial statistics in 1955.

FIGURE 10

pots and woven baskets. Only with large urban concentrations and improved transport does it pay to establish bakeries and jam factories, to manufacture clothing and to set up shoe factories. Even the increased wealth generated by the mines and greater purchasing power in consumers' hands did not at first stimulate local manufacturing, but gave rise instead to larger imports of consumer goods, the foreign exchange for which was met from gold exports. Indeed mining developments were so rapid during the latter part of the nineteenth century that they absorbed all available capital, skilled manpower and entrepreneurship. For these and other reasons the growth of large-scale manufacturing was essentially a phenomenon of the twentieth century. It should also be remembered that even as late as 1911 about half the whites, coloured people and Asians and 87 per cent of the Africans were rural dwellers, and that the urban population numbered altogether only $1\frac{1}{2}$ million, widely distributed between four main centres and some fifty smaller towns and villages.

Industrial development falls naturally into certain well-defined stages.

1910–25

Because of the difficulties of importation, the First World War stimulated the local manufacture of certain consumer goods, but when importation became easier after the war there was a setback. Tariffs in the colonial days were essentially for revenue purposes, but in 1906 the Cape Colony introduced mild protection of a number of consumer goods like boots, shoes, blankets, confectionery, soap, sugar, etc., with a view to stimulating local production. In 1910 the Cullinan Commission was appointed to investigate the possibility of developing local industries, and it recommended tariff protection if there were a reasonable chance of the industry becoming efficient when once established. The first Union Customs Tariff Act, no. 26 of 1914, was mainly a revenue measure, but gave limited protection on a number of articles. In 1921 a Board of Trade and Industries was appointed with the functions of receiving representations on tariff matters, reporting on anomalies, and advising the government about assistance to South African industries.

1925–9

There was a change of government in 1924, and the new coalition of the National and Labour parties adopted a more positive attitude towards industrial development, motivated partly by the desire to create employment opportunities for the large number of poverty-stricken whites who were leaving the land and drifting into towns, and partly, in the knowledge that gold was a wasting asset, by the desire to have a developed manufacturing industry to support the economy when the gold mines were depleted of ore. The Board of Trade and Industries was reconstituted and specifically charged with the task of revising tariffs to give more positive assistance to South African manufacturers. As a consequence the Customs Tariff and Excise Duties Amendment Act, no. 36 of 1925, considerably extended protection and included in its scope a number of industries which had previously enjoyed no protection. Twenty years later, a report of the Board of Trade and Industries stated: 'The policy of protection inaugurated in 1925 has been continued ever since and, except in the case of industries supplying mining and agricultural requirements, the vast majority of existing industries in the Union enjoy protection to a greater or lesser degree.'[2]

Manufacturing industry grew significantly during the period 1925 to 1929 as shown in the table below:

	1924–5	1928–9	Increase between 1925 and 1929 %
Number of establishments	6 009	6 238	4
Number of workers:			
all races (thousands)	115	141	22
whites only (thousands)	41	54	32
others (thousands)	74	87	18
Value of gross output (R millions)	115	161	39
Value of net output (R millions)	49	67	37

Based on p. L–3, *Union Statistics for Fifty Years.*

Many of the new factories were producing final consumer goods, often from imported raw materials or from semi-finished products. For example clothing manufacture from imported textiles preceded by many years the growth of a textile industry, in spite of the fact that South Africa was a major producer of wool. This bias towards the production of consumer goods rather than the processing of South African materials is to be explained by the size of the market, the

[2] Board of Trade and Industries, Report 282: *Investigation into Manufacturing Industries*, 1945, para. 329.

relative amount of capital required and by certain technical factors. A notable exception to this trend was the relatively early development of an iron and steel industry based upon local materials. Before Union there had been several small works using scrap iron,[3] but after 1916 three had been experimenting with the use of South African ores.[4] Attempts were made between 1920 and 1924 to amalgamate the various interests and to raise the necessary capital to establish by private enterprise a large-scale iron and steel works based on local materials. These attempts failed and after the general election of 1924, the new government favoured the development of the industry under State auspices. Meanwhile a detailed survey of the prospects for the industry[5] had been published, stating, *inter alia*, that a sound economic basis existed for the industry, and that Pretoria was the best site. In 1928 the South African Iron and Steel Industrial Corporation (Iscor) was established by the Iron and Steel Industry Act, no. 11 of 1928, with a capital of R7 million, divided into 500 000 'A' shares of R2 each, held by the Governor-General and carrying 51 percent of the voting rights, and the balance of the capital in 'B' shares was to be offered to the public. There were also government guaranteed debentures of R3 million. There were to be seven directors, four appointed by the government and three by shareholders. The capital offered to the public was taken up to a very limited extent only, and by an amending act of 1931 the unissued shares were taken by the government. Thus Iscor, which has played such a major role in industrial development of the country, is a public utility corporation almost wholly government-owned.

1930–3

Many industrial concerns were hit by the great depression, and although the number of establishments increased slightly between 1930 and 1933, the total employment, value of gross output and net output all declined.

---

[3] The Witwatersrand Co-operative Smelting Works, 1909; George Holt & Co. Ltd., 1910; Cartwright & Eaton Ltd. (later the Dunswart Iron & Steel Works), 1911; Union Steel Corporation, 1911.

[4] The Pretoria Iron Mines Ltd. set up by C. F. Delfos in 1916, and Messrs. Lewis & Marks in Vereeniging and M. Eaton at Newcastle in Natal. Mr. Eaton's blast furnace at Newcastle was the first to produce pig-iron on a commercial basis. This was later acquired by the Union Steel Corporation of South Africa.

[5] By Gutehoffnungshütte, a German steel firm.

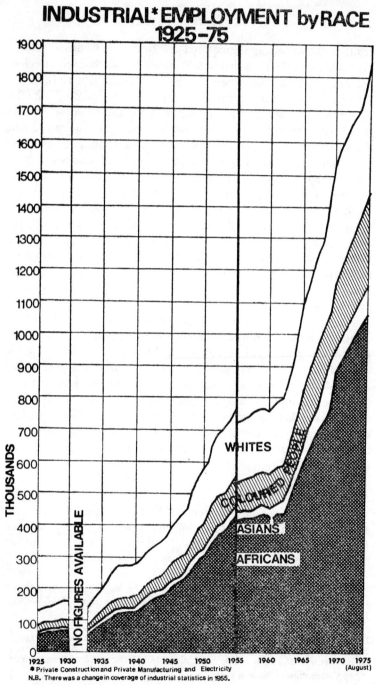

INDUSTRIAL* EMPLOYMENT by RACE
1925-75

THOUSANDS

NO FIGURES AVAILABLE

WHITES

COLOURED PEOPLE

ASIANS

AFRICANS

1925 1930 1935 1940 1945 1950 1955 1960 1965 1970 1975
(August)

* Private Construction and Private Manufacturing and Electricity
N.B. There was a change in coverage of industrial statistics in 1955.

FIGURE 11

	1929–30	1932–3	Change 1930–3 %
Number of establishments	6 472	6 543	+ 1
Number of workers:			
all races (thousands)	142	133	− 6
whites only (thousands)	55	57	+ 4
others (thousands)	87	76	−12
Value of gross output (R millions)	157	135	−14
Value of net output (R millions)	68	61	−10

The anomalous increase in the number of white workers is explained by the government's so-called 'civilized labour policy', which was in effect the substitution of white workers for non-white wherever possible. This was consistent with the view that manufacturing industries were a white man's preserve, but it meant that the full weight of the great depression fell upon the non-white industrial workers.[6]

1933–9

The gold-mining boom which followed devaluation of the South African pound rapidly lifted the country out of the depression, and manufacturing industry made great forward strides between 1933 and 1939.

	1932–3	1938–9	Change 1933–9 %
Number of establishments	6 543	8 614	32
Number of workers:			
all races (thousands)	133	236	77
whites only (thousands)	57	93	63
others (thousands)	76	143	88
Value of gross output (R millions)	135	281	108
Value of net output (R millions)	61	128	110

During the six-year period the value of both gross and net output more than doubled and the total labour force increased by 77 per cent. Part of this increase represented a cyclical recovery from the depth of the depression, but notwithstanding, there was a general advance of manufacturing industry during the period. It is of interest

---

[6] It was argued that unemployed African workers could return to the subsistence economy of the reserves, but this was not true of those industrial workers who had become permanent urban dwellers.

that in contrast to earlier periods non-white employment increased more rapidly than white, from 76 thousand to 143 thousand, or about 88 per cent compared with the 63 per cent increase in white workers. This is normal in periods of rapid expansion because the supply of African labour is much more elastic than that of white.

1939–45

The period from 1939 to 1945 presented a great challenge to South African manufacturing industry. For one reason the war caused some major disruptions. For example the skilled staff at Iscor were almost all Germans, there on contract to train South African workers. They were interned on the outbreak of war, leaving only the as yet untrained South Africans to keep the works going. The fact that they were not merely able to do so, but soon increased output, speaks highly of their resourcefulness and adaptability.[7] Then too throughout industry many skilled workers were drawn into the army,[8] although attempts were made to keep key men at their civilian jobs. The shortage of skilled men was acute and industrial output was enabled to expand only by the increased employment of non-white workers in semi-skilled and skilled jobs. There were also other difficulties on the supply side, because importation of tools, machine parts and semi-processed components was often impossible, and great ingenuity was displayed in the engineering industry in overcoming these bottlenecks. On the demand side there was a great increase in the consumption of the products of South African factories. Not only was the normal civilian demand cut off from overseas sources of supply, but South African industry also made a substantial contribution to the allied war effort in ship-repair work,[9] manufacture of munitions and the production of armoured cars. This was possible only because of the increased output of high-grade steel from Iscor. The table below reflects in statistical form the growth of manufacturing during the war.

[7] Even the highest executives like Dr. H. J. v. d. Byl and Dr. F. Meyer rolled up their shirt sleeves and took their turn in the works.

[8] There were 309 000 South African men in the armed forces: 186 000 whites and 123 000 others. Source: *Union of South Africa and the War*, Govt. Printer, Pretoria, 1948.

[9] Total number of ships repaired, 1941–4, was 10 648, and at the peak over 2 500 men were employed. *Official Year Book of the Union of South Africa*, no. 29, 1955, p. 878.

	1938–9	1944–5	Increase 1939–45 %
Number of establishments	8 614	9 316	8
Number of workers:			
all races (thousands)	236	361	53
whites only (thousands)	93	112	20
others (thousands)	143	249	74
Value of gross output (R millions)	281	608	116
Value of net output (R millions)	128	276	116

The extent to which the wartime expansion of manufacturing industry was dependent upon increased employment of non-white labour is seen from the fact that white employees increased by 20 per cent and non-white by 74 per cent. The Second World War found South African industry much better equipped to meet the challenge of temporary isolation that it was in 1914, and the rapid expansion to meet wartime demand was proof that it was more broadly based and more mature.

Since 1945

Since the war, manufacturing industry has made further rapid growth, and increased employment of both white and other workers continued at a rapid rate. Unfortunately, it is not possible to give comparable statistics beyond 1954–5, because in that year there was a change in the coverage of the industrial census. Growth between 1945 and 1955 is shown below.

	1944–5	1954–5	Increase 1945–55 %
Number of establishments	9 316	13 725	47
Number of workers:			
all races (thousands)	361	653	81
whites (thousands)	112	184	64
others (thousands)	249	469	88
Value of gross output (R millions)	608	2 221	266
Value of net output (R millions)	276	964	249

In terms of the new industrial census classification the figures for the period 1955 to 1970[10] were as follows:

[10] Source: *Statistical News Release* 20/1/71 and 7/8/70. The figures for 1969–70 are provisional.

	1954–5	1969–70	*Increase* 1955–70
			%
Number of establishments	10 126	13 142	30
Number of workers:			
all races (thousands)	610	1 164	91
whites (thousands)	158	278	76
others (thousands)	452	886	96
Value of gross output (R millions)	2 154	5 983	178
Value of net output (R millions)	852	2 398	181

It may be of interest to compare the rates of growth during the different periods that have been considered. This is set out below.

Average Annual Change in Each Period as Percentage

	1925–9	1929–33	1933–9	1939–45	1944–55	1955–70
Number of establishments	1,0	0,3	5,3	1,3	4,7	1,9
All workers	5,5	−2,0	12,8	8,8	8,1	5,7
White workers	8,0	1,3	10,5	3,3	6,4	4,8
Other workers	4,5	−4,0	14,7	12,3	8,8	6,0
Value of gross output	9,8	−4,6	18,0	19,3	26,6	11,1
Value of net output	9,3	−3,3	15,0	19,3	24,9	11,3

The expansion of the private manufacturing sector from relative insignificance in 1911–12 to the largest single component of the national income is undoubtedly the greatest structural change that has taken place in the South African economy during the last fifty years.

Private Manufacturing* as Percentage of the National Income

1911–2	1921–2	1931–2	1941–2	1951–2	1971
6,7	11,9	15,4	18,4	25,0	31,0

*Including *construction*, and *electricity, gas and water*.

Although protective tariffs have played some part in stimulating industrial development, the main cause has undoubtedly been the expansion of the South African market. Based initially upon the gold mines and the urban population which grew up around them, the manufacturing developments have had a cumulative effect in expanding the market, because each successful phase of industrial expansion generates more income and increases the urban population, and this in turn stimulates further expansion.

One of the great handicaps of manufacturing firms in South Africa has been the small scale upon which the majority of them have had to operate owing to the limited size of the domestic and export markets, but improvement, as shown by the table below, has taken place, although the average size is still regrettably small.

*Manufacturing Firms in South Africa**

	Number of firms	Average value of net output R	Average fixed capital R	Average number of employees
1924–5	6 009	8 230	10 000	19
1938–9	8 614	14 800	14 000	28
1954–5	13 725	70 200	63 000	48
1967–8	13 142	182 000	172 000	80
1970	13 121	236 000	191 000	83

*Sources: *Union Statistics for Fifty Years,* p. L–3 up to 1960; *South African Statistics 1974* for later years.

The total number of firms has tended to decline in recent years but the average size firm has quadrupled in terms of labour and increased nineteenfold in terms of capital, but averages can be misleading and these figures do not fully indicate the advance that has been made, because an increasing percentage of total production now comes from a relatively small number of large concerns. Nevertheless, in many instances the size of the market is still the main factor preventing fuller benefits from the economies of scale. This matter will be referred to again in a later section of this chapter.

MAIN CLASSES OF INDUSTRY

The industrial census classifies private manufacturing industry under nineteen major groups[11] but this is too many to consider in detail here.[12] Instead main classes of related industries will be selected, of which the iron, steel and engineering group, the food and drink group, the clothing and textile group, and the chemical industries group are the most important.

Metal products and engineering (comprising groups 14, 15, 16, 17, 18)
This industry has its origin in the needs of the mines, and engineering repair shops soon developed on the Witwatersrand, but it

[11] Group 1 Food, Group 2 Beverages, Group 3 Tobacco, Group 4 Textiles, Group 5 Wearing apparel, Group 6 Wood and wood products, Group 7 Furniture, Group 8 Paper and paper products, Group 9 Printing and publishing, Group 10 Leather and leather products, Group 11 Rubber products, Group 12 Chemicals and chemical products, Group 13 Non-metallic mineral products, Group 14 Basic metal industries, Group 15 Metal products, Group 16 Machinery, Group 17 Electrical machinery, Group 18 Transport equipment, Group 19 Miscellaneous.

[12] Statistics of the full nineteen groups (in 1968) are given in table 17 with totals for 1970.

was undoubtedly the establishment of Iscor in 1928 which laid the foundations for later expansion of what has now become the largest branch of manufacturing in South Africa. It would appear to have great growth-potential and to be soundly based upon local materials, and cheap coal gives it a comparative advantage which may enable an increasing volume of exports. Data relating to the growth of this sector are given in table 18 of the statistical appendix. Between 1925 and 1970 employment increased about eighteenfold and net value of output rose from R8,2 million to R1 150 million; between 1945 and 1955 the physical volume of output of this group of industries more than doubled[13] and in the decade from 1963 to 1973 it increased by about 50 per cent. In 1970 it employed 387 000 workers.[14]

Major expansion at Iscor was announced in 1962 involving new capital expenditure of R574 million on the extension programme, and by 1970 steel output had reached 3 384 000 metric tons. For the growth of Iscor capacity see the table opposite.[15] Increased exports of selected products of the metals and engineering industry are forecast with reasonable confidence; recent experience indicates that in certain lines South African products are competitive in cost and quality with the major steel-producing countries, and recent contracts with Japanese buyers have expanded the export market.

Iscor's Productive Capacity
Steel Products

Financial year	Metric tons	Percentage of country's requirements
1935	142 147	17,2
1940	319 572	35,5
1945	456 629	58,3
1950	604 689	48,3
1955	1 287 193	70,6
1960	1 586 237	79,3
1965	2 588 440	66,4
1970	3 384 896	74,8

It is estimated that when the new works come into full production Iscor should have an annual capacity by 1980 of over 8 000 000 tons.

Until a relatively short time ago the automobile industry was primarily the assembly of motor vehicles from imported components,

[13] *Union Statistics for Fifty Years*, p. L-27.
[14] See statistical appendix, table 18.
[15] Iscor, *Annual Report*, 1970.

but under fiscal and other pressures the proportion of South African manufactured components is increasing markedly. Many of the major producers are now using South African chassis, engine blocks, bodies, wheels, tyres and other components. In 1968 there were 1 034 firms engaged in the transport equipment industry employing over 65 000 workers and having a gross output of R485 million. Rapid development is also taking place in the aircraft industry, both manufacture and repair.

Food, beverages and tobacco (groups 1, 2 and 3)[16]

Industries processing South African agricultural produce were some of the earliest to arise, and in 1924 this group of industries accounted for no less than 32,2 per cent of the value of net output of all manufacturing industries. Although this group of industries has expanded greatly from a net output of R15,8 million in 1925 to R438 million in 1970, the percentage of the total represented by this group has declined steadily. The percentage decline reflects the more rapid expansion of other sectors rather than a lack of growth in this particular field. Between 1963 and 1973 the physical volume of output of the food-processing industry increased by about 57 per cent. In 1970 this group of industries employed 155 000 workers and was an important contributor to the nation's exports.

Textile and clothing industries (groups 4 and 5)[17]

As mentioned earlier, the clothing factories were the first to develop, and the production of textiles is largely a feature of the post-war development. In many countries textiles and clothing develop at an early stage of industrialization because of an assured consumer demand. Even countries with low *per capita* income provide a relatively large market because clothing of some sort is normally an essential item of consumption. Moreover, textile manufacture is a relatively 'easy' industry to establish in an undeveloped country. For one thing, modern machinery is largely automatic and can be operated by semi-skilled labour, and only a few highly skilled men are required for setting up the machinery and for maintenance. Also, the initial capital required is not as great as in many other branches of industry.

---

[16] For groups see footnote 11.
[17] See tables 17 and 18.

In 1970 the value of net output of textiles and clothing together was R382 million, of which clothing accounted for R197 million and textiles for R185 million. Together they employed 213 000 workers. Although the textile industry made great forward strides between 1945 and 1959, in which latter year there was a total of 156 textile units, operating 264 000 spindles, 5 000 looms and 2 776 knitting machines, there would still seem to be scope for expansion in certain fields. South African production in 1959 accounted for only 38 per cent of the South African consumption of textiles.[18]

Chemicals and chemical products (group 12)[19]
The chemicals industry in South Africa can be divided into five main types of products. Since it was the foundation of the industry in its early days, the manufacture of explosives for the mines should be the first to be mentioned. South Africa has at Modderfontein what is probably the largest privately owned explosives factory in the world. In 1959 the gross value of output of explosives was R31 million and net value R12 million. Equally important is the fertilizer-manufacturing industry, which is playing an increasingly important role in agricultural development. The gross value of its output in 1959 was R30 million. In the same year basic industrial chemicals had a gross value of R40 million and the manufacture of products of petroleum and coal showed a gross value of R65 000 million. To these basic four there must of course be added the pharmacy industry, and the manufacture of things such as soap etc.

The chemicals industry was developed by private initiative; a series of mergers in the inter-war period led to the huge organization, African Explosives and Chemical Industries, which is jointly owned by De Beers Industrial and Imperial Chemical Industries. This link with I.C.I. of Britain has been invaluable in providing the latest technical knowledge. Other large chemical manufacturers like Fisons and National Chemical Products have similar overseas links. Since 1950 the government has played an active role, either directly or through the Industrial Development Corporation, in the expansion of the chemicals industry.

The establishment of a plant for the synthesis of oil from coal was

[18] Board of Trade and Industries, Industrial Development Series No. 1: *The Industrial Potential of the Textile Industry in the Union of South Africa*, p. 2.
[19] For groups see footnote 11.

a major landmark in the chemical industry, and Sasol – the largest oil-from-coal plant in the world – has opened up a new era of expansion. It was estimated to cost R50 million, but the actual figure was almost twice this figure. Based upon cheap coal from its own coal mine it is producing a wide and increasing range of chemical products, including petrol, diesel fuel, ammonium sulphate, tars, waxes, solvents and plastics. This is only the beginning, and great expansion is expected in the quantity and in the variety of products which can be derived from the cheap coal. Already, numerous firms have come into being for the manufacture of the derivatives of the main products.

The net value of the output of the chemicals industry as a whole was R306 million in 1970 and it employed over 60 000 persons. Its present rate of growth is rapid – from a net output of only R12 million after the war to over R300 million; and its potentialities are great, both as providing new lines of export and in making the national economy less dependent on certain strategic products formerly imported, notably petrol and rubber. In the ten years from 1949 to 1959 the value of chemical exports increased from R11 million to R39 million and a further expansion to R78 million had occurred by 1972.

These four groups – iron, steel and engineering; food; clothing and textiles; and chemicals – are the most important groups in the manufacturing sector of the economy, but there are many more with large outputs and potentiality for expansion. Table 17 lists the nineteen major groups of manufacturing industry and gives the value of output and the employment of each for the year 1968.

Building and Construction

Clearly related to manufacturing, and together with it constituting the secondary sector of the economy, is the important group of building and construction. Expansion of this activity has been very rapid since 1945 because of the growth of the national economy.

Building and Construction

	Employment (thousands)	Contribution to G.D.P. (R millions)
1945	34,5	36
1950	79,0	80
1960	117,4	152
1970	367,8	507

These figures indicate that since the war there has been a more than tenfold increase in employment, and a thirteenfold increase in the value of output. Construction is, however, particularly sensitive to changes in the *rate of growth* of the national economy, and any reductions in the growth rate would have severe consequences for this sector.

If to the employment in manufacturing proper be added employment in building and construction and in the supply of electricity, gas and water, the total employment in the secondary sector of the economy in 1970 exceeded one and a half million people or about one-fifth of the total economically active population, and its contribution to the G.D.P. was about thirty per cent.

ASPECTS OF GOVERNMENT POLICY TOWARDS MANUFACTURING

Although there has been this phenomenal increase in manufacturing industry in South Africa, aspects of industrial policy have at times been a matter of controversy and there has been much discussion about the role which manufacturing should be called upon to fill in the national economy. Several government reports[20] have stressed the importance of building up a powerful and diversified manufacturing industry, both to provide employment for the increasing population and to replace the income generated by the gold mines as these became exhausted. The *Third Interim Report of the Industrial and Agricultural Requirements Commission* (1941) was an important landmark in the evolution of official industrial policy, for it stressed the fact that industrial development can only be a substitute for gold mining, if manufacturing is ultimately established on a self-supporting basis.[21] It recommended that greater emphasis should be placed on efficiency and on optimum resource allocation throughout the whole economy. Measures for the general rationalization of South Africa's manufacturing industries were proposed, including, *inter alia:*

(*a*) that certain South African raw materials at present exported in an unprocessed state be conserved for future industrial use;

[20] *Report of the Customs Tariff Commission,* 1934–5, U.G. 5/1936; *Third Interim Report of the Industrial and Agricultural Requirements Commission* U.G. 40/1941; Board of Trade and Industries Report 282: *Investigation into Manufacturing Industries,* 1945; *Report of the Commission of Enquiry into Policy Relating to the Protection of Industries,* U.G. 36/1958.

[21] Para. 163. See also C. S. Richards, 'Fundamentals of Economic Policy in the Union', *S.A.J.E.,* vol. 10 no. 1, March 1942, p. 56.

(b) that greater emphasis in establishing manufacturing industries be placed upon the processing of South African materials, particularly important being the development of iron and steel products, where owing to the cheap price of coal South Africa would appear to have marked comparative advantage;

(c) that better use be made of labour, including the increased use of Africans in industry, and the provision of technical training for all classes of labour;

(d) that there should be a more equitable distribution of the national income because great inequality, such as prevailed when the wages of whites in mining and manufacturing were respectively 8 times and between 4 and 5 times those of other groups, was prejudicial to the whole society and severely limited the domestic market for consumption goods;

(e) that, however, remuneration should remain linked to effort and ability and that, therefore, active steps should be taken to increase the productivity of labour;

(f) that more strenuous efforts should be made to expand South African exports of manufactured goods;

(g) that in granting assistance to manufacturing care be taken not to raise costs in gold mining or the other major export industries.

Two years later S. H. Frankel[22] showed that, in spite of the impressive expansion that had taken place in manufacturing, it was not a substitute for gold mining, but was in a sense a parasite, because the gold-mining industry provided the foreign exchange without which manufacturing industries would be unable to function.

'In this connection,' he wrote, 'it is only necessary to mention the significant fact that although 50 per cent of all raw materials used in manufacturing industry still had to be imported before the war, manufacturing industry did not supply more than 2,5 per cent of the Union's total exports. For every £100 of goods imported by manufacturing (exclusive of imports of machinery and equipment) only £7,6 of goods were exported by manufacturing industry.'

In 1950 H. F. Oppenheimer quoted figures to show that in 1946-7 raw materials for industry to the value of R208 million were imported

---

[22] S. H. Frankel and H. Herzfeld, 'An Analysis of the Growth of the National Income of the Union in the Period of Prosperity before the War', *S.A.J.E.*, vol. 12 no. 2, June 1944.

while exports of manufactured goods in 1946 amounted to only R48 million. The export deficit of the manufacturing sector was therefore R160 million.

'Far, therefore, from secondary industry offering an alternative to take the place of mining in our economy, the fact is that the prosperity of gold mining and the other primary exporting industries is a prerequisite and a condition of our industrial development . . . Manufacturing industry will only be able to serve as a substitute for the wasting asset of our mining industry if it is able to increase substantially its contribution to our export trade. This is really another way of saying, that as a whole, industry in South Africa, if it is to be able to stand on its own feet, must reduce costs. And in order to reduce costs the principal requirements are greater efficiency and a large internal market.'[23]

The Viljoen Commission[24] of 1958 recognized that the small size of the market was a major impediment to efficient production and listed various measures to overcome this difficulty, *inter alia:*

(1) that the domestic demand can be expanded only by increasing the purchasing power of the population as a whole and particularly that of the lower-income groups;

(2) this depends upon increasing the productivity and employment opportunities of the whole population;

(3) greater specialization of plants and economies of scale would be realized if there were greater standardization of products and in the specification of requirements of major government departments;

(4) the share in the home market available to the South African producer should be kept as large as was consistent with efficient production by a system of selective protection, and by reasonable preferences for South African products in the placing of government orders;

(5) every effort should be made to expand exports so that the total market, domestic and foreign, for South African products should expand to the point where unit costs will be reduced by large-scale production. In this connection the adjacent markets of South Africa

[23] H. F. Oppenheimer, *The Future of Industry in South Africa*, S.A. Institute of Race Relations, 1950, pp. 3 and 4.

[24] *Report of the Commission of Enquiry into Policy Relating to the Protection of Industries*, U.G. 36/1958, para. 376.

and the Rhodesias complement one another, and the tariff between the two countries should be kept as low as possible.

South African manufacturing industry is at present passing through a difficult period of reassessment and reorientation. Manufacturing started with the production of certain products for the mining industry and for a small and protected home market in consumers' goods. Its very success in industrial expansion has however created problems, and it is now universally acknowledged that if manufacturing is to assume the role of the leading sector of the economy it must be oriented increasingly towards export, and instead of producing for a small protected home market it must face the keen winds of international competition. The importance of manufacturing in the future economic development of South Africa cannot be too greatly stressed because all the indications are that it must be the cornerstone of future expansion. Agriculture at present employs the great mass of the people, but more modern methods of production and, in particular, reform of peasant farming in the reserves are likely to release large numbers of workers for whom alternative employment opportunities will have to be found. Mining is still a very important and expanding sector; but, barring major new mineral discoveries, employment in mining is unlikely to increase much beyond the present level. It is therefore to an expansion of manufacturing and tertiary activities that one must look for the employment opportunities and income generation for *the whole of the natural increase of the population.*

The long-term prospects are good. South Africa is richly endowed with many essential raw materials. Cheap coal and iron ore could be the basis of very great expansion of iron, steel and engineering industry. South Africa is today by far the most highly developed economy in the continent of Africa, and has the most highly trained and industrially conscious population – white and black – in this continent.

Transport and communications are adequate to support major industrial expansion, and the adjacent countries in Africa may offer an expanding market for industrial products. Moreover, recent experience would indicate that in certain lines of manufacture, South Africa has, or can develop, a comparative advantage sufficient to promote exports to Europe, America and other world markets.

In the immediate present, however, certain very real difficulties present themselves. In some branches of industry the South African market is too small to warrant the introduction of the most modern machinery throughout the plant, or to justify sufficiently long production runs to take full advantage of the economies of scale. Thus a relatively high cost structure is imposed by the limitations of the market. If a large volume of exports could be attained, the total market (exports plus domestic consumption) would bring about considerable economies of scale. The expansion of exports demands high productive efficiency and low unit costs, but these are difficult to achieve owing to the restricted size of the domestic demand, which thus adversely affects the competitive position of South African products on world markets. Hence there is strong pressure to expand the domestic market.

The small domestic market is in part due to the size of South Africa's population in comparison with that of many of the major industrial countries,[25] and little can be done about this except to atttempt to expand the area of free trade in southern Africa. The limited domestic market is, however, also due to the fact that a majority of the South African population has only a very low level of consumption. Most of the four-and-a-quarter million whites and not more than three quarters of a million others, have a relatively high standard of living but the twenty million remaining citizens live for the most part very little above a bare minimum standard. If the average level of consumption could be raised to the present level of the whites this would lead to at least threefold increase in the South African domestic market. There is, therefore what might be described as a symbiotic relationship between the advancement of the standard of living of the non-white section of the population and the general progress of manufacturing for the home market, which rests upon the fact that mass-production methods necessarily imply mass-consumption of their products. Any increase in the incomes of the poorer section must, however, be related to over-all increases in productivity because, unless this were so, unit costs of production would rise and impair the position of exports to world markets.

Difficulties of a different kind also arise from the fact that many factories were originally set up to manufacture consumer goods out of imported semi-processed or raw materials, and these were allowed

[25] United States 183 million, Soviet Union 218 million, European Economic Community 222 million.

in duty-free or on rebate. With the increasing emphasis on the need to stimulate the use of local raw materials, protective tariffs are being demanded by factories engaged upon the *earlier* stages of the productive process. This tends to raise costs for the manufacturer at the final stage, and he in turn tends to pass them on in higher prices to the consumer. Yet it is essential to prevent any rise in price levels that will adversely affect the cost structure of the major export industries. Illustrative of this situation is the fact that the protection given to the textile industry tends to raise costs in the clothing industry; tariffs on leather assist the tanner, but hurt the footwear manufacturer. The dilemma facing the automobile industry is that factories were established at the ports to assemble vehicles from foreign components. Now pressure is being brought to bear upon them to use a progressively greater proportion of South African-made components, until eventually the whole car will be of local manufacture. With the sound basis of an indigenous iron and steel industry this is probably wise policy in the long run, but it raises great difficulties in costs, location and markets at the present time.

Difficulties of this nature have given rise to a more detailed analysis of specific industries to estimate their growth potential and their backward and forward linkage with other sectors of the economy. This will enable *selective* tariff protection to be granted where it is likely to be most effective in stimulating sound industrial expansion and at the same time to have the minimum adverse effect upon the general cost structure. Three classes of industry seem particularly favoured: industries with a high input of local materials, which when once established, appear likely to have a comparative advantage and an export potential; import replacement industries; and industries which from an economic or military viewpoint have strategic importance.

The need to export has been given wide publicity, and the government and leading industrialists are doing much to promote the export trade. It is, however, a difficult reorientation for the average industrialist to make, because for years he has looked towards a protected home market, but now he is being required to face about, and must learn to sell his products abroad, with all the implications which this has in matters of industrial efficiency and competitive pricing, not to mention the need to develop overseas selling agencies and the detailed study of foreign market requirements. It also raises important problems for the best location of the industries.

THE LOCATION OF INDUSTRY

Industries based upon the processing of perishable agricultural commodities (the canning of fruit, vegetables and fish, the making of wine, the saw-mills etc.) are normally situated at the source of their materials and are fairly widely distributed geographically. Apart from these, however, the industries of South Africa have tended to be very highly concentrated in four main areas – the southern Transvaal, Cape Town, Durban and Port Elizabeth. The southern Transvaal represents by far the largest concentration of population in southern Africa and is therefore the major market for manufactured goods. The other three industrial areas are seaports, and transportation between them can be effected relatively cheaply by sea. Thus in some measure the ports, which can collectively be regarded as a second large market, are not as highly concentrated as that of the southern Transvaal. Although each of the ports has its particular features, the locational advantages for industry at all of them have certain things in common. Therefore the analysis of locational advantage can be simplified without great distortion if we regard the ports as together forming a single entity. Thus there are two major alternative sites for setting up a new factory – the southern Transvaal or one of the ports.

Some industries were established primarily to serve the needs of the mining industry. These, like the explosives industry, were naturally located in the southern Transvaal. But, as we saw in an earlier section of this chapter, many factories were initially set up to manufacture consumer goods from imported raw materials or semi-processed components. For these factories, the ports offer some advantage. Thus a factory using mainly imported materials and producing for a nation-wide market would probably find its optimum location at one of the ports, because there it would not have to pay railage on its imported materials, although the railage on that portion of its output sent inland might be heavy. Had the factory been situated inland, it would have had to pay railage from the ports on the whole of its imported materials and in addition face the cost of transporting back to the coast that portion of its final output sold at the ports or destined for export.

An additional complication is introduced by the tariff schedules of the railways. On the principle of 'charging what the traffic will bear', railway freight rates are usually much higher on manufactured goods than on raw materials.[26] This differential tariff system thus tends to strengthen the pull of the market vis-à-vis the pull to the source of the raw materials. Therefore, a firm producing primarily for the southern Transvaal market might find it better to be located inland although it was using mainly imported materials, because it would be cheaper to transport these inland as low-rated goods than to manufacture at the ports and face the high railway rates on the finished product. The optimum location for a factory depends. therefore, upon a combination of the proportion of its output destined for the inland markets and the difference between the railway tariff on its raw materials and its finished product. Other things being equal, the railway tariff system would tend to favour the southern Transvaal. Nevertheless, the fact remains that many industries were successfully established at the ports.

With the more recent tendency to develop the processing of South African raw materials, so strikingly illustrated by the development of Iscor and Sasol, the situation is being rapidly transformed. As the manufacturers of consumer goods increasingly depend upon South African rather than imported materials the locational advantage of the ports diminishes greatly, and manufacturing is becoming more and more concentrated in the southern Transvaal. This process is shown clearly in the following table.

*Output and Employment of Industrial Regions as a Percentage of the South African Total**

	1916–17	1928–9	1938–9	1945–6	1949–50	1953–4	1967–8
Southern Transvaal							
Value of net output	37,4	34,7	44,0	47,1	45,6	48,0	50,5
Total employment	28,2	34,1	43,9	44,9	44,1	45,2	46,3
Western Cape							
Value of net output	22,1	22,4	18,6	17,4	17,1	15,3	11,2
Total employment	20,9	19,6	16,5	16,2	15,8	14,3	12,1
Durban and Pinetown							
Value of net output	11,7	11,6	12,2	12,5	12,3	11,4	13,1
Total employment	11,1	11,5	10,9	11,2	11,1	10,8	13,2
Port Elizabeth†							
Value of net output	3,1	5,8	5,7	5,4	7,6†	7,0†	6,9†
Total employment	3,4	5,0	4,6	4,6	5,8†	5,8†	5,9†
The rest of the Republic							
Value of net output	25,7	25,6	19,5	17,6	17,4	18,3	18,1
Total employment	36,4	30,0	24,7	23,1	23,2	23,9	24,4

* Industrial census for relevant years.
† Uitenhage added to Port Elizabeth.
Source: *Census of Manufacturing, 1967–68* No. 10–21–18.

[26] There are fourteen classes of goods, and freight rates on Class 1 are at least ten times and often more than 10 times higher than on Class 14.

The tendency is for there to be a decline in the relative importance of all areas other than the southern Transvaal, and industry of the southern Transvaal has increased until it now supplies about half of the total output of the country. The actual figures from the 1967-68 census were:

Region	Number of Estabs.	Employment (thousands)	Output Gross	(R million) Net
Cape (0101)	1 755	120	650	279
P.E. (0301)	491	58	449	164
Durban (0801)	1 441	131	833	316
S. Transvaal (1001 to 1007)	5 765	458	2 792	1 222
Rest of Republic	3 690	222	1 259	437
S.A. Total	13 142	989	5 983	2 418

Moreover, it is a movement which, if unchecked, is likely to accelerate as time goes on. There are many instances of manufacturing firms formerly located at the ports which have moved inland, and there are many more that would do so, but for the heavy new capital investment this would involve.

Decentralization of industries

This concentration in the southern Transvaal has given rise to a desire for State intervention to bring about a wider dispersal of manufacturing industry. The ports are increasingly alarmed at their relative decline. It is also argued that the large concentration in the southern Transvaal is economically and socially undesirable. Although the market and raw materials available may make the southern Transvaal the optimum location from the point of the profitability of private industry, it is argued that there are hidden social costs in the provision of increased services – transport, sanitation, water supply and health and recreational facilities and the maintenance of law and order – and that these are overlooked. As long ago as 1949 H. R. Raikes[27] drew attention to the fact that availability of water was the limiting factor to the expansion of the industry in this area, arguing that the ever-increasing demands being made upon the Vaal River were an aspect which could no longer be

[27] H. R. Raikes, 'Liquid Fuel from Coal', *S.A.J.E.*, vol. 17 no. 1, Marc h 1949, p. 41 et seq.

neglected in planning future developments. Surely it is better to take steps now to divert suitable industries elsewhere than to wait until a critical situation has developed. The military argument is also advanced, namely that in this age of nuclear weapons it is foolish to permit the concentration of nearly half the industry and a quarter of the population of a country of 1 222 000 square kilometres in one locality, where all could be destroyed by a single hydrogen bomb.[28]

A contrary view is also strongly held, namely, that what the country as a whole requires above all else at the present time is rapid industrial expansion to absorb the growing population, and that the southern Transvaal is at present the area where greatest growth is taking place. State intervention to secure decentralization may well check the rate of growth, not only of the southern Transvaal, but also of the country as a whole, by introducing a new and unpredictable element, and by persuading industry to be established at a site which does not offer the maximum locational advantage. Such factories would for ever be burdened with additional costs which would reduce their economic efficiency, be a hindrance to the expansion of exports and be a perpetual burden upon the economy. Moreover, it is pointed out that the concentration may be large in relation to the size of the national economy, but that the Transvaal industrial complex is small relative to some great industrial areas in other countries. An additional argument against deflecting industry from the Witwatersrand is that some of the older gold mines will have to close down in the near future, and it is essential to prevent these reef towns from becoming 'ghost cities' by attracting manufacturing industries there to replace the mines.

If the drive to increase the volume of manufactured goods exported is successful, this introduces a further complication into the problems of industrial location. A factory at present producing for the home market may find itself well located in the Transvaal, but if it is successful in its export drive the inland location may eventually prove to be a handicap because of the railage to the coast. Had the export possibilities been envisaged when the factory was erected, one of the ports might have been selected as the appropriate site.

The already complicated problem of location is made yet more difficult by the consideration of providing employment opportunities

[28] A foreign visitor who had flown over most of South Africa commented upon the Witwatersrand industrial complex, that it looked as if all South Africans were playing that children's game known as 'sardines'.

for the population in the African homelands, who, as was shown in chapter 3, must be displaced from the land if agricultural progress is to be rendered possible. The migratory-labour system described in chapter 4 is almost universally admitted to be economically inefficient and socially destructive, but it will be expanded and its evils intensified unless new employment opportunities other than as perpetual migratory labourers can be found for these 300 000 to 500 000 displaced families. The objective should be to absorb them into factories which are near their homes, so that normal family relationships can be restored, and they can be encouraged to become permanent and fully committed industrial workers. If some 500 000 families of the present migrant workers are to be transported to the existing industrial areas, the cost of providing housing and other essentials will be exceedingly great in areas where land values and other costs are already high.

As an alternative the Tomlinson Commission recommended the establishment of industries in or near the existing African areas. Provided the factories located there are not faced with locational disadvantages (other than temporary ones which will be overcome as development of the area proceeds), there is much to be said in support of bringing industries to where the people live. Some industries are of course quite unsuited to the African areas, but there are others, particularly those which by their nature are labour-intensive, which might successfully be induced to go to these areas. In many respects this scheme is similar to attempts in other countries to promote industrial development in certain areas, like Northern Ireland and southern Italy, but unfortunately it has been associated with the government's policy of separate development of the races, and it has thus become emotionally charged both to supporters and opponents of the government's ideological plans. Thus objective economic assessment of these proposals is difficult to achieve.

The government rejected the Tomlinson Commission's recommendation for industries within the reserves, for the somewhat spurious reason that 'Bantu enterprise, unimpeded by European competition, should be enabled to develop its own industries',[29] proposing instead

---

[29] White Paper on the government's decisions on the recommendations on the Tomlinson Report: W.P.F/1956. This reason appears spurious, because any undeveloped area like the reserves requires capital and industrial know-how, and these can only be effectively supplied by white entrepreneurs. Safeguards to prevent exploitation of the Africans could have been imposed.

the establishment of industries in white areas on the periphery of the reserves. There are several sound reasons for preferring these areas for industrial development at the present time. Deep in the reserves there are few essential services: in most areas rail transport, electricity, water storage and sanitation services are lacking and could only be installed at great capital cost; while in some of the 'border areas', the essential infrastructure to support large industrial expansion is already developed. Moreover, two of these border areas also have advantages for the development of export industries since they are near ports. Three areas have been selected for the location of border industries – in the Transvaal north of Pretoria, in Natal along the railway line from Durban to Pietermaritzburg, and in the eastern Cape on the railway line from East London to the north. All three are close to large African areas, and the last two are close to the ports of Durban and East London respectively, and are therefore well situated for exporting or for receiving imported raw materials, but they are far from the main inland market. This is especially true of East London. Manufacturers establishing factories in these border areas are offered special inducements to offset any initial locational disadvantage, in the form of capital assistance for buildings and layout of industrial sites, remission of taxation in the initial years, possible exemption from certain provisions of industrial labour laws,[30] and concessions in the matter of railway freight rates. The Physical Planning and Utilization of Resources Act of 1967 conferred Draconian powers upon the Minister of Planning to impose restrictions upon expansion of manufacturing activity in the established industrial areas.[31]

Manufacturers with established factories in the main industrial areas expressed concern lest the concessions to be granted in the border areas might expose them to unfair competition from newly established factories in the border areas, but were assured that it was the government's intention that these concessions would merely offset any initial locational disadvantage. Opposition to the provisions of the Physical Planning Act was widespread, and the restrictions upon African employment led to such dissatisfaction that an inter-departmental committee under the chairmanship of Dr. P. J. Riekert was appointed to report upon the matter, and in July 1971

[30] This aspect is related to industrial legislation, discussed in chapter 7.
[31] Act 88, 1967.

the government issued a White Paper reaffirming the intention to implement the policy of industrial decentralization, but making the enforcement of the policy somewhat less rigid.[32]

The somewhat dramatic announcement early in 1962 that the government was granting self-government to the Transkei has added a further complicating factor in assessing industrial development and location, which affects particularly the East London area. It is still too early to see clearly the implications of 'self-government'. If it were to develop into any form of political independence which might result in restrictions upon the free movement of goods and labour between the Transkei and the rest of the Republic it would be most injurious to industrial development in general and to the border industries in particular. If on the other hand it is merely a form of local government, or political independence within a common customs union similar to the present position of Botswana, Lesotho and Swaziland, it should not affect the economy adversely. Nevertheless it introduces another element of uncertainty especially when many people believe that the present boundaries of the Bantu areas are by no means immutable.

Enough has been said to indicate the complicated and interacting factors affecting industrial location at the present time. A much fuller account is to be found in a book by Trevor Bell.[33] The major switch from imported to South African components in manufacture, the great pull of the southern Transvaal, the drive to expand exports of manufactured goods, the move for the greater decentralization of industry, and the policy of establishing industries in the border areas to provide employment for African peasants displaced from the land, are all elements in the very intricate balance of economic and political forces. The outcome will be observed with interest.

On the more general question whether secondary industry will continue to grow towards a situation where it is fully self-supporting, past development and available resources give a confident answer that this goal can be reached. Provided adverse political events – in the Republic, in the rest of the African continent or in the world at large – do not intervene, the continued expansion of manufacturing industry can be regarded as an economic certainty.

[32] Other aspects of the White Paper are referred to on page 231.
[33] R. T. Bell, *Industrial Decentralisation in South Africa*.

7 Labour, Wages & Standards of Living

THE EVOLUTION OF POLICY

In the 1860s there was little wage-paid labour in South Africa. Apart from a small number of persons engaged in trade, commerce and transport, the mass of the population was supported by agriculture. In the tribal areas the Africans continued to practise their traditional subsistence farming in small family units and there was no wage-labour because cultivation in the reserves was done by members of the family. Most of the white farmers were also largely engaged in subsistence farming. In the Cape Colony farm labour was provided by the Hottentots, by the coloured descendants of the slaves who had been liberated in 1834, and, particularly after the 'cattle killing' of 1857,[1] by Xhosa refugees who settled on white farms in the eastern Cape. Cash wages were low or non-existent, because few farmers earned a significant cash income, and most remuneration was in kind. This generally took the form of payment in cattle (usually one beast per annum), grazing rights, permission to erect a hut for the man's family and the granting of a piece of arable land for his wife to cultivate. Indeed the African on the white farms lived very much as his brethren in the tribal areas, save that he had to devote a portion of his time to working for his white master in return for the benefit he received. In Natal, the Orange Free State and the Transvaal very similar conditions prevailed except that there were few coloured people or Hottentots and almost all the labourers were black

---

[1] In 1857, under the influence of a young girl of 16, Nongqause, who claimed that she had spoken with ancestral spirits, the Xhosa chiefs ordered their followers to kill all their cattle and destroy their grain, in the belief that on an appointed day the ancestors would arise from the dead and drive the white man from the land. When the miracle failed to occur, famine swept through the country. How many died beyond the Kei will never be known, but the population of the Ciskei was estimated to have been reduced by death or dispersion from 105 000 to 37 000. Many entered the colony to work on white farms.

Africans. In Natal indentured Indian labour was also used on the cane plantations.[2] Throughout South Africa share-cropping was widely practised. Many farm servants owned ten or more cattle, and in this sense they might be regarded as relatively wealthy; but the standard of living of the majority of farm servants, and of their masters, was low by modern standards. The relationship was essentially that of master and servant tempered by mutual interdependence and a large measure of paternalism on the part of the employer. The whole association was still largely within the confines of a subsistence economy, and cash payments played only a very minor part.

The mineral discoveries in the latter part of the nineteenth century introduced a wholly new element by giving rise to an almost insatiable demand for labour and by offering a hitherto unprecedented opportunity for earning cash wages. Skilled labour was imported from Europe, America and Australia; and high wages had to be offered in order to secure it. Unskilled labour was obtained from local sources and, although the African mine worker was paid more than he could have earned on white farms or in subsistence tribal agriculture, his wage was only a fraction of that paid to the skilled worker. Initially the disparity between skilled and unskilled rates was the natural reflection of the relative supply-and-demand situations, and was caused by the great scarcity of skilled workers in an underdeveloped economy. But the distinction between skilled and unskilled soon came to be more or less identified with the distinction between the races, and the operation of market forces came in some measure to be replaced by the convention that a white man's wage was usually five to ten times the wage of a black man. This convention was reinforced by trade-union pressure, for the white workers were more articulate and soon came to be better organized than the black. Moreover, the whites in the Transvaal had the franchise and the blacks had not, so that political power was used to support economic privilege. The process by which this more or less rigid racial stratification of the labour force has come about has been described by several South African economists,[3] and only the main events can be mentioned here.

[2] First introduced in 1860, recruitment was suspended in 1866, but was reintroduced in 1874 and continued until 1911, when it was stopped by the government of India in retaliation for prohibition of Indian emigration to South Africa.

[3] Sheila T. van der Horst, *Native Labour in South Africa;* also 'The Economic Implications of Political Democracy', supplement to *Optima,* June 1960; and G. V. Doxey, *The Industrial Colour Bar in South Africa.*

Trade unionism was introduced into South Africa from Britain in the 1880s.[4] At that time the 'new model' trade union, composed of skilled craftsmen associated to maintain and advance their position in modern industrial society, dominated the British scene. It was not until after the London dock strike of 1899 that British unionism came to include the unskilled worker. The craft-union pattern fitted naturally into the South African setting, and its objectives of furthering the interests of skilled workers soon became associated with a policy of preventing the position of the white worker from being undermined by the use of black or coloured workers in any but unskilled jobs. British trade unionism of the 1880s thus reinforced South African convention in these matters.

The Anglo-Boer War of 1899–1902 disrupted the economy of the whole of southern Africa and brought the gold-mining industry to a standstill. The large labour force had been dispersed, and the demand for labour for the reconstruction of the country and the rebuilding of farms led to an acute labour shortage. When the gold mines were reopened in 1902 progress was restricted by the shortage of African labour. Lord Milner realized that the rehabilitation of the Transvaal after the war depended upon a rapid expansion of gold output; and, to overcome the labour shortage, indentured Chinese workers were imported in 1904. Their introduction was strongly opposed by many in South Africa and particularly by a group of white miners led by F. H. Creswell, who proposed an alternative policy of recruiting white miners from Europe. He claimed that it would be possible to operate the mines efficiently on an all-white basis. Meanwhile in Britain there was strong opposition to 'Chinese slavery in the Transvaal', which became a slogan in the election of 1906. As a result of the Liberal party victory, the importation of Chinese workers was discontinued, and those in the country were all repatriated to China; but, as the figures below indicate, they had served their purpose, because by 1910 Africans had again been recruited in sufficient numbers to expand gold production; nevertheless the 'Chinese interlude' had important consequences.

---

[4] The first union in South Africa is believed to have been a branch of the English union of Carpenters and Joiners, formed at Cape Town in 1881.

Employees in the Gold Mines*

	Whites	Africans	Chinese	Total
1899	12 000	107 000	–	119 000
1902	10 000	45 000	–	55 000
1906	18 000	94 000	51 000	163 000
1910	25 000	195 000	305	220 000

* M. H. de Kock, p. 440.

In the early days of mining most of the white mine workers were immigrants from abroad; and even as late as 1910 there were only 7 285 South African-born white miners, representing 27,2 per cent of the white labour force, while 62,8 per cent of the white miners came from Britain and 10 per cent from other countries.[5] Trade unionism began to develop in the gold-mining industry about the time of the Chinese importations, as the white miners increasingly felt the need to unite to protect their position as skilled workers. African labour had not previously been a serious threat because the cultural gulf and difference in skill between the whites and Africans was so great that there was little possibility of substitution. With the Chinese, however, it was different and, under pressure from the white miners, Ordinance no. 17 of 1904 (Transvaal) limited the employment of non-European immigrants to unskilled labour,[6] thereby introducing the first statutory colour bar in South African industry. Three years later there occurred a strike of white mine workers in opposition to an attempt to increase the ratio of non-white to white workers by requiring each white miner to take charge of three drilling machines instead of the customary two.[7] Thus in the Transvaal the two main methods for protecting the white skilled workers had emerged before Union. These were measures designed to reserve certain occupations for whites only, and pressure to resist any attempts by employers to alter the over-all ratio of non-white to white workers. The former principle was entrenched in Union legislation by the Mines and Works Act, no. 12 of 1911, through the prohibition – allegedly in the interests of safety – of the issue of blasting certificates to Africans, and the latter by specifying in regulations under the Act the number of African miners a white foreman could supervise.

[5] M. H. de Kock, p. 442.

[6] See Sheila T. van der Horst, *Native Labour in South Africa*, p. 171.

[7] E. Gitsham and J. F. Trembath, *A First Account of Labour Organization in South Africa*, 1926, p. 28.

The trade-union movement among white workers was growing in strength, and in July 1913 a general strike was called in which some 19 000 men came out. Later in the year when a similar general strike was planned, the government called out the newly created defence force, declared martial law and summarily arrested and deported nine leaders of the trade-union movement. It was, however, not until 1922 that the labour situation on the Witwatersrand reached its real climax. Also in 1913, the first successful organization of non-white workers occurred when the Indians in Natal, led by a young Indian lawyer, M. K. Gandhi,[8] who had been trained in England, called a general strike of all Indian workers in Natal. Gandhi advocated passive resistance, and in general the strike was without violence. He and several other leaders were arrested and imprisoned, but were soon released, and the publicity given to the Indians' grievances led to some amelioration of the causes of their discontent.

There was growing industrial unrest in South Africa from 1918 onwards. The price of gold had risen and so had costs and wages, but the prospect of Britain's return to the gold standard at the pre-war gold parity precipitated a major crisis in the mining industry.[9] It was estimated that unless costs were reduced, twenty-four out of the thirty-nine producing gold mines might have to close down and discharge some 10 000 white miners and many thousands of Africans. To avoid this the Chamber of Mines proposed major reorganization designed to reduce labour costs. Between 1913 and 1918 wages of Africans had increased by only some 9 per cent, but white miners' wages had risen 60 per cent.[10] It was not proposed to reduce the wages of the white miners, but to effect the economy by substituting a certain number of Africans for whites, and altering the proportion of highly paid white workers and low paid Africans. This involved a modification of the *status quo* agreement, which was a wartime measure by which the Chamber of Mines undertook to maintain 'the *status quo* as existed on each mine with regard to the relative scope of employment of Europeans and coloured employees'. In

[8] Subsequently world famous as Mahatma Gandhi, the liberator of India. See M. K. Gandhi, *Satyagraha in South Africa* (trans. V. G. Desai), Ganesan, Madras, 1928.

[9] The price of gold would fall from a peak of R13,00 to the statutory price of R8,50.

[10] Doxey, p. 124.

order to allay the fears of the white miners the Chamber of Mines offered a fixed ratio of 1 white to 10,5 non-white miners, but reserved the right to make any changes it thought necessary within this over-all ratio. The South African Industrial Federation, which represent-ed the white miners, rejected the proposal and demanded a ratio of one white to 3,5 non-whites, not only in mining, but throughout the whole national economy except in agriculture. It was estimated that had the Chamber's proposals been accepted some 2 000 white miners would temporarily have lost their jobs, but it was hoped that they would speedily be reabsorbed with the expansion of mining consequent upon the reduction of costs.[11]

Led by a more extreme section known as the Action Group, whose members included persons associated with the Third Inter-national, the white mine workers armed themselves and went on strike, calling for general support to protect the white workers. The strikers were in possession of a large part of the Witwatersrand and the government had to mobilize police and defence forces, and use aeroplanes, and artillery, before what was known as the Rand Rebel-lion was suppressed.[12] The Rand Rebellion is a focal point in the South African labour movement because it highlights many of the underlying tensions and contradictions in the labour situation. In it we have the curious spectacle of Communist-inspired leaders calling upon the workers of the world to unite to protect the privileged position of white workers.[13]

The action of the government in putting down the rebellion, and the severity of the sentences imposed,[14] turned the white workers against the South African party led by General J. C. Smuts, which had governed the country since Union; and paved the way for a *rapprochement* between the Labour party under Col. F. H. Creswell

---

[11] E. A. Walker, *A History of Southern Africa.*

[12] For a detailed but somewhat partisan account of these events see *2 000 Casualties* by Ivan L. Walker and Ben Weinbrun, S.A. Trades Union Council, Johannesburg, 1961.

[13] Lang, Hull and Lewis went to the gallows singing 'The Red Flag', ibid., p. 157. Colonel F. H. Creswell, leader of the Labour party, said in January 1922 that he 'believed the kernel of the dispute to be the proposals of the Chamber of Mines to carry a big step forward the process of restricting the opportunities of civilized men to earn a living in the industries of the country. On this question of the colour bar, he believed the workers to be absolutely right' (p. 101).

[14] As a result of these disturbances forty-six persons were charged with high treason and murder, of whom eighteen were convicted and sentenced to death; of these, four were hanged, the remainder being reprieved (p. 150).

(whose members were still predominantly English speaking and whose political faith was socialist) and the Nationalist party led by General J. B. M. Hertzog (which represented the hard core of anti-British sentiment and whose objective was an independent republic for South Africa). The outcome was an election pact between the two parties whereby each undertook to put its principles into cold storage for the duration of the pact – the socialists agreed not to press for socialism, and the republicans not to press for a republic. They were successful in the general election of 1924 and the Nationalist-Labour Pact government took office. This event did much to give positive direction to the traditional sentiment towards African, Coloured and Asian workers.

The labour leaders were mainly concerned with the protection of the skilled white workers in mining and industry who were largely English speaking and the majority of whom had been born outside South Africa. The Nationalist party leaders were particularly concerned with the unskilled whites who were drifting into the towns from the country. These 'poor whites', as they were called, numbered somewhere between 200 000 and 300 000 and were a major social problem.[15] They were mainly Afrikaans speaking, and their plight was in part due to the legacy of the Anglo-Boer War, but mainly to population increase and to the reconstruction in agriculture which was changing from subsistence farming to production for the growing urban markets and for export. The difficulties were enhanced by the violent fluctuations in the price of agricultural products on the international markets in the 1920s to which reference was made in the chapter on agriculture. Drifting into the towns, these Afrikaners from the *platteland* lacked knowledge of urban ways, possessed no industrial skills, and laboured under the additional handicap that mining and industry were largely controlled by English-speaking people and were conducted in what to them was a foreign language. In the unskilled labour market they found themselves in competition with non-white people whose wages were too low to support a civilized way of life.

The Pact government embarked upon a policy of encouraging manufacturing industries in order to provide a new field of employment for the whites displaced from the rural areas, and introduced

[15] See Carnegie Commission Report on *The Poor White Problem in South Africa*, vol. 1: 'Rural Impoverishment and Rural Exodus' by J. F. W. Grosskopf, 1932.

labour legislation designed to protect white workers. Three major Acts, which have been the foundation upon which future policy has been built, were the Industrial Conciliation Act, no. 11 of 1924, the Wages Act, no. 27 of 1925, and the Mines and Works Amendment Act, no. 25 of 1926. The first of these was in many respects an admirable piece of legislation providing machinery for consultation between employers' organizations and trade unions for the determination of wages and conditions of work by collective bargaining; and providing for arbitration in the case of disputes. It applied only to those industries in which labour was organized; but by its definition of an employee it excluded the vast majority of Africans. Thus the white workers were empowered to negotiate with the employers for an industrial agreement which fixed the wages of all grades of labour, including unskilled, but the mass of unskilled workers, though bound by its terms, had no part in the negotiations. The Wage Act was complementary to the Industrial Conciliation Act, and was operative in all those industries and trades in which the workers were not sufficiently organized to engage in collective bargaining with the employers. It set up a Wage Board consisting of three members, appointed by the Minister of Labour, to investigate conditions of work and rates of pay in the industries falling within its jurisdiction and to recommend minimum rates of pay where this was deemed desirable. Upon the Minister's consent these minimum-wage determinations had the force of law. The third of these Acts – the Mines and Works Amendment Act of 1926 – reiterated and reinforced the principle of the original Act of 1911, certain provisions of which had been declared *ultra vires* by the courts, and firmly established the principle of race discrimination in certain jobs related to mining.

Besides these three Acts other measures contributed to the protection of the white workers. The Apprenticeship Act, no. 26 of 1922, and its amending Act, no. 37 of 1944, although they did not specifically impose any racial discrimination, laid down conditions for apprenticeship which made it difficult for many Africans, coloured people and Asians to qualify as skilled workers. Then too the Native Labour Regulation Act of 1911, no. 15 of 1911, and the various Natives (Urban Areas) Acts[16] and, in relation to the right

[16] The first was Act 21 of 1923 which was replaced by Act 25 of 1945 and this in turn has been amended from time to time.

to own land outside the reserves, the Land Act of 1913, imposed a multitude of restraints upon free movement of Africans which had important consequences on the labour market through restriction of their mobility. In addition the 'civilized labour policy' of the government in the 1920s tended to stimulate the employment of whites in preference to other races by preferential tariff duties and by the placing of government contracts with firms employing a high proportion of 'civilized' labour, and by the replacement of Africans, coloured people and Asians in unskilled jobs in the government service and on the railways by whites at a higher rate of pay.[17] The effects of these policies in manufacturing industry were discussed in the last chapter. It was there seen that in the 1920s, especially during the great depression, white employment was maintained at the expense of the African, coloured and Asian workers, but that in the period of rapid expansion of the economy in the 1930s and during and after the war, the employment of non-white people expanded more rapidly than the employment of whites. It would appear that in periods of rapid economic growth the restrictions on non-white employment tend to be relaxed owing to the need to maintain output. In such periods non-white people can even move into more highly skilled occupations, replacing white workers who have moved into preferred avenues of employment elsewhere.

Since 1948 the government has introduced further measures for the protection of white workers in industry, the most important of which was the Industrial Conciliation Act, no. 28 of 1956. This Act retained the general principles of the earlier Industrial Conciliation Acts, no. 11 of 1924 and no. 36 of 1937 – but contained two new and highly contentious provisions. The first was the principle of job reservation. The Act provided for the establishment of an Industrial Tribunal consisting of five members appointed by the Minister of Labour, and section 77 (as amended by Act 41 of 1959) gave the Minister wide powers to reserve, on the recommendation of the tribunal, certain jobs for members of a particular race, or to specify the percentage of workers of a particular race to be employed.

The second new provision was the principle of enforced racial separation in the trade unions. Trade unionism began among the

---

[17] For an excellent analysis of the cumulative effect of these measures upon the employment opportunities of Africans see Sheila T. van der Horst, *Native Labour in South Africa*.

skilled white workers, but there was no legislative restriction upon members of any race joining the unions, and in the Cape Province racially mixed unions were common until this Act. Africans formed a huge all-African union in the 1920s when Clements Kadalie launched the Industrial and Commercial Workers Union, which included African workers in industry and commerce and even some agricultural workers. It had a meteoric career, claiming at one time to have over 100 000 members; and in many aspects it resembled Robert Owen's Grand National Consolidated Trades Union in Britain in the 1830s. It collapsed for much the same reasons – lack of coherent organization, lack of financial integrity and experience in its officials, strong and determined opposition by employers and the State. Since then various African unions on a smaller scale have been formed, but African unions have never enjoyed official recognition carrying with it immunity from breach of contract. They have thus been denied the strike weapon, and this has greatly militated against their effective growth. The Industrial Conciliation Acts excluded Africans from participation in the machinery of collective bargaining, and the 1953 Native Labour (Settlement of Disputes) Act, no. 48 of 1953, as amended, set up special machinery for African workers. This Act forbade strikes and lock-outs. It provided for the establishment of Regional Native Labour Committees under the chairmanship of the native labour officer of the area, with not less than three Africans nominated by the Minister to represent the interests of African workers. Provision was also made for a Central Native Labour Board. The whole structure was essentially paternalistic, and did not go as far as the 1951 Industrial Legislation Commission[18] had recommended, namely that, subject to special measures for their control and guidance, African unions should be granted official recognition. The Industrial Legislation Commission found that in 1949 there were 199 registered trade unions,[19] of which 63 were genuinely multi-racial; 76, though registered as multi-racial, were in fact confined to members of one race only (54 whites only and 22 non-whites only); 36 were registered as being for whites only; and 22 for non-whites only. A further 8 unions did not furnish clear

---

[8] U.G. 62/1951.

[19] This of course excludes African unions which, not having official recognition, were not registered.

information.[20] A study[21] undertaken by Muriel Horrell revealed that in 1958 in 159 unions investigated the position was that:

68 were all-white unions with a membership of	210 679
18 were coloured or Indian unions with a membership of	18 422
51 were 'mixed' unions with a membership of	183 762
22 were African unions (officially unrecognized) with a membership of	20 175

The purpose of the Industrial Conciliation Act of 1956 was to achieve racial separation in the 'mixed' unions and section 4(*b*) provided that no trade union might be registered for both white and coloured workers, nor might it be registered if membership was open to white and coloured workers unless total membership was so small that the formation of separate unions was impracticable. In this case the Minister might give special permission for the registration of a 'mixed' union, but it must hold separate meetings for its white and coloured members.

An attempt has been made to trace briefly the main stages through which the present labour structure of South Africa has evolved into what S. H. Frankel has described[22] as 'multi-racial teams of non-competing workers'. To an increasing extent the type of work which a man may perform was determined by his race rather than by his productive capacity, and an industrial labour caste system was in process of evolution. There have been many outspoken critics of this policy, and economists and others of all shades of political opinion, have stressed the danger of the growing rigidities in the labour market, and the way these rigidities hamper the industrial progress of the country and militate against optimum resource allocation.[23]

Apart from any possible long-term political consequences arising from the frustration it engenders, the industrial colour bar has a number of immediate consequences which adversely affect national productivity. In so far as it prevents any man from performing a task for which he is competent, and confines him to one which is less skilled, there is economic waste of scarce resources. For many years there has been a marked shortage of skilled workers, and

[20] U.G. 62/1951. Quoted in Doxey, p. 148.

[21] Muriel Horrell, *South African Trade Unionism*, S.A Institute of Race Relations, 1961, p. 160.

[22] S. H. Frankel, 'Whither South Africa? An Economic Approach', *S.A.J.E.*, vol. 15 no. 1, March, 1947.

[23] For comment on this danger in official documents see especially the Van Eck report (U.G. 40/1941) and the Viljoen report (U.G. 36/1958), and for other criticism see Sheila T. van der Horst, *Native Labour in South Africa*.

efforts have been made to recruit people for these posts from abroad; but, until recently, the obvious solution of training Africans, coloured people and Asians for more highly skilled jobs was precluded in large measure by the colour bar. The rapid industrial expansion in the 1930s and in the immediate post-war period, described in the last chapter, was possible only because of a tacit relaxation of restrictive practices. This was particularly marked in the newer industries where traditional work-spheres for the various racial groups had not as yet crystallized. In the textile industry, for example, the African has been enabled to prove himself a highly competent industrial operative and has shown that under efficient management he can become an industrial worker whose output compares favourably with labour in other industrial countries. In the denial of opportunities to Africans, coloured people and Asians waste is incurred not only in the jobs they are precluded from performing, but also because of the effect this has upon their incentive to excel in the work they are permitted to perform. The ceiling placed upon their industrial advancement,[24] though difficult to measure in statistical terms, undoubtedly has a marked effect upon the efficiency of the African industrial workers, particularly upon the abler and more ambitious in their ranks. On the other side, the artificial protection afforded to some white workers tends also to lower efficiency because they lack the incentive afforded by healthy competition.

A further important consequence of the colour-bar policy is its effect upon the incomes of Africans, coloured people and Asians and upon their power to consume.[25] Although in recent years the industrial colour bar has been considerably relaxed and members of other races are increasingly moving into work-spheres traditionally reserved for whites, the lower average incomes of some 19,5 million non-whites in a total population of 25,5 million has a significant effect upon the size of the domestic market for manufactured products; and, as noted in the previous chapter, is an important factor in reducing economies of scale and preventing the lowering of unit costs of manufacturing output.

This aspect should, however, not be overstressed, because although the industrial colour bar is an important element in depressing the

---

[24] This aspect was noted by the Tomlinson Commission and was one of the reasons prompting them to recommend territorial racial separation.

[25] This aspect is frequently stressed: see in particular F. P. Spooner, *South African Predicament* (1960).

earnings of Africans, it is at present not the only, nor probably the most important, cause. Low earnings are largely due to the imperfect adaptation of the African from subsistence farming to a modern economy[26] and to the very elastic supply of African labour. More will be said of this in a later section on wages and standards of living.

Employers in both mining and manufacturing find themselves severely hampered in their business by the growing rigidity in the labour market, which not only restricts their freedom in planning a least-cost-combination of factors, but has introduced a new and arbitrary political element into their calculations. A firm may have planned production on the basis of a given type of labour and installed its machinery with this intention in mind, but a new job reservation can upset its whole programme. Moreover, there have been suggestions that in the new industries which the government is trying to encourage on the periphery of the African areas – the 'Border Industries' – some relaxations of industrial regulations may be permitted. Desirable though this may be from the over-all national viewpoint, it has caused some consternation to industrialists in the established industrial areas who fear competition from the more privileged factories in the new areas.

In no country does one find a perfect labour market because differences in skills and training automatically make for imperfections, but in South Africa these are multiplied and are reinforced by custom and legislation. One can distinguish some five different markets for labour in South Africa, each representing a group of workers who are largely non-competing with those in the other groups. There are some $3\frac{1}{2}$ million African peasants in the reserves. Strictly speaking these do not represent a labour 'market'; but, together with African immigrants from other African states, they represent a reservoir of labour which in varying degree may find its way into one or other of the labour markets proper. The first distinct market for labour is in agriculture (mainly employment on farms owned by whites), where labour consists almost entirely of Africans, except in the western Cape, where a large number of coloured people have always been employed. The coloured people and many of the African families have lived on farms for generations, but the farm labour supply is also augmented by recruitment in the reserves and

---

[26] The colour bar, of course, tends to impede this adaptation, but it is not the cause of the disparity.

by the influx of Africans from these areas coming on their own initiative to seek work. Wages in agriculture tend to be depressed by restrictions on the movement of farm workers into mining,[27] and by the very severe restrictions upon their entry into urban areas to seek employment in manufacturing, commerce or other urban occupation.[28] The demand for labour in agriculture has increased slowly in the past, but there are indications that it is likely to remain static or actually decline in the future owing to increased mechanization.

The second and third labour markets are in mining, where the labour force consists of two almost wholly separate markets, the one for skilled white labour, the other for unskilled black labour. It is interesting to observe in table 19 that average white earnings in mining are greater than average white earnings in manufacturing, but that the reverse holds for African earnings. African mine workers are almost wholly migrants whose homes are either in the reserves or outside the Republic.

The fourth and fifth labour markets are in the manufacturing and commercial sectors of the economy. This too is a dual or dualistic market, with white workers mostly in the skilled ranks and other workers mostly in the unskilled or semi-skilled categories, but the rigidities are not nearly as great as in mining. There are, as we have seen, great impediments to the vertical mobility of African, coloured and Asian workers in industry, but by far the most important impediment is that which protects the urban African worker from competition through the exclusion of immigrants from farms, reserves and adjacent countries. Exactly how effective these stringent influx control measures are in practice is a matter of debate because the scale of evasion is difficult to assess. Restriction of African immigration to urban areas was instituted initially to protect the white workers, but the rapid industrial development has rendered this largely unnecessary and its main function at present would appear to be to protect the second generation of urban African workers from the competition of Africans from the reserves and farms, and in the western Cape to protect the coloured workers from an influx of Africans.

---

[27] Owing to the opposition of farmers, recruitment for the mines is not undertaken in certain farming areas.

[28] For a short account of the legal restrictions on African farm labour see Margaret Roberts, *Labour in the Farm Economy*, S.A. Institute of Race Relations, pp. 121–9.

The whole structure of the labour market is most complex. There are these five major non-competing groups largely insulated from one another – farm labour, white mine labour, non-white mine labour, white skilled industrial labour, and unskilled and semi-skilled industrial labour (mostly coloured and African). In a somewhat broader context there are the skilled white workers enjoying a privileged position as a result of the policy whose evolution we have attempted to outline. At the other extreme there are between 500 000 and one million migrant African workers, many from outside the Republic, who are mainly employed in mining but some of whom also find work in farming and in manufacturing. They come from the subsistence and traditional African economy largely as 'target workers' in the sense that their supply price is affected more by conditions in their tribal homes (about half of them outside the Republic) than by costs and standards of living in the modern sector. In between these two extreme groups there lies a large and growing group of non-white workers – coloured, Indian and African – who have become fully committed to the industrial way of life and are permanent and stable industrial workers, mostly in unskilled and semi-skilled occupations, but increasingly moving into operative and even skilled ranks in spite of the impediments to their advancement.

No simple solution to the problem presents itself. The extreme *laissez-faire* policy of the removal of all restrictions on mobility and employment, which is sometimes advanced by theoretical economists, is somewhat unrealistic in view of the fact that even in racially homogeneous societies skilled workers resent 'dilution' and organize themselves to protect their skilled position. In South Africa the racial cleavage and the great disparity between present earnings of skilled and unskilled workers tend to enhance these fears. There is perhaps some parallel between the mass immigration of Africans into the Republic from adjacent countries (and even from the Homelands within the Republic, since although these latter still form a geographical part of the Republic, they are not part of its modern exchange economy) and the movement of peoples from poor countries to those that are economically more prosperous. In this respect South Africa's problem is analogous to one of the great international problems of today, and it is interesting to reflect that even countries that are much richer and are more easily able to absorb such an influx, such as the United States and Britain, have seen fit to impose very strict immigration control.

A large section of the trade-union movement[29] has expressed itself against a colour bar in industry and in particular against the principle of racial job reservation, and puts its faith in the principle of 'the rate for the job' irrespective of the worker's race or colour. Much, of course, would depend upon the difficult matter of determining the appropriate rate for each particular job and the details of job classification. If this does not correspond fairly closely to the actual skill required and the disutility of the type of labour involved, it could easily become a major restrictive force. There is also the vexed question of whether a less proficient worker – and many Africans, coloured people and Asians are at present less proficient than whites – should be allowed to accept lower remuneration in order to offset his lower efficiency.

Perhaps the greatest difficulty in the rate-for-the-job approach is the problem of the incompetent white worker. In all racial groups there is a normal distribution curve of ability, and inevitably some whites will be found in the lower range. If a privileged position is to be maintained for whites of low intelligence or those with grave defects of character, at the expense of competent people of other races, grave injustice and economic waste is inevitable. The rate-for-the-job principle carries the implication that the less competent whites will have to be satisfied with the lower-paid jobs. The prevailing great disparity between skilled and unskilled rates of pay, which was the underlying cause of the poor-white problem of the 1920s, raises major humanitarian and political issues. Ultimately it is to be hoped that the growth of the real national income will provide for an unskilled wage which would be adequate for people of all races to live decently, but in the meanwhile a special tax upon all white South Africans to support or to provide 'sheltered employment' for the less competent whites would be sounder policy than an economically wasteful colour bar. In spite of all difficulties, developments along the lines of the rate-for-the-job are likely to prove more fruitful than either complete *laissez-faire* or racial separation, but they are likely to be frustrated by the complete domination of the political machine by an all-white electorate, unless that electorate can be prevailed upon to take an unusually far-sighted view of its own best interests.

[29] The Trade Union Council, representing about 150 000 workers, and the S.A. Congress of Trade Unions, representing some 30 000 (mainly African, coloured and Indian).

Sectional interests and political expediency often neglect, and sometimes even conceal, the basic economic reality that in the long-term national interest it is essential for the welfare of all South Africans, irrespective of race, that productive efficiency of all industrial workers be increased as much as possible so that manufactured products may be able to complete in world markets. With the inevitable fact that gold is a wasting asset the standard of living of the people of South Africa must ultimately depend upon the productivity of their labour in other industries.

THE COMPOSITION OF THE LABOUR FORCE

The South African labour force at the time of the 1970 Census is shown in Figure 3 (p. 000) when the economically active population was given as 7 986 220 out of a total population of 21 402 470 or 37,3 per cent.

Previous Censuses
Comparison with previous censuses is as follows:

	1970	1960	1951	1946
		(*in thousands*)		
Whites	1 497	1 151	983	887
Africans	5 605	3 890	3 110	2 905
Coloured people	704	554	405	349
Asians	180	126	94	79
All races	7 986	5 721	4 593	4 221

By 1975 the economically active population is estimated to have increased from the 1970 figure of 7 986 000 to 9 801 000 out of a total population of 25½ million.

The number of persons employed in each of the main sectors of the economy is given by race and sex for 1970, and by race only for 1960 and 1951 in Table 2 (p. 271). It will be observed that in 1970 Africans formed 70,2 per cent of the work force, and that with Coloured persons and Asians this rose to 81,3 per cent, while Whites constituted a mere 18,7 per cent.

The three main sectors of the economy are agriculture, mining and manufacturing. A comparison of the figures in each from the last three censuses, with the estimated position in 1975 is shown below (in thousands):

	1975[1]	1970[2]	1960[2]	1951[2]
Agriculture	1 451[3]	2 239	1 698	1 509
Mining	619	676	605	510
Manufacturing[4]	1 762	1 520	996	767
Total economically active	9 801	7 986	5 691	4 592
Total population	25 471	21 402	15 981	12 671

[1] Source *Statistics in Brief 1976.*
[2] Source *South African Statistics, 1974* p. 1.33.
[3] Figure for 1974.
[4] Manufacturing, construction and electricity.

During the decade 1960 to 1970 the economically occupied population increased from 5 691 000 to 7 986 000, and it is estimated to have increased by a further 1,9 million between 1970 and 1975. The figure for agriculture for 1970 is baffling, being over half a million greater than the previous census and the subsequent estimate, and it is probably explained by a change in the statistical treatment of African peasant family labour. Taking the 1975 estimate as more accurately reflecting the position, it is seen that there has been a slight falling-off in employment in agriculture.

Employment in mining has increased from 510 000 in 1951 to 605 000 in 1960, and to 676 000 in 1970 but there has been no great change in the racial proportions. The increase in employment has been most marked in manufacturing and construction – from 258 000 in 1936 to 996 000 in 1960, 1 520 000 in 1970 and 1 762 000 in 1975, with all racial groups participating in the increase. The percentage of white workers, however, declined from 41 per cent in 1932–3 to 31 per cent in 1960, 22 per cent in 1970, and 21 per cent in 1975.[30]

General economic considerations would seem to suggest that no further large expansion of employment is likely in either agriculture or mining, and that it is therefore to manufacturing and tertiary activities that one must look for the future employment of the expanding population of all races.

WAGES AND STANDARDS OF LIVING

It is best to begin by speaking in very general terms and to consider the average income of the population as a whole, ignoring for the present the details of its distribution. In 1970 the net national income of South Africa was R9 913 million, and the population recorded in

[30] *Bulletin of Statistics* June, 1975 pp. 2.4, 2.7.

the 1970 census was 21 485 000, so that the average national income per head of the population was approximately R460 per annum. In terms of average income per head this places South Africa in the middle group of countries of the world, lying between the very rich and the very poor. South Africa's *per capita* income is thus about one-sixth that of the United States, and rather less than half that of Great Britain, but on the other hand, it is four times that of Brazil and over five times that of India or Pakistan or many African countries.

International comparisons of national incomes in money values are notoriously unreliable, because exchange rates seldom accurately reflect differences in cost of living, and it may be of interest to compare the average daily intake of calories per person as a rough check. In 1955, the position was:[31]

High-intake countries		Medium-intake countries		Low-intake countries	
New Zealand	3 390	France	2 890	Portugal	2 450
United Kingdom	3 250	Turkey	2 790	Mexico	2 420
Australia	3 230	*South Africa*	2 590	Ceylon	2 060
United States	3 150	Italy	2 550	Pakistan	2 000
		Brazil	2 520	India	1 880

This comparison also places South Africa in a middle position between the rich and the poor countries.

In the continent of Africa the Republic of South Africa was easily the richest country, with a *per capita* income in 1965 over one and a half that of Ghana (the next richest after it), more than twice that of Rhodesia, five times that of Botswana and Nigeria and seven times that of Malawi.

Net National Income per capita of African Countries
(U.S. $ per annum: 1965)

South Africa	*439*
Ghana	233
Rhodesia	196
Ivory Coast	192
Zambia	175
Botswana	82
Nigeria	68
Lesotho	66
Tanzania	60
Malawi	58

[31] *Food and Agricultural Organization Year Book, 1956.*

Income in South Africa is not evenly distributed. It was estimated that in 1952 the average income of the whites was ten times that of the Africans, eight times that of coloured people and five times that of the Asians.[32]

In 1960 Stephen Enke took average non-white earnings at one-fifth of white earnings,[33] but he is presumably excluding the subsistence section. Much depends upon the treatment of the subsistence income of the African peasants in the reserves and the money value placed upon their income in kind, for which estimates may vary by over 80 per cent.[34]

Valuable contributions have been made in this field by the Bureau of Market Research of the University of South Africa and others who have investigated family incomes and expenditure of various racial groups in several major cities. There is however no definitive account of the distribution of the national income by race and by economic sector,[35] and the migratory labour system makes it difficult to impute earnings to a particular sector. For example, when we speak of 'the average earnings of Africans', we ignore the marked difference between those employed in the modern sector of the economy and those still engaged in subsistence farming. In a study undertaken in the eastern Cape in 1952, the earnings of urban Africans were found to be about five times those of rural Africans,[36] and in the large industrial centres like Johannesburg and Cape Town the disparity must be even greater.

Despite these uncertainties, it is clear that there is a very unequal

[32] Tomlinson Report, vol. 10, ch. 24, pp. 43–7. On these proportions the annual *per capita* incomes of the various groups in 1952 would have been: whites R631, Asians R133, coloured people R86, and Africans R63. The percentage of the total national income accruing to each group would have been: whites 71 per cent, Africans 23 per cent, coloured people 4 per cent and Asians 2 per cent.

[33] Stephen Enke, 'South African Growth: A Macro-Economic Analysis', *S.A.J.E.*, vol. 30 no. 1, March 1962, p. 37. He writes, 'After a consideration of the available published statistics relating to labour and wage income in manufacturing, mining and transport, it appeared that a ratio of five to one could reasonably be assumed.'

[34] The Tomlinson Report (Summary), p. 98, estimated African peasant family income at R84 per annum by the conventional methods, and at R194 when various allowances were made.

[35] See, however, A. M. K. M. Spandau, 'Income Distribution and Economic Growth in South Africa 1971' (2 vols.), unpublished thesis, UNISA, Pretoria.

[36] D. Hobart Houghton (ed.), *Economic Development in a Plural Society*, p. 252, gives incomes of rural Africans at R14 per head per annum, compared with average *per capita* African income in the town of East London of R90 per annum.

distribution of income in South Africa, and that the average earnings of whites are several times higher than those of other races. Table 19 (p. 289) gives employment, and aggregate and average earnings in the main sectors of the economy by race for the years 1950, 1960 and 1970. The white group generally receive the greatest income, followed by the Asian and then the coloured, and in all sectors the African is at the bottom of the log.

Average Earnings in September 1970
(Rands per annum)

	Mining	Manufacturing	Construction	Public authorities
Whites	4 370	3 643	3 833	3 234
Asians	1 667	936	1 840	1 314
Coloured people	875	878	1 301	1 148
Africans	217	626	589	514
Average all races	608	1 397	1 226	1 594

It must be noted that these were cash earnings and do not include free food, quarters and other benefits and that these were considerable in the case of the African mine worker. None the less these do little to mitigate the wide disparity in cash earnings between white and African mine workers.[37]

White earnings in mining were the highest of any sector and African earnings were the lowest. Average white earnings were some 20 times those of Africans in mining. In manufacturing, in which sector African earnings were higher than in any other sector, white earnings were only 5,8 times as high. In interpreting these figures it is important to remember that these aggregate earnings include the wages and salaries paid to the higher ranking employees from the manager downwards; so that it is incorrect to say, for example, that white *wages* in manufacturing were 5,8 times those of Africans. Indeed the 'rate for the job' is increasingly being applied. The real reason for the discrepancy is to be found not solely in the wage-rate, but also in the fact that the more highly skilled and responsible positions (which are also the more highly paid) are usually performed by white people, and that Africans generally fill the lower paid positions.

Since 1970 there has been a considerable rise in the wages of all groups. Professor P. A. Nel in an article, 'The Non-White Worker in South Africa' in *Finance and Trade Review*, December, 1975, gives

---

[37] A comprehensive study of mine wages is to be found in Francis Wilson's book, *Labour in the South African Gold Mines 1911-69.*

the percentage increases in wages between May, 1973 and February, 1975, as follows:

	Whites	Coloureds	Asians	Africans
Mining	33,5	44,6	45,5	122,8
Manufacturing	24,4	31,4	28,3	35,8
Construction	13,1	31,3	19,5	35,5

In mining the percentage increase in black wages is over three times that of whites; and in both manufacturing and construction, wages of Africans increased by a larger percentage than wages of whites. This however, does not mean that the absolute gap between the higher and lower-paid is closing: indeed the reverse is the case because the difference is so great that a much larger percentage increase would be necessary to reduce the absolute wage-gap between white and black.

Difference in earning capacity should not be attributed so much to innate inferiority in ability, as to the deficiencies in social environment and educational systems which fail to provide large sections of the population with technical training and the opportunities to develop those qualities of leadership so essential to success in a modern industrial society. Added to this are the customary and legislative restraints upon the vertical movement of non-white people, and Africans in particular, which go under the comprehensive designation of the 'industrial colour bar'. Although these are being rapidly modified or removed, they are still a factor of significance in certain cases.

The fact that the rich are white and the poor are black has tended to focus attention upon the racial inequality of distribution and to lead to the facile assumption that these disparities are due solely to some form of racial discrimination. That this is not so is clear from the fact that there are as great, or greater, inequalities in some of the all-African states elsewhere in Africa. Inequalities of earnings can often be explained merely in terms of the relative scarcity of skilled manpower in a predominantly primitive population.

While it is true that the average earnings of whites are several times higher than those of Africans, it should not be forgotten that not all whites are rich, and that poverty among a section of the white population is a real social problem, although it is not of the same magnitude as poverty among people of other racial groups. It is also true that in South Africa a larger proportion of the African population has been drawn into the modern sector of the economy than anywhere else south of the Sahara, and in consequence Africans in the Republic are generally better off materially than in most other African countries.

The influx of between half a million and a million Africans from adjacent territories is clear demonstration of this fact, but this influx must necessarily have a depressing effect upon the earnings of Africans in the Republic, especially in mining where the impact is most keenly felt.

Mine Wages

In mining most of the African labour is provided by migratory workers, many from outside the Republic. They are housed and fed by the mining companies and the value of this is not included in the calculations which follow. Table 19 shows the average cash earnings of whites and other groups (mainly Africans) employed in mining in 1950, 1960 and 1970. In 1935 whites received R684 and others R61. White earnings were thus 11 times those of other groups. In 1950 the figures were: whites R1 427, others R98 (14,5 times); in 1960, whites R2 312, others R167 (13,9 times); and in 1970 the figures were whites R4 370, others R224 (15 times). It must, however, be remembered that, as in farming, the African engaged in mining receives many benefits in addition to his cash wage, such as housing, food, medical attention and various other amenities. Even when these are taken into account, the gap between white and non-white earnings in mining would appear to have increased. Sheila van der Horst, using figures from the International Labour Office[38] has estimated that 'in 1924 African wages, including the value of food and housing on the basis of cost to the gold mines of such provision, averaged just less than one-eighth of white earnings; in 1957 they were less than one-ninth'.[39]

Five factors appear to have combined to depress the wages of African mine workers. First, the powerful monopsonist position of the Chamber of Mines through its two native recruiting organizations[40] has largely insulated African mine-workers' wages from the

[38] International Labour Office, *African Labour Survey*, 1959, p. 281.

[39] Sheila T. van der Horst, 'The Economic Implications of Political Democracy', supplement to *Optima*, vol. 10, June 1960.

[40] The Witwatersrand Native Labour Organization and the Native Recruiting Corporation.

operation of supply and demand, and has prevented competition for labour between different mining companies from forcing up wages. Second, the rigidity imposed by statute upon the work-spheres of people of different races has greatly restricted the mining companies in making the most effective use of the available labour force. Thirdly there were peculiar conditions in the supply of migrant workers who were concerned primarily with the support of their families in the subsistence economy. This gave rise to the belief that the supply curve of such labour was backward-sloping if wages exceeded a given level. Although this proposition is of very doubtful validity,[41] it has made mining companies reluctant to raise wages and has often been advanced in evidence to commissions of inquiry.[42] Finally, perhaps one of the most powerful forces of all is the fact that legislation restricting the movement of Africans into urban areas does not apply to mine workers. Thus general influx control, by diverting to mining men who might otherwise have sought employment in some other field, tends to increase the supply of mine workers and thus to depress wages in mining.

Wages in manufacturing

Earnings in manufacturing and construction are also shown in table 19. It will be noticed that although the difference between white and non-white earnings is not as great as in mining it is nevertheless considerable.

Although African earnings in manufacturing are nearly three times their earnings in mining, and have advanced considerably from R232 in 1950 to R626 in 1970, nevertheless expressed as a percentage of white earnings they have declined relatively from 23,8 per cent to 17,2 per cent. Thus the great industrial upsurge of the last twenty years has increased the earnings of all groups but has done nothing to reduce the gap between the higher and lower groups. Indeed the gap appears to have become wider.

The average earnings of Asians and coloured people is considerably higher than that of Africans but even in their case their position relative to whites shows a decline.

[41] For an excellent analysis of the supply curve of migrant labour see Elliot J. Berg, 'Backward-Sloping Labor Supply Functions in Dual Economies – the Africa Case', *Quarterly Journal of Economics*, vol. 80 no. 3, August 1961.

[42] See especially *Report of the Witwatersrand Mine Natives' Wages Commission*, U.G. 21/1944, p. 16.

Average Earnings in Construction
(Rands per annum)

	1950	1960	1970
Whites	1 058	1 870	3 833
Asians	500	1 000	1 841
Coloured people	468	665	1 301
Africans	204	315	589
Asian earnings as % of white	47,3	53,5	48,0
Coloured earnings as % of white	44,2	35,6	33,9
African earnings as % of white	19,3	16,8	15,4

In many countries of western Europe the average unskilled wage is between 70 to 80 per cent of the skilled wage.[43] In the United States and Canada the unskilled wage is generally between 50 to 60 per cent of the skilled rate. In South Africa, however, it is only round about 20 per cent of the skilled wage.

ATTEMPTS TO RAISE THE INCOMES OF THE POORER SECTION OF THE POPULATION

In the 1920s the poor white problem dominated the social and political scene. The industrial expansion, combined with better educational facilities and, perhaps, assisted by some of the protective measures discussed earlier, has done much to alleviate poverty among the white section of the population; and present attention is increasingly focused upon poverty among other races. A number of recent studies of the family budgets of Africans in the 1970s in the main urban areas[44] have drawn attention to the gap between the family income and what are estimated to be the minimum requirements for an adequate standard of living for Africans in urban areas,[45] where their needs in relation to food, housing, transport and clothing are changing from those in the tribal economy, and are becoming similar to those of white urban dwellers. The Institue for Planning Research[45] of the University of Port Elizabeth in 1975 calculated the Primary Household Subsistence level for a black family of size – two adults, two teenagers and two younger children –

[43] Some people regard this ratio as too high and as affording too small a premium for skill.

[44] Publications of the Bureau of Market Research University of South Africa, Institute of Planning Research, University of Port Elizabeth, and the Department of Economics at Cape Town, Durban and Witwatersrand Universities.

[45] *The Household Subsistence Level in the Major Urban Centres of the Republic of South Africa: 1975*

and arrived at a monthly figure ranging from R124,97 in Cape Town (the highest) to R112,46 in King William's Town (the lowest). In December, 1974 average earnings of black persons in manufacturing were R96. Therefore the average household cannot make ends meet unless there is more than one breadwinner in the home. For humanitarian and for economic reasons many leading industrialists have urged that earnings of the poorer section of the population should be raised. A private organization with which many large manufacturing concerns are associated – the Bantu Wages and Productivity Association – has the object of attempting to raise both the productivity and earnings of African workers and claims to have been instrumental in bringing about considerable wage increases in recent years. In 1961 the National Development Foundation organized a conference of industrialists and economists on 'The economics of increased Bantu wages and productivity'. A powerful motive behind this movement is the recognition by manufacturers that the small size of the domestic market for their products is due to the general poverty of the non-white section of the population. *Per capita* consumption by the whites is already relatively high, and if South Africa is to move towards the era of high mass-consumption it is the non-white people whose incomes and purchasing power will have to be increased. That in an urbanized population it is not *race* but *income* that is important in determining the expenditure pattern is demonstrated in the following figures from an investigation in the East London and King William's Town urban areas in 1955.

Expenditure of White and African Families, 1955[46]

	Income group	Percentage of income devoted to:	
		food	*clothing and footwear*
African families	Less than R200	61,7	nil
	R200 to R400	43,1	4,9
	R400 to R600	35,8	7,6
	Over R600	30,8	11,2
White families	Less than R1 500	30,0	11,5
	R1 500 to R2 000	28,6	11,9
	R2 000 to R2 500	24,5	12,6
	R2 500 to R3 000	24,0	13,8
	R3 000 to R4 000	19,8	11,4
	Over R4 000	17,8	11,5

[46] D. Hobart Houghton, *Report to the Members of the Footwear Federation of South Africa* (private circulation). The African expenditure was based upon data collected by the author, and the white expenditure was derived from a survey of income and expenditure conducted by the Bureau of Census and Statistics.

There have been demands for minimum wage legislation to accelerate the rise in non-white earnings,[47] and economists have stressed the need to reduce the gap between skilled and unskilled rates of pay, but there are certain aspects of the situation that must not be overlooked. Wage increases unless related to either *ex ante* or *ex post* increases in productivity[48] will tend to impair South Africa's export position and may give rise to serious unemployment. The needs to maintain a high rate of expansion of manufacturing industry to absorb the natural increases of the population of all races, and to give employment to those who are expected to move out of subsistence agriculture in the reserves, place certain limitations on measures designed to raise wages of African workers.[49]

After the meeting of the Economic Advisory Council in March 1962 the Prime Minister issued a statement[50] in which he said these matters had received careful consideration. He summed up the arguments for and against a rapid increase in minimum wages, pointing out that 'drastic action might lead to the ruin of many undertakings and seriously hamper the establishment of new industries which is of great importance to the country's future prosperity . . . However, the government supports the endeavours to establish a wage level which will enable all low-paid workers (white as well as non-white) to meet at least their minimum subsistence requirements. To achieve this object the existing machinery for the determination of minimum wages is being used to an increasing extent.'

Before concluding this chapter on wages and standards of living, we must refer to the increasingly automatic processes which are being adopted in modern industry. Automation in the United States is rendering millions of workers redundant, and a huge programme of retraining workers is in progress. If South Africa

[47] L. B. Katzen, 'The Case for Minimum Wage Legislation in South Africa', *S.A.J.E.*, vol 29 no. 3, September 1961.

[48] It is sometimes argued that it is not necessary for productivity to have risen *before* the wage increase takes place, because in the present situation wage increases will themselves bring about increase in productivity because of the improvement in nutritional standards of the workers and for other reasons.

[49] Some of these matters are discussed by Dr. S. P. Viljoen, 'Higher Productivity and Higher Wages of Native Labour in South Africa', *S.A.J.E.*, vol. 29 no. 1, March 1961. The African wages problem is ably presented by two articles: W. F. J. Steenkamp, 'Bantu Wages in South Africa', and O. P. F. Horwood, 'Is Minimum Wage Legislation the Answer for South Africa?', both in *S.A.J.E.*, vol. 30 no. 2, June 1962.

[50] Press release on 26 April 1962.

is to expand manufacturing industries, it is essential to adopt the most modern processes. Attempts to compete with automated industry by using labour-intensive processes seem doomed to failure and must certainly force wages down to the bare subsistence level. Moreover, in a labour force lacking a high degree of manual dexterity and craftsmanship, automation has been found to improve quality and reduce cost. This has certainly been the experience in textile factories in South Africa. Automation in industry, however, renders most unskilled labour redundant. It has been observed earlier in this chapter that the labour requirements of agriculture and mining are unlikely to expand, so that the whole of the natural increase of the population of all races must look largely to manufacturing industry for their employment. Thus if automation is introduced increasingly in South Africa – and it seems inevitable that it will be – an immense programme of training, not only for white workers, but also for hundreds of thousands of coloured people and Africans will have to be speedily undertaken to make them productive workers in the modern age.

8 Foreign Trade & Balance of Payments

The greater part of South African exports have always been primary products. Exports during the nineteenth century (shown in the table on page 13) were limited to raw materials of agricultural origin, diamonds and gold; and at the beginning of the twentieth century, gold accounted for half the total. Imports were in two main categories – (1) consumers' goods of all sorts, (2) mining machinery and other capital goods. The great structural change in the South African economy during the last fifty years, to which reference has repeatedly been made, was the development of manufacturing industries to provide goods for the domestic market. This has affected foreign trade in various ways. In the first place the proportion of the requirements of both gold mining and manufacturing obtained from foreign sources has shown a downward trend.

There has been a marked increase in the extent to which South Africa has been able to supply consumer goods for the population and both the capital goods and other requirements of the mines and industries of the country. Thus, for any given output of gold, the import requirements have been considerably reduced over recent years. A similar trend is observable in the raw materials for manufacturing industry, but the proportion imported has declined to a lesser extent than for gold mining. The proportion of the capital equipment for manufacturing which has to be derived from external sources, is certainly much higher than for the gold-mining industry. Thus, although there is a tendency in both gold-mining and manufacturing industry for the dependence upon imports to decline, the growth in relative importance of manufacturing (which is more heavily dependent upon imports) has prevented any general decline in the country's imports. In 1910 total imports to the value of R68 million were 26 per cent of the national income, by 1958 imports to the

175

value of R1 111 million were a higher percentage of the national income, namely 28 per cent, but, by 1974, the percentage returned to 26, with imports at R5 733 million and Gross Domestic Product at R22 382 million.

It thus appears that the process of rapid industrialization that occurred over the past fifty years made the country *more*, not *less*, dependent upon imports. The volume of goods imported increased greatly although the percentage of the national income which these represent remained fairly constant. There is, of course, no harm in this, provided the efficiency in the exporting industries is such that they are able to earn the increased foreign exchange necessary to finance the increased imports. Indeed, it merely indicates fuller participation by South Africa in world trade, which should be accompanied by a rising standard of living. The periodic difficulties which South Africa has experienced since 1945 in balancing her international payments indicate, however, that the high degree of dependence of manufacturing industry upon imports is a factor that should not be neglected.

In consequence of this situation increasing emphasis was placed upon the encouragement of import-replacement industries, particularly in the fields of textiles, chemicals, metal manufactures and machinery, where the volume of imports was high and the conditions for local manufacture appeared favourable. This was an attempt to accelerate a process which had been proceeding steadily since the 1920s. In 1910 imports of food and drink constituted 17 per cent of all imports; in 1973 about 5 per cent. In 1910 clothing and textile imports were 29 per cent of total imports; in 1973 about 6 per cent. The proportion of imports to the national income had remained relatively constant, but the character of goods imported had altered greatly.

In table 22 South African exports are shown for 1973 in terms of the international classification. Items 1, 2 and 8 represent farming products of R383 million; items 5, 13 and 14 represent products of mining to a value of R707 million; and items 9 and 10 products of forestry of R70 million. Therefore the primary sectors of the economy are more or less directly responsible for exports of R1 160 million to which gold amounting to R1 789 million should be added. Total exports, including gold, in 1973 amounted to R4 216 million, of which the primary sector contributed R2 960 million, or about 67 per cent of all exports. This classification is only approximate, but it indicates clearly the extent to which South African foreign trade still depends upon exports of the primary sectors and, bearing in mind the limited future prospects of gold mining, demonstrates clearly the need for a marked increase in the export of manufactured goods. The Republic is still vulnerable to adverse fluctuations in the world price of primary products and in recent years it has suffered from price declines in wool, maize and copper.

THE DIRECTION OF SOUTH AFRICAN EXPORTS

The origin of imports and the destination of South African exports (excluding gold, atomic energy materials and ships' stores) is shown in table 21 for the years 1970 and 1973. The United Kingdom is still, and has always been, South Africa's best customer, taking, in 1970, R466 million worth of goods, or 30,2 per cent of our total exports. This is partly the result of the close political association between the two countries, going back to the early colonial days, and partly because for over a century the United Kingdom has been the major world market for agricultural products and raw materials. In view of recent political events one might have expected a lessening of the trade ties between the two countries, but this has not been the case. During the last fourteen years South African exports to Britain have increased in absolute value from R116 million in 1950 to R466 million in 1970, and the proportion this represents of South Africa's export trade has risen from 26 to 30,2 per cent. Nevertheless, there is some concern about the future of South Africa's markets in Britain. The entry of the United Kingdom into the European Common Market may raise difficulties. Until policy is known it is impossible to forecast the economic consequences of this event, but it cannot be expected that any special concessions that may be arranged for members of the Commonwealth would also apply to South Africa. The South African products most likely to be adversely affected are agricultural products, fresh and canned fruits and wine. In these Australia is already a keen competitor.

Much will depend upon the direction in which the European Community moves. If the emphasis is upon lowering tariffs between members and upon an expansion of economic activity, South Africa may benefit through an expanding market; if, on the other hand, the emphasis is upon a high common external tariff, and towards European economic isolationism, there is a distinct possibility that the consequences for South Africa – and for the rest of the world – will be adverse.

Exports to western Europe[1] in 1970 were of considerable importance, amounting to R337 million, or 21,8 per cent of total export. This was an increase of R173 million from the level of R164 million in 1950. In 1970 major sales were to German Federal Republic R109 million (R58 million), Italy R42 million (R40 million), France R40 million (R36 million), Belgium R55 million (R36 million), and the Netherlands R35 million (R24 million). Figures in brackets indicate the 1950 position.

A significant development since World War II has been the expansion of trade with other countries in Africa, particularly with Rhodesia. The Rhodesian trade grew rapidly from 1945 onwards, rising from R5,2 million in 1938 to R169 million in 1957, and was of special value to South Africa because, as the most highly industrialized nation on the continent, it was able to find an outlet for manufactured goods. Trade with African states reached a high level in 1957. Thereafter owing to political uncertainties in many parts of the continent which retarded the rate of economic growth, and because of the boycotting of South African goods, exports to some African countries declined; but by 1970 the total had risen, although the percentage this represents is less than in 1957.

South African Exports to African Countries
(in R millions with percentage of total South African
exports in parentheses)

	1938	1950	1957	1964	1970
All African countries	5 (8%)	69 (16%)	153 (19%)	114 (12%)	264 (17%)

In 1957 the Federation of Rhodesia and Nyasaland ranked second only to the United Kingdom as an export market for South African products but since that date exports to African countries are not given except as a global African total. It is reasonably certain that Rhodesia still ranks high.

A significant development has been the expansion of trade with Asian countries,[2] exports to which increased from R17 million in 1955 to R118 million in 1964 and to R219 million in 1970. Most

---

[1] Austria, Belgium, Denmark, France, Finland, German Federal Republic, Italy, Netherlands, Norway, Portugal, Republic of Ireland, Spain, Sweden, Switzerland.

[2] Trade commissions were dispatched in 1961 to Europe, the Americas and the Far East, and in a statement on 26 April 1962, the Prime Minister said that these areas appeared to offer fruitful opportunities for trade expansion.

spectacular has been trade with Japan. Exports to Japan rose from R1,3 million in 1950 to over R180 million in 1970 – a hundred-and-forty-fold increase. During this period great economic expansion occurred in Japan, and South Africa was able to supply many products that country required, notably pig-iron, steel, sugar and maize. Imports from Japan also increased greatly to R221 million in 1970 but the unfavourable balance was not as great as in the case of the United States from which South Africa imported R424 million worth of goods in 1970, but exported only R129 million.

In 1970 South Africa's main trading partners, in descending order of importance of exports, were:

	Exports to (R millions)	Imports from (R millions)
United Kingdom	466 (30,2%)	561 (22,0%)
Africa (mainly Rhodesia)	264 (17,1%)	131 (5,1%)
Japan	181 (11,7%)	221 (8,7%)
U.S.	129 (8,4%)	423 (16,6%)
West Germany	109 (7,1%)	372 (14,6%)

SOUTH AFRICA'S BALANCE OF PAYMENTS

South Africa's balance of payments with the rest of the world for the years 1955 to 1970 is shown in table 23.[3] This is divided into two main parts – current account and capital account. The former represents the result of all current trading during the year and the latter reflects capital movements, both private and official, and includes the ultimate balancing item 'changes in reserves of gold and foreign exchange'. It is sometimes said that the balance on current account shows the result of the year's trading, and the capital account the methods by which this was financed. In the sense that the balance on capital account must always be equal (but opposite in sign) to the current account, this is true, but it should not be taken to imply that capital movements may not themselves initiate changes which have important repercussions upon the current account items. Thus, in years of large capital inflow, imports of merchandise may greatly exceed the current earnings of foreign exchange without causing a decrease in holdings of gold and foreign exchange. Conversely, in years of large capital outflow, declining reserves may necessitate monetary contraction and fiscal measures which reduce the volume of imports below current earnings of foreign exchange.

[3] Source: S.A.R.B., *A Statistical Presentation of South Africa's Balance of Payments for the Period 1946–1970.*

There is normally a high marginal propensity to import, and increases in export earnings which raise the national income usually result in an increase in imports after the appropriate time lag.[4] This high propensity to import applies not only to consumer goods but also to capital goods, particularly in the case of increases in investment in manufacturing industries.[5] This high propensity to import places severe strains upon the balance-of-payments position not only as a result of inflationary tendencies resulting from monetary factors, but also as a result of rapid industrial expansion, and sometimes as the result of quite fortuitous events.[6] In consequence, currency- and import-control measures have been resorted to at various times since the war. These in turn have introduced a further element of instability. If merchants and others expect import regulations to be imposed or made more stringent, there tends to be heavy over-importing in anticipation of the restrictions. Thus any pressure upon the foreign reserves tends to be reinforced by speculative action.

The current account

Table 23 shows four major items in the current account – merchandise imports, merchandise exports, gold output, and 'other current items'. Merchandise imports have shown a general upward trend from R972 million in 1955 to R2 578 million in 1970 and R5 723 million in 1974 but there have been several abrupt increases from one year to the next due to increased importation as a result of an expansion of consumption or investment, or abrupt reductions due to the imposition of control measures. Exports of merchandise have also shown a general upward trend, from R737 million in 1955 to R1 413 million in 1970 and R3 218 million in 1974; and the rise in exports has been more consistent than the rise in imports, each succeeding year being greater than the previous one, except for the decline in the years 1958, 1959 and 1960 compared with the high figure for 1957 and a similar decline in 1969 and 1970.[7]

---

[4] S.A.R.B., *Review of the South African Economy*, 1961, p. 13, shows a close correlation between export earnings and imports allowing for an eight-month time lag.

[5] See Franzsen, pp. 20, 21.

[6] Such as the phenomenal rise in the price of wool in 1951, which stimulated the purchase of expensive American motor-cars by wool farmers.

[7] This was mainly due to a decline in the world price of some of our major exports.

Because South Africa is a major gold producer, gold output must be included in the current balance of payments. Ever since 1947 gold output has shown a remarkably steady and pronounced upward trend, rising from R195 million in 1947 to R837 million in 1970, and since then the higher free market price has pushed the value of gold output up to R2 565 million in 1974. It has played an invaluable role in helping to meet the cost of our imports.

'Other current items' include invisible imports such as payment for banking, transport, insurance and other services and payment of dividends, interest and wages[8] to foreign-owned factors of production employed in South Africa. South Africa is a debtor nation and net foreign liabilities exceeded net foreign assets by over R2 000 million[9] in 1969. Therefore, interest and dividends is always a minus item in the current balance of payments. It should be noted that South Africa has been a debtor-borrower, and the balance on current account was a minus quantity up to 1958 and again in most years since 1964. This deficit had in general been met by a substantial inflow of foreign capital. The adverse balance on current account has fluctuated considerably. For the years 1946 to 1953 it averaged R225 million per annum; in 1954 and 1955 it averaged R110 million; in the following two years the average was only R11 million; but in 1958 it rose suddenly to R129 million. During the years 1959 to 1963 it changed from an adverse to a favourable balance on current account averaging R180 million per annum over the five year period. This marked general improvement in the current account, from large deficits to surplus, was the result of expanding exports of merchandise and increased gold output, while imports had been held to a more or less constant level.

After 1963 the balance of payments reverted to one of deficits in every year except 1968[10] and 1973; and in 1971 the deficit amounted to no less than R1 003 million. As a result of the rapid industrial expansion described later in chapter 10 there was heavy importation of capital goods and mounting inflationary pressures, and imports expanded rapidly to reach an all-time record of R3 218 million in 1974. Imports in millions of rands per annum were:

---

[8] Wages to foreign labour employed largely in the gold mines – see ch. 5.

[9] Foreign liabilities R4 990 million; foreign assets R2 449 million.

[10] Unusually large exports of maize and a high price for copper were largely responsible for the surplus in this year.

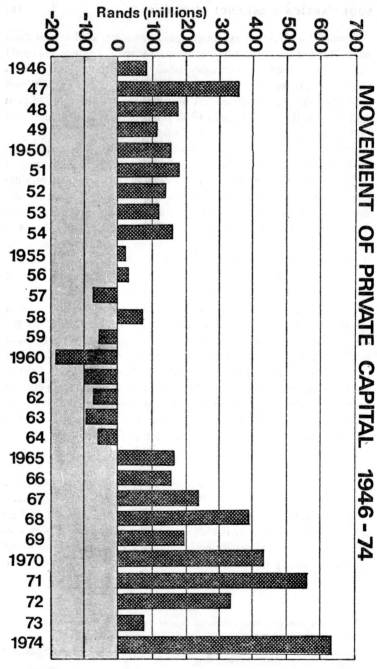

FIGURE 12

1963	1964	1965	1966	1967	1968	1969	1970	1971	1972	1973	1974
1 283	1 578	1 799	1 645	1 942	1 885	2 149	2 578	1 556	2 218	2 550	3 218

and the consequences might have been disastrous had it not been for large capital inflows, and the higher price of gold.

The Capital account

Foreign investment in South Africa has been of considerable magnitude ever since the discovery of diamonds and gold in the last century, and in the years immediately following the Second World War the capital inflow was large, particularly in 1947 when it reached R357 million.[11] The movements of private capital during the years 1946 to 1974 are shown in figure 12, p. 182. The average annual inflow over the years 1947 to 1954 was R176 million. In the following four years it fell to an annual average inflow of R15 million.[12] In the six years 1959 to 1964 there was an outflow of capital, which reached a peak of R152 million in 1960, and averaged R96 million per annum over the period.

An abrupt change occurred in 1965 and from then to 1970 capital poured in at a very high rate except in 1973. Total capital inflow, private and government, in millions of rands per annum was as follows:

1965	1966	1967	1968	1969	1970	1971	1972	1973	1974
255	141	162	459	197	501	764	415	–110	775

giving a total accretion of capital from abroad of R3 559 million in the ten years.

Crises in the balance of payments

Figure 13 shows the total holdings of gold and foreign exchange reserves. The four low points in the years 1948–9, 1953–4, 1957–8 and 1960–1 are all associated with more or less severe crises in the balance-of-payments position, but there is an important difference between the first three and that of 1960–1. In so far as it is ever possible to isolate the causes of complex economic phenomena, it may be said that the crises of 1948–9 and 1953–4 had their origins wholly in items which enter into the current trading account. That of 1948–9 was due to imports in excess of the country's export

[11] This large figure was partly due to a flight of capital from Britain, where a capital levy was feared.
[12] There was in fact an outflow of R61 million in 1957, almost counteracted by an inflow of R59 million in the next year.

earnings so large that even a capital inflow of R357 million, R173 million and R151 million, respectively, in the years 1947, 1948 and 1949, was inadequate to offset the deficit in the balance of payments. Devaluation of the South African pound, in concert with devaluation by other countries in the sterling area, restored the position by checking imports from the non-sterling area and by raising the price of gold from R17,25 to R24,82 per oz. As a consequence the country's reserves of foreign exchange rose during 1950 by about R142 million.

Similarly the crisis of 1953–4 was due to excessive importation in relation to export earnings, and it occurred in spite of a considerable capital inflow. It was generally agreed that inflationary pressures caused by the rapid expansion of the economy and in particular by a high rate of investment in both the private and public sectors of the economy were the cause of the strain upon the foreign exchange position; and monetary and fiscal restraints were imposed. These relieved the position and in 1954 imports were only R29 million above the figure for 1953, but exports of merchandise and gold had risen by R91 million, and the balance of payments was further relieved by an increase in the capital inflow of R57 million. The over-all result was a rise of R88 million in the country's reserves of foreign exchange.

The next few years were a period of somewhat unstable equilibrium. The exchange position was well maintained and, for the first time in South Africa's history, there was virtually a balanced position in the current account,[13] and export earnings were sufficient to meet both the merchandise imports and the invisible items. On the other hand, the anti-inflationary measures had slowed down the economic growth of the country and, in particular, the rate of industrial expansion. The view was expressed in 1956[14] that 'the rate of economic expansion, which had slowed down considerably in 1955, was somewhat further reduced in 1956. . . . Considered on a monthly basis, it would appear that the monetary value of economic activity still showed an upward tendency in 1956, but that the physical volume of activity, on the whole, tended to remain relatively stable.' A foreign-exchange crisis developed again in 1957–8. A substantial net outflow of private capital of R61 million during 1957 and a fall

---

[13] In 1956 the estimated balance was zero, but allowing for errors and omissions there was an adverse balance of only R1 million.

[14] By the head of the statistical department of the South African Reserve Bank, see *Quarterly Bulletin*, March 1957, p. xii.

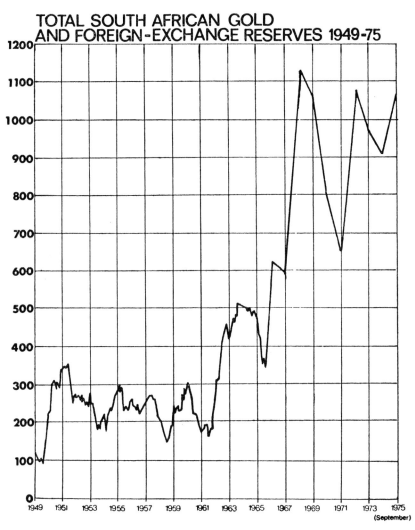

TOTAL SOUTH AFRICAN GOLD
AND FOREIGN-EXCHANGE RESERVES 1949-75

FIGURE 13

in the value of exports from R903 million in 1957 to R774 million
in 1958 together combined to bring about a depletion of reserves
which required drastic fiscal and monetary measures. The position
was however restored; and in 1959, despite an outflow of private
capital, the favourable balance on current account of R151 million
was sufficient to augment exchange reserves by R80 million.

The crisis of 1960–1 was of a different character from all the
preceding ones in that the current trading position was favourable,[15]
and at the end of 1959 it appeared as if the national economy were
about to recommence its upward course. This time the crisis was
provoked by a loss of confidence on the part of private investors
and the large capital outflow was greater than the favourable balance
on current account could cover. A decline in foreign confidence in
South Africa may perhaps have been implied by the reduced capital
inflow as early as 1955, which changed to an outflow of capital in
1957. This was reversed in 1958, but the outflow recommenced in
1959 and various events occurring in the Republic and in the continent of Africa precipitated a huge capital outflow of over R12
million per month during 1960 and the early part of 1961. Reserves
of gold and foreign exchange were reduced to less than half, falling
from R312 million in January 1960 to less than R153 million in
May 1961, and there was the danger that fears of devaluation might
accelerate the capital outflow. South Africa faced a balance-of-
payments crisis more severe than any experienced since 1932. During
May 1961 the bank rate was raised, import controls were intensified,
restrictions were imposed upon commercial bank loans for hire-
purchase and stock-exchange dealings, and foreign-exchange facilities were reduced. Finally, in June, foreign-exchange control was
extended to stock-exchange transactions, South African residents
being prohibited from remitting funds for the purchase of securities
abroad, and non-residents, though permitted to sell securities on the
Johannesburg Stock Exchange, were prohibited from repatriating
their capital. Repatriation of dividends was permitted to continue.
The result was that South African shares were quoted on the London
Stock Exchange at levels considerably below their Johannesburg
prices. These restrictive measures led to a spectacular improvement
in the foreign-exchange position, a favourable balance on current

[15] The three years 1959, 1960 and 1961 showed a favourable balance on current
account of R166 million, R21 million and R201 million respectively, totalling
for the three years R388 million.

account for the year 1961 of R190 million; and, despite a capital outflow of R72 million during the year, a recovery in the foreign-exchange reserve from R153 million in May 1961 to over R316 million in February 1962 – the reserves of gold and foreign exchange thus exceeding the figure at which they had stood in January 1960.

Weighing the alternatives

The recovery of the economy from the desperate situation of May 1961 indicated the inherent strength of its foundations, which enabled an increase in export earnings of R87 million[16] above the previous year's figure to be achieved during 1961 in spite of the large capital withdrawals. This, together with a saving of R116 million on imports, brought the year to a close with a favourable balance on current account of R190 million. The large capital withdrawals during the three years from 1959 to 1961 had, however, retarded the growth of the national economy and caused a recession in certain sectors, particularly in building and construction. The recovery in the foreign-exchange position in the second half of 1961, therefore, raised difficult problems of priorities. On the one hand it was argued that first priority should, in the long-term interests of the country, be the restoration of foreign confidence in South Africa in order to revive foreign investment, and that this would best be done by using the rising reserves for the relaxation of the controls upon foreign-exchange dealings. Nothing, it was argued, would do more to restore international confidence than making the rand once more fully and freely convertible. A contrary opinion was also expressed, namely, that the restoration of the earlier rate of growth in the domestic economy should be the first priority. Early relaxation of exchange control was held to be inadvisable for several reasons. Firstly, it was thought that this would probably necessitate continued credit restrictions and high interest rates at home, which would retard industrial expansion and might perpetuate or increase unemployment. This might create an explosive situation within the country which would do more to shake the confidence of the foreign investor than convertibility of the currency would restore it. Further, the flight of capital was due to panic caused by political events in the African continent and was not based upon an assessment of the

---

[16] Exports of merchandise increased by R47 million, and gold output rose by R40 million.

basic economic situation, which was essentially sound. Doubts were expressed as to the probability of a renewed capital inflow until the whole position in the continent of Africa became more stable, and the benefit to South Africa of encouraging non-direct foreign investments,[17] which might suddenly be withdrawn in a moment of panic, was questioned. Too rapid a return to free convertibility was condemned on the ground that there were still nearly R1 000 million of foreign funds invested in the South African share market, and that this was all potentially 'hot money' susceptible to panic withdrawal caused by political fears. Thus free convertibility could only be restored with success if reserves of gold and foreign exchange were raised to unprecedented levels. Direct investments, however, were to be welcomed, especially when a foreign firm was prepared to co-operate in the establishment of factories and was prepared to supply a part of the capital and the necessary technical knowledge. This type of direct investment was more likely to be attracted by an expanding market and economic prosperity in South Africa than by the mere fact of complete currency convertibility. The right to remit dividends was, of course, recognized as sacrosanct.

After 1962, official policy appeared to lie between these two extremes of absolute priority for free convertibility on the one hand, and sole concern for the expansion of the domestic economy on the other. By various monetary and fiscal measures and by a bold policy of expansion of industries falling within the state-controlled sector of the national economy, the government stimulated expansion and restored the high rate of growth that had prevailed in the past. At the same time it made it clear that it was fully conscious of the dangers – so apparent in the recent history of certain South American countries – of using exchange control, tariffs and import control to bring about a spurious prosperity by insulating the country from the world economy. Some relaxation of currency control was introduced, and the emphasis placed on the need to expand exports and to make South African goods fully competitive in world markets, coupled with categorical statements that import control should be

---

[17] *Direct investment* means that the foreigner participates in the ownership and management of the enterprise. *Non-direct investment* is a more liquid form of foreign investment ranging from deposits with South African banks to shares purchased on the stock exchange, which may easily be realized and withdrawn. The latter is more likely to be affected by the possibility of short-term capital gains or losses; the former (direct investment) is more concerned with the long-term dividend prospects.

regarded only as a temporary expedient and not as a permanent instrument of policy. Economic policy in South Africa has never been isolationist. For the past hundred years it has ranked high among those countries in which international trade represents a major portion of total economic activity,[18] and in future imports and exports are likely to assume greater not lesser importance as South Africa is drawn ever more fully into the international economy.

The measures adopted in 1961 and 1962, and the recovery of the economy to which they gave rise, led to a revival in confidence on the part of the international investor. In 1965 a massive and somewhat unexpected inflow of foreign capital commenced, and this was maintained up to 1974 during which period no less than R3 559 million of new funds entered the country. This is to be seen in figure 12 (page 182) and its consequences for the gold and foreign reserves are shown in figure 13 (page 185). Imports rose very markedly and the trade gap widened to unprecedented size but the adverse balance on current account was covered by the capital inflow except for 1971 and 1973. In 1971 the adverse balance on current account reached the figure of R1 003 million against a capital inflow of R764 million, and in 1973, there was actually a capital outflow of R110 million. This massive foreign investment in South Africa greatly hindered the anti-inflationary measures which the government and the Reserve Bank were attempting to impose. These matters are more fully discussed in chapter 10.

[18] In 1961 South African exports (including gold) amounted to R1 502 million, imports to R1 021 million. Exports plus imports were R2 523 million, or 53 per cent of the national product.

9 Laying the Foundations of a Modern Economy

English economists often speak of 'social overheads', and French economists use the term 'infrastructure'; but, however it may be described, it is clear that a modern industrial economy cannot be developed without an appropriate institutional framework in which it can operate. In the industrialized modern economies of the western world the appropriate political and economic institutions have developed *pari passu* with the growth of the economy in a gradual evolution since medieval times, and therefore they tend to be taken for granted – so much so, indeed, that the difficulties of creating the appropriate infrastructure for a modern economy in countries where this does not yet exist are usually underestimated by western writers. In its widest aspect the problem is that of developing the whole range of institutions and of stimulating the mental attitudes of modern civilized man. Therefore, the tasks confronting the emergent African nations are both difficult and intricate. First there is the creation of political institutions, which will guarantee the maintenance of law and order, provide efficient and incorruptible administration, and give the mass of the population a sense of creative purpose. Then there are those social institutions, such as education, both of the masses and of an elite (which must provide the political and economic leadership), and health services and other aids to human welfare. Finally there are the more strictly economic institutions such as banking, transport, communications, power and water. Within the last hundred years South Africa has gone far towards providing many of these basic services. Education, initially pioneered by the churches and by missionary bodies, is today mainly run by the State, and there were in 1975 some 5 427 000 pupils at school,[1] and 153 000

---

[1] Of these 3 698 000 were Africans, 903 000 whites and 824 600 coloured people and Asians (*Statistics in Brief, 1976*)

190

at teacher-training colleges, technical colleges, and universities. In the field of health there were in 1962 10 000 doctors, 30 000 nurses, and 717 hospitals with beds for 22 000 white and 66 000 non-white patients. During that year some 593 000 white and 1 394 000 non-white people were treated at these hospitals.[2] There are also other welfare services for all racial groups which include old-age and dis-ability pensions; and although these still lag far behind what might be deemed desirable, particularly in the case of the non-whites, they are at least a recognition of the need for the State to concern itself with the welfare of all persons.

It is, however, with the more strictly economic aspects of the infrastructure that this chapter is concerned, and attention must therefore be directed to the provision of banking and financial facilities, transport, communications and other measures directly conducive to the growth of a modern exchange economy.

THE EVOLUTION OF BANKING AND FINANCIAL INSTITUTIONS

The first private commercial bank to be established in South Africa was the Cape of Good Hope Bank, which commenced business in 1837. Prior to this, banking had been a government monopoly. Between 1838 and 1862 banking progress was rapid and by this latter year there were no less than twenty-eight banks in the Cape. They were, however, generally small local affairs, and their aggregate paid-up capital did not reach R1 million. A new phase in banking was initiated by the advent of the so-called 'imperial banks', which were incorporated in London and, being able to avail themselves of the facilities of the London money market, were in a stronger position to withstand temporary setbacks than were the local banks. A severe drought and excessive credit creation hit the smaller banks in 1865, and in the years following many were absorbed by the larger banks, which established branches and introduced branch-banking on the English model in place of the traditional local unit-bank system. By 1891 there were eight banks: the Standard, the Bank of Africa, the African Banking Corporation, the National Bank of the South African Republic, the Robinson South African Bank, the Netherlands Bank, the Natal Bank and the Stellenbosch and District Bank. By 1926 further amalgamations had reduced the number to four – the Standard Bank, Barclays Bank D.C.O. (which took

[2] *Statistical Year Book, 1965,* section D.

over the National Bank), the Netherlands Bank and the Stellenbosch and District Bank. This last was, and still is, an interesting survival of the early local unit-banks. The other three all had their head offices abroad, the first two in England and the third in Holland; and there were fears both that banking was becoming too monopolistic and that South African interests were not always best served by institutions whose head offices were abroad. A new bank, Volkskas, with its head office in South Africa was founded in 1941, and four further banks made their appearance by 1961 – one French, one Greek and two American. The following figures represent the number of commercial banks, branches, sub-branches and agencies in August 1961 and the local liabilities to the public at 31 May 1961.

Name of bank	Liabilities to the public (R millions)	Number of branches	Number of sub-branches	Number of agencies
Barclays D.C.O.	467,60	340	14	309
Standard	410,94	350	18	272
Volkskas	151,40	160	—	96
Netherlands	63,84	42	2	36
French Bank of S.A.	8,53	5	—	—
Stellenbosch & District	4,26	1	—	2
First National City	4,19	2	—	—
Chase Manhattan	2,34	3	—	—
S.A. Bank of Athens	2,09	2	—	—
TOTALS	1 115,20	905	34	715

By 1970 the situation had altered in several important respects. The Banks Act of 1965 made provision for the registration with the Registrar of Banks of six categories of financial institutions: (a) Commercial banks, (b) General banks, (c) Merchant banks, (d) Discount houses, (e) Hire-purchase banks, and (f) Savings banks. In 1971 there were nine commercial banks registered in the Republic as shown below.

Name of bank	Liabilities to the public at 31 March 1971 (R millions)
Barclays National Bank	1 274,2
The Standard Bank of South Africa	1 097,3
Volkskas	619,9
Nederlandse Bank van Suid-Afrika	322,9
French Bank of Southern Africa	52,5
The First National City Bank of New York	43,3
The Bank of Lisbon and South Africa	30,2
Die Stellenbosche Distriksbank	11,9
South African Bank of Athens	10,8
	3 463,0

Source: Totals based on information kindly supplied by the Registrar of Banks.

At the time of union in 1910, banking legislation differed among the four provinces, but some measure of uniformity was introduced by the Banks Act of 1917. The first major development, however, came in 1920, when legislation was passed for the establishment of a central bank[3] – the South African Reserve Bank. The constitution of the Reserve Bank was that of a privately owned institution subject to a large measure of State control. The whole of the capital of R2 million was subscribed by the public,[4] and shareholders elected six of the eleven members of the Board of Directors, in whom management of the Bank was vested. The remaining five were appointed by the government, and included the Governor and Deputy-Governor. Thus the representatives of private shareholders were in a majority of six to five over those nominated by the State.[5]

The Reserve Bank was given a monopoly of the right to issue notes, and from a specified date[6] commercial banks were prohibited from issuing or reissuing bank notes within South Africa. Moreover, the commercial banks were by law required to hold on deposit with the Reserve Bank a reserve amounting to a prescribed percentage of their demand and time liabilities to the public.[7]

The Reserve Bank was initially required to hold a gold reserve of

[3] The Currency and Banking Act, no. 31 of 1920, subsequently replaced by the South African Reserve Bank Act, no. 29 of 1944.

[4] After the precedent of the American Federal Reserve System, provision was originally made for half the capital to be subscribed by the commercial banks, who could elect three of the six representatives of the shareholders, but this was changed by Act no. 22 of 1923. In his annual address to shareholders the governor said: 'The chief reason for recommending this alteration is that the Reserve Bank's business is almost entirely with the other banks and it was found by the great majority of the Board that it was very difficult to discuss the business of the Bank in the presence of customers who were moreover between themselves competitors. It was also felt strongly that the Reserve Bank would occupy a higher position vis-à-vis the public and command more confidence in its decisions if it stood on its own basis independent of the other banks.'

[5] In 1960 a second deputy-governor was appointed and this had the result of equalizing the number of officially nominated and privately-elected members of the Board, and a third deputy-governor in 1970.

[6] Subsequently fixed as 30 June 1922.

[7] Initially 13 per cent of demand liabilities plus 3 per cent of time liabilities. The former percentage was reduced from 13 to 10 per cent (Act no. 9 of 1933). Act no. 45 of 1956 empowered the Reserve Bank to prescribe additional reserve requirements. This supplementary reserve was limited to 10 per cent of the commercial banks' demand liabilities, not more than 2 per cent increase being permitted in any one month. This provision was first invoked in 1958 and has greatly increased the Reserve Bank's control of credit creation.

40 per cent against its notes and liabilities, but this was reduced to 30 percent in 1933[8] and 25 per cent in 1948.[9]

At its inception the Reserve Bank was in a relatively weak position, especially in relation to the powerful and long established commercial banks but the transference to it of the government accounts in 1927 considerably enhanced its prestige, and an agreement with the Chamber of Mines in 1925, by which it became the channel for the sale of all South African gold, increased its power to control the foreign-exchange rate.

In the original Act of 1920 the type of security and currency of bills in which the Reserve Bank was entitled to deal was severely circumscribed, but there was progressive relaxation of these restrictions, and the Reserve Bank Act of 1944 has been described as 'completing the process of liberating the Bank from the strait-jacket in which it was originally clothed'.

Apart from the Act establishing the Reserve Bank, the most important Act affecting commercial banking was the Banking Act, no. 38 of 1942, which consolidated and unified banking legislation throughout the country and introduced important innovations. The most far-reaching of these was the requirement that all commercial banks in South Africa must maintain a balance between their assets and liabilities *in South Africa*. In the 1920s it had been the practice of some banks to avail themselves of the advantages of the London money market for investment of short-term assets, with the result that although there was an over-all balance of assets and liabilities, this was not necessarily true of their position *in South Africa*. As long as the South African currency remained at par with Britain this was not of grave concern, but when Britain devalued the pound sterling in 1931 and South Africa remained upon the gold standard, the banks found that their assets had depreciated in relation to their liabilities. This therefore exerted strong pressure for the devaluation of the South African currency in opposition to the policy of the government at that time. The 1942 Act ensured that such a position would not recur by requiring all banks operating in this country to maintain a balance between their assets in South Africa and their liabilities in South Africa. Two other important provisions of the

---

[8] Act no. 9 of 1933.

[9] In terms of Act no. 49 of 1948 the statutory reserve was based upon the Reserve Bank's liabilities to the public minus the amount of its foreign assets.

1942 Act were the institution of a Registrar of Banks (with whom all banks had to be registered and to whom they had to make monthly, quarterly and annual reports), and the introduction of stricter provisions governing the banks' capital and reserve requirements.[10] A further important provision was that in addition to the cash-reserve requirements (of 10 per cent of demand plus 3 per cent of time liabilities) every commercial bank was required to maintain in South Africa liquid assets equal to 30 per cent of their total liabilities in South Africa. This provision focused a spotlight upon what had long been a serious deficiency in the South African financial structure; namely, the lack of an effective short-term money market.

Ever since the Kemmerer and Vissering Report of 1925 attention had repeatedly been drawn to the adverse consequences of the lack of an active market for short-term funds. Conditions in the South African money market prior to 1949 have been summarized by G. F. D. Palmer[11] as characterized by:

(1) No organized outlet for temporary surplus funds.

(2) Prevalence of open account and overdraft as sources of credit.

(3) The absence of specialist dealers in short-term securities.

(4) The issue of treasury bills at fixed rates, and in certain years a complete cessation of their issue.

(5) Lack of accepting houses providing bills of high quality.

(6) A relatively unresponsive interest-rate structure.

(7) The ability of the larger commercial banks to insulate themselves from changes in credit policy by virtue of their large cash reserves.

In 1949 the establishment of the National Finance Corporation[12] marked the first step towards creating a short-term money market. This new Corporation aimed at the promotion of such a market and provided an institution whereby idle money could be used in the national interest. It was empowered to accept deposits at call and short notice and to pay interest on them, to invest in treasury bills and short and medium-dated gilt-edged securities, and to deal in these securities. Building societies, banks and insurance companies

---

[10] Every commercial bank was required to maintain within South Africa a paid-up capital and reserve fund not less than *either* R100 000 plus R10 000 for every branch in excess of five, *or* 10 per cent of its total liabilities in South Africa, whichever was the greater.

[11] G. F. D. Palmer, "The Development of a South African Money Market", *S.A.J.E.*, vol. 26 no. 4, December 1958.

[12] Act no. 33 of 1949.

were empowered by legislation to deposit their surplus cash with the Corporation and to regard such deposits as liquid assets for their reserve and liquidity regulations. The liquidity of the Corporation was itself guaranteed by the Reserve Bank. The National Finance Corporation proved an immediate success and obviously fulfilled a real need, for during its first year deposits rose to almost R140 million, and within three years it had an annual turnover of R2 000 million. Other institutions followed: in 1955 the first South African accepting house was opened; in 1957 the first discount house; from 1958 treasury bills were offered on tender; and since then other specialized institutions have come into being.[13] Although it cannot yet be said that South Africa possesses a developed and fully competitive short-term money market, substantial progress in this direction has undoubtedly been made.

As a result of the growth of these various types of financial institutions with greater or lesser power to create credit, concern was expressed that the Reserve Bank might lack adequate powers effectively to control the quantity of money and 'near-money'; and a Technical Committee on Banking and Building Society Legislation was appointed. Its report (R.P. 50/1964) was followed by the far-reaching Act to Amend the Banking Act (Act No. 61/1964) and the associated Act to Amend the Building Societies Act (Act No. 62/1964). The former was a complicated and highly technical piece of legislation; but, in brief, its main provisions were as follows:

(1) Banking legislation was extended to cover all types of deposit-receiving institutions, of which six categories were recognized: commercial banks, merchant banks (accepting houses), discount houses, hire-purchase banks, savings banks, and a 'general' category (which covered trust banks, boards of executors, &c.).

(2) The requirement to hold balances with the Reserve Bank, formerly obligatory on commercial banks only, was extended to all banking institutions except discount houses. In place of the reserve of 10 per cent of demand liabilities and 3 per cent of time liabilities, a new reserve ratio of 8 per cent of short-term liabilities (other than liabilities under acceptances and loans from other banking institutions) was introduced.

(3) The legal definition of 'liquid assets' was tightened up, and

[13] In January 1962 there were two discount houses (total assets R132 million) and four accepting houses (total assets R96 million). Source: *Quarterly Bulletin*, S.A.R.B., March 1962, pp. 9, 10.

every banking institution, other than a discount house, was required to maintain within the Republic liquid assets equal to (*a*) 30 per cent of its short-term liabilities to the public; (*b*) 20 per cent of its medium-term liabilities; (*c*) 5 per cent of its long-term liabilities (all excluding acceptance liabilities); plus (*d*) 10 per cent of its liabilities under acceptances. Moreover, the Reserve Bank might with the consent of the Treasury vary the reserves under (*a*) and (*b*) between a maximum of 40 per cent and 30 per cent, and a minimum of 20 per cent and 10 per cent respectively. There was also a provision whereby the Reserve Bank might require supplementary liquid assets equal to not more than 70 per cent and 80 per cent of any *increase* after a given date in an institution's short-term and medium-term liabilities, respectively.

(4) A new category of 'prescribed investments' was introduced. These consist of all liquid assets (as elsewhere defined in the Act) plus safe assets which, though not strictly liquid, could be realized without undue loss, and these were listed in the Act. All banking institutions, other than discount houses, were required to maintain within South Africa prescribed investments equal to 15 per cent of their total liabilities to the public. The purpose of this provision was to safeguard depositors, particularly in the case of those institutions which have mainly long-term liabilities and which, accordingly, will not be required to maintain much more than 5 per cent of their total liabilities to the public in the form of *liquid* assets.

(5) Special provisions were laid down for discount houses to ensure that they remained highly specialized institutions fulfilling their primary function of discounting.

(6) Building Societies were not required to keep a statutory reserve with the South African Reserve Bank, but had to maintain certain liquidity ratios in respect of short-, medium- and long-term liabilities (at lower rates than those applying to banking institutions).

The Banking Amendment Act of 1964 was replaced by the comprehensive Banks Act (No. 23 of 1965).

A temporary disadvantage of the new legislation was that it applied initially only to the commercial banks, other institutions being given a year's grace – from January to December 1965 – before having to comply with its provisions. The effectiveness of the new provisions was at once put to the severe test of restraining the inflationary pressures that had built up within the economy. This matter is discussed in the next chapter.

By 1970 there were fifty-six registered banking institutions:

	Number	Assets December 1970[14] (R millions)
Commercial banks	9	3 826,5
Merchant banks	5	347,4
Discount houses	2	362,6
General banks	26 ⎫	
Hire-purchase banks	6 ⎬	1 792,1
Savings banks	8 ⎭	
TOTALS	56	6 328,6

In 1967 a Commission of Enquiry into Fiscal and Monetary Policy in South Africa was appointed under the chairmanship of Dr. D. G. Franzsen and its Third Report[15] made some far-reaching recommendations on banking structure and policy. The chief of these was concerned with the large measure of control exercised by non-nationals of South Africa. In June, 1970, foreign controlled commercial banks had possession of 73,2 per cent of all South African commercial banks' assets, when 'foreign controlled' is defined as a bank with more than 50 per cent of its shares held by foreigners. The Commission recommended that steps be taken to reduce the foreign control of such a vital part of the national economy; and legislation to this effect was introduced in 1976, requiring the gradual transfer of ownership of shares in excess of 50 per cent to South Africans.

It is not possible to trace in detail the evolution of a modern banking system, and its associated institutions in South Africa,[16] but enough has been said to indicate the remarkable progress that has been made during the past fifty years. In addition to the banking institutions there is of course the highly developed market for stocks and shares provided by the Johannesburg Stock Exchange, together with a variety of other financial institutions like trust banks and deposit-receiving institutions, building societies,[17] and for the provision of credit to agriculture, the Land Bank.[18] There are also the

[14] S.A.R.B., *Quarterly Review*, March 1971, pp. S-7, 14, 17, 19.

[15] R.P. 87/1970.

[16] For a fuller account see Report of the Social and Economic Planning Council no. 12, *Central and Commercial Banking in South Africa*, U.G. 42/1948; and G. de Kock, *A History of the South African Reserve Bank (1920–52)*, and other sources cited in the bibliography.

[17] Total assets December 1970, R3 061,5 million.

[18] Total assets December 1970, R635,1 million.

large mining corporations, which have combined financial and investment functions with co-ordination of technical and managerial provision for the mines within their 'group'. For manufacturing industry there is the Industrial Development Corporation and since 1957 the Industrial Finance Corporation.

The currency of South Africa from 1910 to 1961 was the South African pound,[19] which was kept approximately at par with the pound sterling, except for the period September 1931 to December 1932, when sterling had been devalued but South Africa remained on the gold standard. Parity was resumed in 1933 and the South African pound was linked to sterling and devalued with it in 1959. In February 1961 South Africa adopted a decimal currency with the 'rand' as the basic monetary unit.[20] The international value of the rand was determined, like its predecessor the pound, by its par value with the International Monetary Fund.[21] This situation prevailed until August 1971 when the world monetary system was shattered by President Nixon's announcement of the suspension of gold payments against United States dollars. The South African government decided that the rand would maintain its former parity with the dollar, and this led to a *de facto* devaluation of the rand in terms of countries whose currencies had 'floated' to higher parities. In December 1971 the Group of Ten Countries announced agreed new currency parities. These included the devaluation of the dollar by 7,89 per cent in terms of gold. The South African government decided to devalue the rand by 12,28 per cent in terms of gold, raising the official South African price of gold from R25 to R28,5 per fine ounce. In September, 1975, there was a further devaluation of the rand by 17,9 per cent.

In general the effectiveness of South Africa's monetary and banking system can be judged by the relative stability of its money over the past sixty years and by the country's reputation for financial integrity. Since 1945 it has, like the majority of other nations, suffered from inflationary pressures, but the price indices in table 24 show

---

[19] £1 = 20s.; 1s = 12d.

[20] R2 = £1. The rand is subdivided into cents; 100c = R1.

[21] In February 1961, this was fixed at a statutory gold price of R24,82 per fine ounce or R1 = $1,4. After devaluation in December 1971 and a period of floating linked to sterling in 1972, the rand was again given a fixed parity in October 1972 with gold at R29,75 per fine ounce. In September, 1975, the rand was again devalued, this time by 17,9 per cent.

that it has been as successful as most in preventing inflation from getting out of control.

TRANSPORT AND COMMUNICATIONS

South Africa has had to overcome natural disadvantages in the development of an effective system of transport and communications. The coastline affords few natural harbours, and most of the existing ports have had to be constructed at great expense; moreover the coastal belt is separated from the interior either by huge tracts of arid or semi-arid land with a sparse population or by great mountain barriers. There are no great navigable rivers to carry ocean traffic to the interior, and the rich mineral deposits of the southern Transvaal have had to be developed without the assistance of a Rhine or St. Lawrence waterway. For over two centuries the economic development of southern Africa was set by the pace of the ox, and it was not until the discovery of diamonds and gold in the later nineteenth century that modern means of transport became an economic proposition. First the railway and the electric telegraph, and later road motor transport, the telephone, wireless, and air transport, have revolutionized transport and communication.

Open lines of railway in kilometres

1861	3
1891	6 680
1911	12 147
1931	21 079
1951	21 478
1961	21 170
1969	21 296

Railway construction began in the 1860s, but although the rate of new construction has declined markedly since the 1920s because of the development of road motor services, the volume of traffic carried by the railways has continued to increase, rising from 4 163 million kg/m in 1929 to 23 125 million in 1969.

Since early times railways have been a public enterprise in South Africa, and the Act of Union made provision for a national railway system – the South African Railways and Harbours – to take over and operate the railways of the four colonies as a public enterprise.

In addition to railways it controls and operates the harbours, air transport, and a large volume of road motor transport. The clause declaring that it was to be run in accordance with business principles seemed clearly to indicate that it was the intention to insulate railway administration from political pressures; but no organization of such basic importance as the national railway system can neglect the broad issues of national economic policy. Undoubtedly the railways have in general performed an excellent service to the country, but certain aspects of their rating policy have from time to time been the object of criticism. On the well-established principle of 'charging what the traffic will bear', to which reference was made earlier, railway freight-rates discriminate between various classes of goods, some being carried at much cheaper rates than others. It has sometimes been suggested that pressures from the farmers' 'lobby' have induced the railways to favour agriculture at the expense of mining and manufacturing. There is also the principle of the tapering rate, whereby the rate per ton-kilometre is reduced as the distance increases. This, in conjunction with various other special rates, such as the special rate to centres of distribution, the nearest-port rate, and the sea-competitive rate have given rise to serious anomalies. A detailed discussion of these matters is to be found in the report of the Newton Commission,[22] which gave rise to certain changes in policy. The situation was still not without critics; evidence of this was the appointment of a commission of inquiry in 1964 under the chairmanship of Professor C. G. W. Schumann, and a further commission in 1969.[23]

Roads in the early days were often only crude tracks over the veld made by the wagons as they travelled into the interior. The advent of the motor vehicle made new demands, and the quality of roads has greatly improved. In 1916 there were 76 000 kilometres of road, of which practically none were bituminous. By 1969 there were over 187 000 kilometres, of which nearly 32 000 were tarred. The responsibility for road maintenance and construction rested with the provincial administrations at the time of Union, but the establishment of the National Road Board and the policy of cen-

[22] *Report of the Committee Appointed to Enquire into Railway Rating Policy in South Africa*, U.G. 32/1950.

[23] *Report of the Committee on Railway Rating Policy and Industrial Location in South Africa (1964)*; and *Report of the Commission of Inquiry into the Co-ordination of Transport*, R.P. 32/1969.

tralized control of the main national roads, which developed in the 1930s, have greatly improved long-distance road travel. The impelling force behind this is seen in the increase in motor-vehicle registrations from 40 000 in 1920 to over 1 366 000 in 1964 and 3 418 000 in 1975.

Motor-vehicle Registrations

Year	Total	Cars	Buses	Commercial vehicles	Motor cycles
1920	40 008	24 064	115	905	14 924
1930	186 075	135 177	1 395	16 012	33 489
1940	390 898	317 958	1 745	49 470	21 725
1950	623 215	471 374	4 433	123 549	23 859
1958	1 025 853	758 657	9 382	197 062	60 752
1964	1 366 000	1 015 000	18 000	243 000	90 000
1970	2 294 000	1 654 000	33 000	428 000	184 000
1975	3 418 000	2 117 000	n.a.	800 000	n.a.

In addition to the railways and roads, air transport (both international and within South Africa) is assuming considerable importance, especially for the transport of passengers, mail and perishable freight. All the major cities are connected by daily air services, and in 1969 these carried over one million passengers and 30 million metric tons of freight and mail on internal services only. In addition there are daily international services from the larger airports to all parts of the world.

A certain portion of South African domestic transport is also handled by coastwise shipping, but for a variety of reasons transport by sea between South African ports has not assumed the major importance which might be expected.[24] In 1969 a total of slightly over 3 million metric tons of coastwise traffic was handled, which is small in relation to the volume carried by other forms of internal transport, and only about one-seventh of the foreign traffic handled by the ports.[25]

In the development and present operation of transport and communications facilities, the State has played, and plays, a dominant role; but, in a country with the great natural difficulties that occur

[24] The basic reason is that the bulk of the traffic is between the interior and the ports rather than from one port to another, but the fact that the ports and the railways are jointly administered may have been a subsidiary cause as railway interests may sometimes have inhibited the development of coastwise shipping traffic.

[25] Foreign traffic handled by South African ports in 1969 was 21 million metric tons.

in South Africa, private enterprise could not have been expected to have had either the resources or the incentive to undertake major national-development programmes. The main criticism has been the effect of the policy of railway freight tariffs upon the location of industry,[26] and the dominating position of the South African Railways and Harbours in the whole transport system, particularly its influence upon the development of alternative and more modern methods of transport such as those by road and air.

In general, however, it may with confidence be said that for a country of its size with a relatively small population, South Africa has today a system of transport and communications which compares favourably with any similar country in the world.

Whatever one's general views may be about the relative merits of private enterprise and public control and ownership, it is inevitable that the State should play a large part in the progress of a relatively undeveloped country by providing at least those essential services without which private initiative cannot effectively operate. This has certainly been so in South Africa.

In addition to the generally accepted functions of government and administration, defence from external attack, and the maintenance of law and order within the country, the central government operates the postal, telephone and telegraph services of the country. Through a public corporation – the South African Broadcasting Corporation – it operates all radio and television services. The central government together with the provincial administrations provides almost all primary, secondary and technical education, and the universities, though still in form autonomous bodies, are heavily subsidized by the State.

The Act of Union made provision for a national railway system; and, as mentioned above, the South African Railways and Harbours has come to dominate the whole transport system of the country. In 1974 it employed 233 000 persons and earned a total revenue of R1 353 million – R1 007 million from railways, R81 million from harbours, R175 million from air services, R31 million from road motor services, and the balance from miscellaneous sources.

---

[26] See comment in ch. 6 p. .141

Prior to 1922 the supply of electricity was in the hands of private concerns or local bodies, but the Electricity Supply Commission (Escom) established in that year has progressively taken over this function, and today provides over 80 per cent of the supply. A regional grid-system has been developed in each of the main regions of South Africa, and these are being linked by a national grid. Electricity supply is at present derived almost entirely from the use of coal, and the cheap price of coal has enabled the average cost of electricity to be kept at a very low rate.[27] There is however considerable difference in the price between different regions, those near the coal fields being markedly lower than those that are more distant. This has important consequences for industrial location. The increase in the consumption of electricity in South Africa is shown in the table below, which gives consumption in kilowatt hours and gross value of output.

Electricity Consumed in South Africa

Years	K.w.h. (millions)	Value in R (millions)
1916–17	851	5,5
1926–7	1 694	9,5
1936–7	4 361	19,5
1946–7	7 494	38,0
1956–7	17 084	111,3
1968	28 885	161,5 (Escom only)
1974	66 413 (units sent out)	

Source: *Union Statistics for Fifty Years*, p. L-34, and *South African Statistics*, *1970*, pp. O-8, 9.

Of the total consumption in 1958–59, mining accounted for approximately 47 per cent, manufacturing industry 26 per cent, domestic consumption 16 per cent, the railways (for traction) 4,5 per cent, and the balance was used for street lighting, trolley buses and other purposes, including agriculture. Rural electrification in most regions is still in its infancy.

In South Africa the storage and supply of water ranks in importance with transport and electricity supply, and climatic factors often make this an expensive and technically difficult task. In this field too, the public authorities have played an essential part. Much of the

---

[27] Average prices of electricity per unit, 1956:

Central Electricity Authority, United Kingdom	1,403	pence
Electricity Supply Commission, S. Rhodesia	1,090	pence
Hydro-Electricity Power Commission, Ontario, Canada	0,8	pence
Escom, South Africa	0,5142	pence

Source: D. G. Franzsen and H. J. J. Reynders (ed.), *Die Ekonomiese Lewe van Suid-Afrika*, p. 143.

work of providing an adequate water supply for urban communities has been undertaken by local authorities, but in the case of the great industrial complex of the Witwatersrand a public-utility corporation – the Rand Water Board – provides from the Vaal River the water supply for Johannesburg, for the gold mines, and for the various other municipalities in the area. In addition the central government has initiated and executed a number of large conservation and irrigation schemes. Two new schemes have recently been undertaken – the Pongola River scheme in Zululand and the Orange-Fish River scheme. This last is the largest enterprise of its kind yet to be attempted, and involved the diversion of a portion of the water-flow of the Orange River from its natural course to the Atlantic Ocean into the Fish River valley where, after being used for irrigation and other purposes, it eventually reaches the Indian Ocean at a point over 1 500 kilometres from its natural outlet.

It will be generally agreed that all the activities mentioned so far are natural and proper spheres for State action; but, since 1928, the State has extended its activities into the more debatable field of manufacturing industry. Beginning with the establishment and growth of the Iron and Steel Industrial Corporation in the 1930s[28] there has been an increasing number of industrial establishments wholly or partly State-owned. Much of this has come about through the Industrial Development Corporation,[29] which in the twenty years from its inception to 1960 lent or invested no less than R171 million in various industrial projects. Of this, some R39 million has been repaid, and there was in 1960 a sum of R132 million representing investments and loans outstanding at that date.[30] Thus the Industrial Development Corporation has built up a very substantial industrial empire, because in addition to various minor concerns, it has substantial interests in ten major industrial undertakings:[31]

(1) South African Pulp and Paper Industries Ltd. (SAPPI).
(2) South African Coal, Oil & Gas Corporation Ltd. (SASOL).
(3) Northern Lime Company Ltd.

[28] See ch. 6, p. 124.

[29] Established by the Industrial Development Act, no. 22 of 1940, with an initial capital of R10 million.

[30] E. Rosenthal, *The Industrial Development Corporation of South Africa Ltd.,* *1940 to 1960.*

[31] Idem.

(4) Phosphate Development Corporation (FOSCOR).
(5) Good Hope Textile Corporation (Pty.) Ltd.
(6) Fisons (Pty.) Ltd. at Sasolburg.
(7) Fine Wool Products of South Africa Ltd.
(8) South African Marine Corporation Ltd.
(9) Masonite (Africa) Ltd.
(10) South African Industrial Cellulose Corporation (Pty.) Ltd.

The degree of State participation in these concerns varies considerably from one undertaking to another, but collectively it represents a considerable encroachment in a sphere often regarded as more appropriately left to private enterprise. Moreover many of these quasi-public concerns, like Iscor, are now expanding their operations by ploughing back their profits, so that there is a measure of self-generated expansion in the activities of the public sector. This process should not, however, be viewed as a conscious movement toward .a socialist state, for socialism is not a part of the present government's party programme. Indeed the reverse is true and the government has repeatedly declared its desire to stimulate private enterprise.[32] It is contended that public enterprise in manufacturing has occurred only in cases where, because of the heavy capital outlay or for some other reason, private enterprise had failed to take the initiative. Iscor, it will be remembered, was launched only after private enterprise had failed to raise the necessary capital. Both Iscor and Sasol were targets for much criticism at the start, but seem to have justified themselves by their subsequent achievements.

Private manufacturing interests generally accept these contentions, but there remain two criticisms of government policy which have considerable force. The first is that, though government enterprise in organizations like Iscor, Sasol and the railways is valuable, the activities of these concerns should not be permitted to expand beyond their basic purpose. For example Iscor should produce steel, but the manufacture of engineering and industrial products from this steel should be left to private enterprise. It is necessary too for the railways to run their own maintenance workshops, but they

[32] This is in interesting contrast with the deliberate policy of nationalization in many developing nations, in some of which, Egypt for example, it is not always easy to decided whether nationalization is motivated by genuine socialist ideology or is merely the most convenient way of acquiring control over foreign-owned enterprises. South African has been fortunate in avoiding the violent xenophobia so prevalent in many new nations today.

should eschew manufacturing activities which could be done by private concerns. Similarly the National Road Board and Provincial Councils should make more use of the private contractor for road construction. No matter of principle is at stake here and government spokesmen have accepted the point. The real danger is that these public and quasi-public concerns tend to expand simply by the operation of Parkinson's Law[33] unless the whole community is perpetually on guard against this danger.

The second complaint of private enterprise is, that by fiscal policy, budget surpluses diverted to loan account, and by its commanding position in the capital market, the public sector may acquire too large a share of the available capital, leaving the private sector with too little capital for development. This is not so serious while there is a large capital inflow from abroad, but in times of a restrictive monetary policy, the resultant shortage of investment funds makes it a matter of grave concern. The function of the rate of interest in a competitive capital market is to ensure optimum resource allocation; but, if by its privileged position the public sector can acquire more than its fair share, there may be a misdirection of resources.

An attempt has been made to indicate the size and importance of the public and quasi-public sector of the South African economy. Central government and provincial administrations, roads, railways, harbours, airways, electricity, and also manufacturing enterprises, in which there is increasing participation, all add up to a considerable portion of the national economy, and the total number of persons employed by public or semi-public bodies is large. Moreover, in 1970, of gross domestic fixed investment of R3 061 million, public authorities and public corporations accounted for R1 414 million, or 46 per cent of the total. The private sector accounted for R1 647 million, or 54 per cent. Twenty years earlier in 1950 the percentages were: public sector 35, private sector 65. In these twenty years gross capital formation by the public sector rose from R191 million to R1 414 million, and the percentage of the total which these figures represent increased from 35 to 46.[34] In 1975, the Central Government and the Provincial and local authorities employed no less than 696 000 persons or 7,1 per cent of the economically occupied population.

[33] C. N. Parkinson, *Parkinson's Law.*
[34] S.A.R.B., *A Statistical Presentation of South Africa's National Accounts for the Period 1946 to 1970*, pp. 26–8.

One last aspect of State activity must receive mention, however brief. It is the promotion of research in institutions like Onderste-poort and various agricultural research stations, the Medical Research Institutes, the Council for Scientific and Industrial Research, the Human Sciences Research Council, the Bureau of Standards, and state-financed research at the universities. Lasting benefits, incalculable in monetary terms, have been derived from the work of these institutions. Considerable sums of money have, in the past, been devoted to these purposes and it is recognized that with many pressing demands upon the limited national product, to increase both investment and consumption levels, too high a priority cannot be given to research. Nevertheless there are many who believe that greater outlay in this field is essential if South Africa is to maintain its leading position in Africa and accelerate its industrial expansion.

THE FINANCING OF GOVERNMENT

In the previous section reference was made to the expansion of the activities of the public sector and a brief account of the financing of government at all levels should now be attempted. This is, however, a vast and complex topic and only the barest outline can be given.

Government in the Republic operates on at least three levels – the central government, the provincial administrations and local government bodies such as municipalities and (in the Cape) divisional councils. The structure of government is made more complex by the emergence of separate national authorities, such as the Transkei government and other territorial authorities. Also falling within the public sector are state enterprises like the Post Office, the South African Railways and Harbours, the Mint and the Government Printer. In addition there are some quasi-independent bodies created by statute like the Atomic Energy Board, the South African Bantu Trust, the National Transport Commission and others, and finally there are the large public corporations like the Electricity Supply Commission and South African Iron and Steel Industrial Corporation.

The Provincial Councils have their origin in the historical developments which led up to the Union of South Africa in 1910, but their existence complicates the structure of government and increases the difficulty of overall financial control because, although they are autonomous taxing bodies, a large portion of their funds is derived by grant from the central government. It is even difficult to give a short description of the inter-relation of the finances of the various parts of government because, for example, care must be exercised to avoid double counting as would occur if central government and provincial expenditures were to be added together without adjustments. Two commissions[35] have investigated the functional and financial relations between the provinces and the central government, and some rationalization may come about. Similar problems arise in the case of other parts of the public sector.

In table 25 of the statistical appendix the current revenue and expenditure of government at all levels is shown for the period 1946 to 1970. The expenditure covers only outlays against the current revenue account and does not include capital expenditure financed by loans. Moreover the figures specifically exclude the business enterprises and trading activities of government at all levels. It will be observed that general government current expenditure rose from R268 million in 1946 to R1 931 million in 1970. This is a vast increase, but expressed as a percentage of the gross national product the increase was very slight, rising from 15,3 per cent in 1946 to 15,5 per cent in 1970.

If, however, we include government outlays financed on loan account and include the activities of public corporations a very different picture emerges. The table below, taken from the Third Report of the Franzsen Commission,[36] reveals an alarming growth in the outlay of the public sector.

Expenditure by the Public Sector as a percentage
of Gross Domestic Product

	R millions			% of G.D.P.			Average annual % growth rate	
	1938	1960	1970	1938	1960	1970	1938–60	1960–70
Central government	70	404	1 302	7,8	7,5	11,2	8,3	13,9
Provincial admin.	38	301	737	4,2	5,6	6,3	9,9	10,5
Local authorities	32	193	395	3,6	3,6	3,4	8,5	5,8
Public corporations	7	63	302	0,8	1,2	2,6	10,5	19,0
TOTAL	147	961	2 736	16,4	17,9	23,5	8,9	12,3

[35] The Borckenhagen Committee of Enquiry into the Financial Relations between the Central Government, the Provinces and Local Authorities, which published eight interim reports and a main report; and the *Report of the Commission of Enquiry into Financial Relations between the Central Government and the Provinces* (Schumann), R.P. 35/1964.

[36] *Fiscal and Monetary Policy in South Africa* (Third Report of Franzsen Commission) R.P. 87/1970.

The last column reveals the fact that in the decade 1960 to 1970 all the branches of the public sector, except local government, have been expanding their outlays at a rate considerably greater than the annual growth of the gross domestic product.

The problems arising from the general tendency of both public and private sectors to spend in excess of the productive output of the economy, and the difficulty in curbing the resultant inflation, are discussed in the next chapter. The effectiveness of controls upon government spending and the procedures for the formation of the budget received much attention in the Franzsen Commission's report.

Since the formation of the Union in 1910 it has been the practice to divide the budget into two parts – the Revenue Account (which was financed from current revenue and against which current expenditure was debited), and the Loan Account (against which items considered to be of a capital nature were charged) which is financed by government borrowing. Criticism of this system of a dual budget arises partly from the difficulty of drawing a clear distinction between items properly financed from revenue and those properly financed by loan, but mainly from the fact that all government outlay, however financed, is a claim against the productive resources of the country. The total permissible government expenditure and the appropriate methods of financing it should be decided on economic arguments related to the overall state of the national economy and not be circumscribed by accounting procedures. To indicate the order of magnitude of the sums involved it should be noted that in 1969 total expenditure of the central government alone amounted to R1 466 million from Revenue Account and R560 million from Loan Account giving a total of R2 026 million.[37] The Franzsen Commission recommended that the existing dual budget system be replaced by an integrated or unitary budget.

The Franzsen Commission also recommended more stringent control in the drawing up of the budget and proposed the formation of a Cabinet Committee for Finance under the chairmanship of the Minister of Finance to perform this control. This committee should also devise a system by which tax action taken by lower authorities could be co-ordinated with that of the central government.[38]

---

[37] *South African Statistics, 1970*, pp. T-6, 7.
[38] Franzsen Commission Third Report, R.P. 87/1970, pp. 33, 88.

In a rapidly expanding economy it is necessary that government expenditure should grow if the necessary political and economic infrastructure is to keep pace with expanding requirements, but the constant need for the exercise of proper restraint is seen from the table below.[39]

Central Government

	Expenditure on Revenue Account (R millions)	Expenditure on Loan Account (R millions)	Provincial Expenditure (R millions)	The National Debt (R millions)
1965	1 008	383	344	3 222
1966	1 075	443	397	3 396
1967	1 242	502	424	3 770
1968	1 404	534	452	4 218
1969	1 466	560	530	4 879

Year ending 31 March	Total Receipts (R millions)	Total Issues (R millions)	Total Surplus (R millions)	National Debt (R millions)
1970	2 142	2 488	−347	5 372
1971	2 319	2 743	−424	6 014
1972	2 729	3 531	−802	7 007
1973	3 182	3 824	−642	7 506
1974	4 202	4 607	−405	7 507
1975	4 983	5 799	−816	7 985

[39] *South African Statistics, 1970*, pp. T-6, 7, 12, 14. and S.A.R.B. *Quarterly Bulletin*, December, 1975, from 1970

10 The Great Boom: 1961 to 1970

The critical position of the balance of payments after the massive flight of capital in 1960–1 was discussed in chapter 8. Although the stringent measures then taken checked the capital outflow and raised the foreign-exchange reserves, few economists at that time would have predicted 1961 as the prelude to one of the greatest waves of economic expansion that this country has experienced. Indeed the course of development has been so remarkable that it merits particular attention as an illustration of the resilient strength of the national economy.[1] It also, particularly in the latter years of the boom, highlights some of the bottlenecks and inherent contradictions in the economic structure.

Perhaps the most remarkable feature of this period was that recovery took place in the latter half of 1961. Political events throughout the African continent, the outbreak of revolutions in the adjacent territories of Angola and Portuguese East Africa, the prospect of the dissolution of the Federation of Rhodesia and Nyasaland, and civil disobedience and the declaration of a state of emergency in the Republic which severed its link with the Commonwealth, did not combine to produce a political climate likely to inspire economic confidence. Indeed there were many, not only in the independent African states and Communist countries, but also in Europe and the United States, who predicted the imminent collapse of white supremacy in southern Africa. There were even some in South Africa who shared these views. Nevertheless, between 1960 and 1970 the gross national product of the Republic increased from about R5 200 million to R12 400 million, rising by some R7 000 million during the eleven year period – an increase of 140

[1] The author has drawn mainly upon the South African Reserve Bank's *Quarterly Bulletin,* the *Annual Economic Report* and *A Statistical Presentation of South Africa's National Accounts for the Period 1946 to 1970,* throughout this chapter and the next. These sources are indispensable to all who desire a more detailed account of events during this period.

per cent. The South African economy with that of Japan probably had the highest growth-rate in the world at that time. How is this expansion to be reconciled with its unfavourable political context? Undoubtedly, the stern measures adopted by the South African government for the maintenace of law and order played their part in restoring confidence, for they demonstrated that it was not prepared lightly to capitulate to the pressures of African national-ism. Many investors, who feared political instability in newly inde-pendent countries, were reassured by these measures. The main cause of the revival, however, probably lay in the inherent strength of the economy which between 1945 and 1957 had shown its capacity for rapid and sustained growth. The gross national product had more than doubled between 1949 and 1957, increasing from R2 290 million to R4 583 million. There was a slowing down during 1958 and 1959; but after this recuperative period the economy was set for a further major advance, which was inhibited by the adverse political events of 1960 and early 1961. By the second half of 1961, however, the position appeared to have been stabilized, and by 1962 forces making for economic expansion were sufficiently strong to force a break-through which gathered momentum as a bullish sentiment developed in the following years.

THE GROWTH OF THE NATIONAL PRODUCT

The gross domestic product (G.D.P.) for the years 1946 to 1975 at current prices and at constant prices is shown in table 4, (p. 274). The figures for the years 1960–70 of the G.D.P. at market prices and at 1963 prices are given below.

Gross Domestic Product 1960 to 1970

| | At current prices | | | At constant 1963 prices | | |
	G.D.P.* R millions	Increase on previous year R millions	%	G.D.P.* R millions	Increase on previous year R millions	%
	(1)	(2)	(3)	(4)	(5)	(6)
1960	5 274	281	5,6	5 551	182	3,4
1961	5 546	272	5,2	5 735	184	3,3
1962	5 912	366	6,9	6 054	319	5,6
1963	6 555	643	10,9	6 547	493	8,1
1964	7 209	654	10,0	6 986	439	6,7
1965	7 879	670	9,5	7 448	462	6,6
1966	8 555	676	8,6	7 799	351	4,7
1967	9 459	904	10,6	8 391	592	7,6
1968	10 152	693	7,3	8 712	321	3,8
1969	11 339	1 187	11,7	9 325	613	7,0
1970	12 404	1 065	9,4	9 797	472	5,1

*Source: S.A.R.B., *A Statistical Presentation of South Africa's National Accounts for the Period 1946 to 1970*, p. 12.

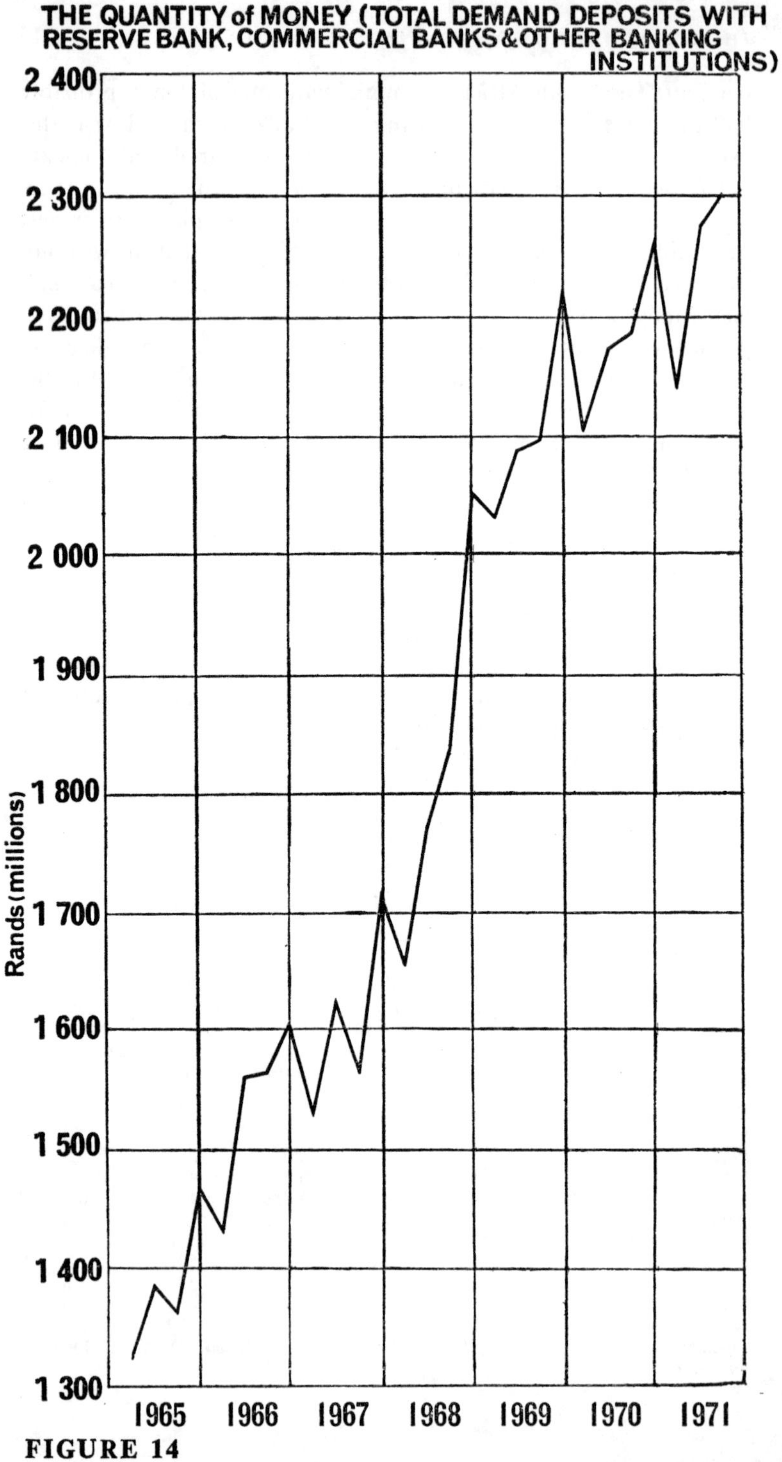
THE QUANTITY of MONEY (TOTAL DEMAND DEPOSITS WITH RESERVE BANK, COMMERCIAL BANKS & OTHER BANKING INSTITUTIONS)
Rands (millions)
2 400
2 300
2 200
2 100
2 000
1 900
1 800
1 700
1 600
1 500
1 400
1 300
1965
1966
1967
1968
1969
1970
1971

FIGURE 14

There had been a falling off in the rate of growth during 1960 and 1961. Indeed the figures conceal the true position somewhat, because they are annual totals and fail to show fully the retardation in the second half of 1960 and the first half of 1961.

The first three columns in the table relate to the gross domestic product at current prices and show the rapid and sustained growth during the decade at the astonishing high annual rate of about 10 per cent in six of the eleven years in the period under review. These figures are however inflated by the price increases that occurred and it is perhaps more rewarding to devote attention to the last three columns which give the gross domestic product at constant (1963) prices. A comparison of the two sets of figures is however instructive as illustrating the degree of inflation in different years.

The real gross national product is given in column 4 and the figures reveal an increase at constant 1963 prices from R5 551 million in 1960 to R9 797 million in 1970 – an increase of 76 per cent over the eleven-year period or an average annual rate of about 7 per cent. Population increased between 1960 and 1970 from 16,0 million to 21, 5 million or by 34 per cent. There was, therefore, a substantial increase in average *per capita* product during the decade.

Column 6 gives the annual percentage real growth, and in every year after 1961 this was significantly above the population increase of 3,0 per cent, so that real *per capita* income increased throughout. In 1960 and 1961 the real increase was 3,4 and 3,3 per cent respectively, but thereafter it rose rapidly and a rate of over 5 per cent was achieved in every year except 1966 and 1968. The rapid rise in 1962, 1963 and 1964 was not surprising as there were unused reserves of labour and capital. That the high rate of real growth continued after 1964 and in general carried through to 1970 demands explanation, because one would have expected the 'slack' to have been fully taken up by the end of 1964. The Economic Development Programme had suggested that the country's labour, capital and foreign exchange resources were capable of maintaining real growth at a rate of 5,5 per cent without imposing undue strain. The fact that rates of 6,6 per cent in 1965, 7,6 per cent in 1967 and 7,0 per cent in 1969 were achieved suggests that the economy had unsuspected productive resources to call upon. As predicted in the Economic Development Programme these rates in excess of 5,5 per cent did lead to inflationary pressures, balance of payments problems and a shortage of skilled labour. These matters will be considered later.

All sectors of the national economy participated in the growing prosperity but agriculture lagged behind the others, adverse climatic conditions causing low crop yields in 1964 and 1968. Gold mining continued to give increased annual outputs despite the persistent pressure of rising costs. There was a tendency for gold production to level off after 1965 but the expanding output of other minerals maintained the strong upward trend for mining activities as a whole. Manufacturing was, however, undoubtedly the leading sector in the economic expansion, the net value of output rising from R1 129 million in 1960 to R2 908 in 1970 – an increase of 158 per cent in the eleven year period.

Inflationary pressures

The inflationary pressures generated by the excessive rate of growth manifested themselves in five ways: (*a*) rising prices; (*b*) pressures on the balance of payments; (*c*) capital shortage and rising interest rates; (*d*) shortage of skilled labour; (*e*) bottlenecks in transport and the supply of certain commodities. Figure 15A shows the total index for consumer prices; price indices for goods and services separately from 1963 to 1970 are given in the table below.

Index of Consumer Prices
(1963 = 100)

	Goods		Services	
	Index	percentage increase	Index	percentage increase
1963	100,0		100,0	
1964	102,5	2,5	103,0	3,0
1965	106,1	3,5	108,0	4,6
1966	109,1	2,8	113,6	4,9
1967	112,2	2,8	118,7	4,3
1968	113,6	1,2	123,2	3,7
1969	115,9	2,0	129,8	5,1
1970	119,5	3,1	137,1	5,3

Prices rose relatively slowly from 1960 to 1963 at less than 2 per cent per annum. In 1964 the cost of living rose more rapidly, largely as a result of poor harvests pushing up food prices. From 1964, however, a more general rise in prices began to show itself as inflationary pressures began to mount showing in 1965 a rise of 3,5 per cent in goods and 4,6 per cent in services. Expansionary monetary policies gave place to more restrictive measures and the rate of inflation was reduced so that by 1968 it appeared that the situation was under control. The rapid inflow of funds from abroad, a relaxa-

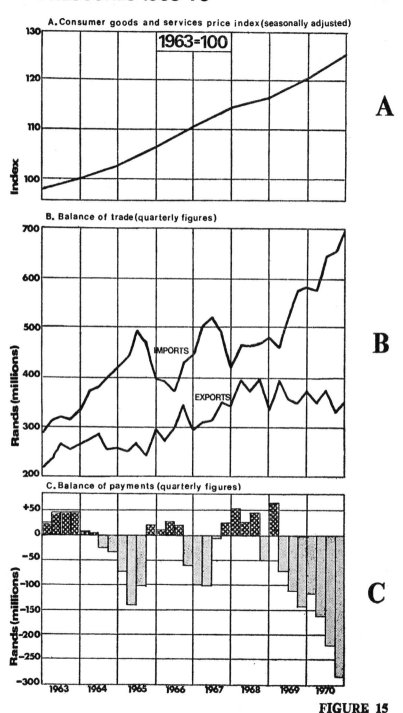

THE EFFECTS of INFLATIONARY PRESSURES 1963-70

A. Consumer goods and services price index (seasonally adjusted)

1963=100

Index

A

B. Balance of trade (quarterly figures)

Rands (millions)

IMPORTS

EXPORTS

B

C. Balance of payments (quarterly figures)

Rands (millions)

C

1963 1964 1965 1966 1967 1968 1969 1970

FIGURE 15

tion of vigilance and some inflationary government spending led to a renewal of the inflationary spiral, and 1970 saw a rise of 3,1 per cent in goods and 5,3 in services and this trend carried on into 1971.

THE BALANCE OF PAYMENTS

The inflationary pressures also made themselves apparent in the balance of payments. Figure 15B shows the growth of the inflationary gap most clearly. While exports were maintained at a more or less constant level, imports show a strong upward movement from 1962 to the middle of 1965. They fell in 1966 by R110 million but rose again in the latter part of 1966 and the first part of 1967 to a level higher than before. They fell somewhat in the second half of 1967 but thereafter resumed their upward course to reach a record of R2 547 million in 1970. (For details see statistical appendix table 20.) Exports showed a steady but unspectacular rise which was quite inadequate to counterbalance the rise in imports. The resultant deficit in the balance of payments on current account is shown in figure 15C. The drought in 1964 and 1965 also aggravated the adverse trade balance by causing, on the one hand, a significant fall in the volume of South African agricultural exports; and, on the other, by increasing imports, as some products normally supplied from domestic sources had to be obtained from abroad.[2] The main cause of the deterioration in the trade balance was, however, the expanding national expenditure. South Africa has always exhibited a high propensity to import, and there is a close correlation between increases in spending power and the volume of imports. In this case the high level of investment by both the private and the public sectors reinforced the general tendency. The deficit in the current account led to a running down of the country's foreign reserves as shown in figure 13 (page 185). These had risen from under R200 million in the trough of 1961 to over R500 million at the end of 1963. Thereafter there was a declining tendency to R320 million in September 1965, but in the latter part of that year as the result of a massive inflow of capital from abroad they improved again to reach R444 million in December 1965 and thereafter soared to the unprecedented level of R1 235 million in March 1969. In 1970 there was a

---

[2] In 1964 agricultural exports dropped by R17,6 million below 1963, and in 1965 there was a further drop of R71,7 million: *Financial Mail*, 21 January 1966, p. 122.

severe contraction in the foreign reserves as a result of the mounting trade gap and balance of payments problems again commanded serious attention.

The decade of the 1960s was one of almost continuous prosperity, but inflationary pressures soon developed and the battle against inflation was waged with varying success. It is perhaps possible to divide the boom into six distinct phases:

1. The recovery period and the beginnings of expansion (mid-1961 to mid-1962).
2. A period of real economic growth (mid-1962 to mid-1964).
3. An inflationary stage with pressure on the balance of payments (mid-1964 to September 1965).
4. A slowing down of inflationary forces at the end of 1965 and the first half of 1966.
5. A renewal of inflationary pressures in 1967 which was not successfully contained, but was somewhat reduced in 1968.
6. A new inflationary wave 1969 and 1970.

Of course, all these stages overlap, and economic indicators are often contradictory from one phase to the next. Moreover the battle against inflation covered several fronts. In 1964–5 the balance of payments appeared to be the critical point, and restrictions on imports were invoked to stem this attack. Then rising domestic prices demanded action, and import restrictions were relaxed to check the rise in prices by permitting more goods from abroad. While it relieved the foreign exchange position, the large inflow of funds from abroad in the latter years of the decade made the battle against rising prices more difficult to restrain by monetary measures.

It must be remembered that all six phases occurred in a rapidly expanding economy and that even in the relatively lean years of 1958, 1959 and 1960 the real domestic product was rising at a relatively rapid rate.

I. The beginnings of expansion (mid-1961 to mid-1962)

In 1961 the main concern was to stem the outflow of capital. When it was apparent that the measures adopted to this end (see page 187) were meeting with success, attention was directed towards stimulating activity in all sectors of the economy. An easy-credit policy was initiated by the monetary authorities. As early as December 1961, bank rate was reduced from 5 to 4½ per cent. There was a general increase in liquidity during the year 1961–2, but there was little increase in personal consumption or private investment. In order to accelerate the rate of spending, which the authorities were confident could safely be done without danger to the balance of payments on current account and without causing internal demand inflation,[3] bank rate was again reduced by ½ per cent in June 1962 and by a further ½ per cent towards the end of the year to 3½ per cent. During 1961–2 gold output and merchandise exports showed a strong upward tendency; these two, assisted by a marked increase in current expenditure by public authorities, provided a strong stimulus to expansion, and the real G.D.P. rose during 1962 by 5,6 per cent. In spite of this, however, the private sector remained sluggish and neither personal consumption nor private investment showed any marked upward trend; so much so, that the slogan 'spend for prosperity' was suggested.

II. Main period of real economic growth (mid-1962 to mid-1964)

Towards the end of 1962, however, the position began to change radically as confidence returned to the private sector. Private fixed investment began to develop a strong upward momentum, and the construction industry, which had been in the doldrums for some years, soon found itself with more orders than it could immediately execute. Figure 16A shows the changes in public and private fixed investment and figure 16B shows building plans passed. The index of building and constructional activity, which stood at about 70 at the beginning of 1962, climbed rapidly through 1963 and 1964 and reached a peak of over 190 in 1965. Capital expenditure on building and construction increased from R585 million in 1962 to R674 million in 1963, and R795 million in 1964, showing an increase of over R200 million in the two-year period.

The contribution of manufacturing industry also rose by some R450 million during these two years and mineral production continued its strong upward trend. Unemployment dropped to a very low level and a state of 'full employment' existed, but there was little sign of inflationary pressure or severe bottlenecks. The consequence was that the real gross domestic product rose by 5,6 per

[3] S.A.R.B., *Annual Economic Report, 1962*, p. 31.

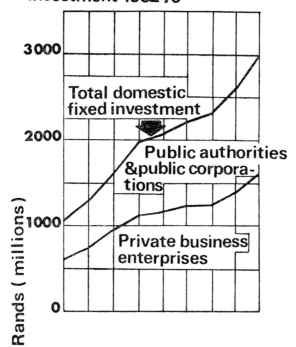

FIXED INVESTMENT 1962-70
A. Gross domestic fixed investment 1962-70

Rands (millions)

Total domestic fixed investment

Public authorities &public corpora- tions

Private business enterprises

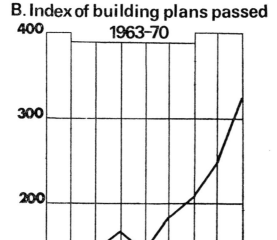

B. Index of building plans passed 1963-70

62 63 64 65 66 67 68 69 70

FIGURE 16

cent in 1962 and a further 8,1 per cent in 1963. There was some rise in prices, but only of the order of 2 per cent per annum. This relatively satisfactory state of affairs carried over into the first half of 1964. Throughout this period interest rates remained low and the commercial banks expanded the credit structure by a policy of easy lending. Indeed the monetary authorities held the view that it was necessary and desirable to assist recovery in economic activity right up to the fourth quarter of 1963.[4]

III. The inflationary phase (mid-1964 to the end of 1965)

The upsurge in the G.D.P. continued during 1964 with unabating vigour and the end of the year showed an increase of 10,0 per cent, with the G.D.P. measured at current prices; but there had been an ominous rise in prices especially in the latter half of the year, and the real G.D.P. increased by only 6,7 per cent, compared with 8,1 per cent in the previous year. Bottlenecks began to appear in steel, building materials, and transport equipment and, above all, in skilled labour. Imports rose steeply during the year, but there was little change in the value of exports. Capital investment, both public and private, continued to rise and the latter was presumably financed in part by the commercial banks, whose loans and advances continued an upward trend with little or no effective curb from the monetary authorities despite a rise in bank rate from $3\frac{1}{2}$ to 4 per cent in July and a further rise from 4 to $4\frac{1}{2}$ per cent in December, and a general hardening of interest rates. As these measures were ineffective in checking the inflationary spiral which continued into 1965, more stringent action was taken in March 1965, and the Minister of Finance issued a warning statement on the inflationary situation. Bank rate was raised from $4\frac{1}{2}$ to 5 per cent, moral suasion was used to its utmost, and various powers were given to the Reserve Bank, the most controversial of which was the power to prescribe maximum rates of interest on various types of deposits.[5] The ratios of liquid assets to be held by commercial banks against their short- and medium-term liabilities in terms of the new Banking Amendment Act were increased to 34 and 24 per cent respectively in March, and these were raised progressively to the statutory limit of 40 and 30 per cent in July. The March budget was mildly disinflationary.

[4] S.A.R.B., *Annual Economic Report, 1964*, p. 36.
[5] Proclamation by the State President 12 March 1965.

In spite of all these measures inflationary tendencies continued during the first half of 1965, and the loans and advances of the commercial banks continued to rise. The deficit on the balance of payments on current account amounted in the second quarter of the year to an annual rate of about R420 million, but the effect on the foreign reserves was cushioned by a substantial inflow of private capital.

The failure of the Reserve Bank's attempts to restrict credit during this period may be attributed to a number of causes. First, there was lack of experience in the practical operation of the Banking Amendment Act, and the commercial banks were able to convert some of their overdrafts into trade bills which qualified as liquid assets,[6] and at the same time some government stock nearing maturity moved into the liquid assets category.[7] Also the unexpected capital inflow neutralized to some extent the disinflationary effect of the adverse balance on current account. A major cause of the failure was, however, the high level of government expenditure (which increased between 1963 and 1965 by over R450 million) and the method by which it was financed. Central government deposits with the Reserve Bank fell from over R200 million in March 1965 to R14 million at the end of October in that year. By this method of financing, additional expenditure was undertaken without any curtailment of expenditure by the private sector such as would have arisen had it been financed by loans or increased taxation. It was thus highly inflationary and tended to counteract the efforts of the monetary authorities to contract the money supply. The ratio of money and near-money to the G.D.P. remained at the exceptionally high figure of about 35 per cent during the first half of 1965.[8]

IV. The slowing down of the inflationary spiral

By the last quarter of 1965 there were signs that the measures taken were beginning to have an effect in checking the inflation. The financial stringency had led to a levelling off, and even to a fall in private investment outlay, and the announcement by the Minister of Finance in September of the steps taken by the government to reduce public expenditure on capital works was taken generally as

[6] S.A.R.B. *Annual Economic Report*, 1965, p. 39.
[7] The government's 1958–68 loan moved into the three-year category and thus qualified as a liquid asset. S.A.R.B. *Annual Economic Report, 1965*, p. 42.
[8] S.A.R.B. *Quarterly Bulletin*, June 1965, XVIII.

an earnest indication of its intention to put its own house in order. The flotation of a twenty-year loan at 6 per cent – the highest rate ever offered on a government loan in South Africa[9] – seemed to indicate that public expenditure would be financed on more orthodox economic principles, and that the rate of interest would again be permitted to perform its essential function in the rationing of scarce resources. A tightening of import control took place in August and this, together with the changes in the domestic economy, led to a lower, though still high, rate of importation in the last quarter of the year. To reinforce all these measures the Reserve Bank at the end of October specifically requested all banking institutions, excluding the Land Bank, to ensure that the total of discounts, loans and advances did not at 31 March 1966 exceed what they had been at 31 March 1965 and to observe certain guiding principles in the creation of credit which were specified in detail.

Many of the economic indicators showed a levelling off and some a downward trend at the end of 1965, so that the Reserve Bank was able to report that 'the latest available evidence confirms that the long cyclical economic upswing in South Africa, which began about the middle of 1961, levelled off about the middle of 1965'.[10] Unfortunately, however, this levelling off did not last long and a new period of inflation commenced in 1966.

V. A period of renewed inflation (1966 to 1968)

The situation of the balance of payments which had been critical in 1965 was relieved by the enforced curtailment of imports and the large capital inflow. In 1965 there had been a net gain of foreign funds of R255 million, and further large inflows occurred in the following years, reaching R501 million in 1970. This counteracted the deflationary efforts of the authorities and militated against effective monetary curbs. Attention now was directed more towards price inflation and less towards the balance of payments aspect. In its *Quarterly Bulletin* the Reserve bank stated,[11] 'the latest available economic statistics show clearly that the new cyclical upswing in the South African economy which began during the second quarter of 1966 continued throughout the year and into the early months of

---

[9] Even so the rate was not attractive to the general public and of the R58 million subscribed, R33 million came from the Public Debt Commissioners.

[10] S.A.R.B., *Quarterly Bulletin*, December 1965, p. XV.

[11] S.A.R.B. *Quarterly Bulletin*, March 1967, p. 5.

1967'. Import control was relaxed in an attempt to arrest the rise in prices and monetary curbs were increased including a rise of bank rate from 4½ to 5 per cent in 1965 and to 6 per cent in 1966. In 1968 the Reserve Bank[12] was able to report that these measures had met with considerable success and that in 1967 excess monetary demand was substantially reduced. The index of the prices of goods which had risen by 2,8 per cent in 1967 rose only 1,2 per cent in 1968 and the real gross domestic product rose 3,8 per cent compared with 7,6 per cent in the previous year.

VI. A new inflationary surge (1969, 1970)

This success in the battle against inflation was however short-lived. Serious labour shortage especially in the skilled categories led to irresistible demands for wage and salary increases and there was a decline in productivity per man. Private consumption expenditure accelerated and private saving declined. Foreign funds still poured into the Republic and the economy resumed its strong upward movement. The Reserve Bank commenting upon the situation said:[13] 'During 1969 and more particularly during 1970, the South African economy became overheated as domestic monetary demands exceeded domestic supply by a margin which increased progressively every quarter . . . a huge deficit was recorded on the current account of the balance of payments, while increases in prices of goods and services began to accelerate and a number of administered prices were also increased in 1971. . . . This imbalance could not, of course be allowed to continue indefinitely and it is, therefore, not surprising that the authorities persistently have been taking steps to curtail most types of domestic spending, while at the same time they have been trying to promote higher production and the creation of additional production capacity.'

South Africa's economic problems were further complicated by President Nixon's announcement in August 1971, that the United States had suspended gold payments on the dollar and imposed a 10 per cent duty upon all imports. The collapse of the dollar had wide repercussions in many countries and particularly affected South Africa as the major gold producer of the world. Moreover, the resulting chaos in the world's foreign exchange markets intensified the

---

[12] S.A.R.B., *Quarterly Bulletin*, March 1968, p. 4.
[13] S.A.R.B., *Quarterly Bulletin*, March 1971, p. 5.

pressures on South Africa's current balance of payments. In these circumstances the South African government in November 1971 tightened import control to protect the rapidly declining foreign reserves.

South Africa had kept the rand at its former parity with the U.S. dollar during the period of exchange instability. In December 1971, however, the Group of Ten announced agreement upon a realignment of currencies in terms of which the mark and yen were to be upgraded, sterling and the franc were to be unchanged, and the dollar was to be devalued by 7,89 per cent in terms of gold. South Africa's response to this was an official announcement of devaluation of the rand by 12,28 per cent in terms of gold, thereby raising the official price of gold from R25 to R28,50 per fine ounce.

These events were perhaps the beginning of a period of international economic disintegration whose effects upon the South African economy are examined in the following chapter. The problems and difficulties of the moment should not however be allowed to obscure the very real economic advance made during the decade of the sixties.

SOME LESSONS TO BE LEARNED FROM THE BOOM

The first lesson to be learned from the course of the boom is the basic economic principle of scarcity or limitation of resources; neither individuals nor countries can continue to live beyond their means without running into serious troubles. In figure 4 the gap between the G.D.P. at current and at constant prices is a rough measure of the extent of inflationary pressure. This gap became most pronounced in the later years and especially in 1970. Gross Domestic Expenditure exceeded Gross Domestic Production: in other words, the country had been consuming more than it was able to produce; hence the adverse trade balance.

It is regrettable that the monetary and fiscal authorities did not apply the curb sooner; but in applying measures of restraint, timing is always difficult. One of the things that undoubtedly influenced the thinking of the government and the monetary authorities was South Africa's urgent need to maintain a high rate of growth in the real G.D.P. They were well aware of the low standard of living of the mass of the population, and the desirability of raising *per capita* incomes. They knew equally well that the population was increasing fairly rapidly, and that annually there were some 128 000 new entrants to the labour market (of these 28 000 were white and 100 000 Africans, coloured people and Asians). For economic, political and humanitarian reasons it was essential to provide jobs for as many of these people as possible by maintaining a high rate of expansion in the economy as a whole. For these reasons they were naturally reluctant to take any *premature* steps to check the rate of growth.

Moreover, until recently, there was a great dearth of up-to-date statistics of the basic economic magnitudes which determine the rate of growth. More adequate statistics for a system of national accounting are now available,[14] but there is still a considerable time-lag. There is also a time-lag between the adoption of measures and their full impact upon the economy, and always some uncertainty about the reactions of those human beings who create the general economic climate. For these reasons monetary control is likely to remain an art based upon experience, judgement and intelligent anticipation, rather than to become an exact science.

Another weakness was the lack of co-ordination and exchange of information about expectations and investment programmes between various government departments and the private sectors of the economy. The institution of an Economic Adviser to the Prime Minister with a small technical staff, and of an Economic Advisory Council appointed by the Prime Minister to represent the main private sectors of the economy, has done much to provide a forum for the exchange of opinions. The Council is also attended by the heads of all major government departments concerned with economic matters, and liaison between the public and private sectors is thus facilitated. More specifically, the staff of the Economic Adviser produced a five-year Economic Development Programme for the Republic.[15] The first was for the period 1964 to 1969, and it was there stated that the Programme would be revised annually and advanced by a further year into the future. This programme is not a hard-and-fast 'plan' to be implemented by all sectors of the economy,[16] but rather an analysis of the implications of specified rates of growth for the various sectors of the economy, and an attempt at

[14] There was a considerable revision of the national accounting statistics at the beginning of 1966.

[15] Government Printer, Pretoria, 1965.

[16] Some doubts have however been expressed on this; see J. Jewkes, "The Perils of Planning", *S.A.J.E.*, vol. 33 no. 4, December 1965.

quantitative formulation of the demands upon resources that will
arise from annual growth-rates of 4½, 5½ and 6 per cent in the real
Gross Domestic Product, and the estimated calls upon the various
major sectors consequential upon these rates of growth. In the process of formulating the Programme consultative committees were
established for the various sectors of private industry and these have
developed into valuable channels for two-way communication.

The first Economic Development Programme indicated that an
average annual growth rate in the Gross Domestic Product of 4½ per
cent was easily possible for the country; that a 5½ per cent rate was
likely to be achieved without undue strain; but that a 6 per cent rate
would encounter difficulties in the skilled-labour supply, the balance
of payments, and certain other fields such as transport and steel
production. After the publication of the Programme in 1965 the
government announced that it accepted a 5½ per cent rate of growth
in the real G.D.P. as an appropriate long-term objective. The second
Economic Development Programme[17] in December 1965 saw
no reason to amend the figure of a 5½ per cent growth rate as a
desirable objective, and pointed out that the actual realized rate in
1964 of 6,3 per cent had encountered the bottlenecks that were to
be expected. The high rate in 1964 meant that the average rate of 5½
per cent over the five-year period could now be obtained with annual
rates somewhat below this figure for the subsequent years. The
calculations for the next quinquennium were based upon a rate of
5,4 per cent growth in the real G.D.P. but once again this rate was
greatly exceeded in the actual course of events.

One of the causes of excessive expenditure was the volume of total
government expenditure on revenue and loan account. The need to
enforce greater economy upon the public sector and to relate the
Consumption and investment demands of all parts of the economy
to the resources available to meet them was stressed by the Franzsen
Commission. It is to be hoped that the Cabinet Committee for
Finance will be successful in bringing this reform into being.

SPOTLIGHT ON LABOUR

The rapid economic growth during the 1960s focused attention
upon the acute shortage of skilled labour. The Economic Develop-

[17] *Economic Development Programme for the Republic of South Africa 1965-70.*

ment Programmes,[18] have highlighted the fact that a major impediment to sustained rapid growth is the shortage of skilled labour.
Indeed their findings bear out much of what was said in chapter 7.
The total economically active population in 1964 was 6 210 500,
and the Programme estimated that it would be 7 077 000 in 1970.
The actual breakdown of the figure in 1964 and the projected
breakdown for 1970 on the assumption of a 5,4 per cent growth
rate are given below.[19]

	Employment (thousands):					
	1964 (actual)			1970 (projected)		
		Other			Other	
	White	races	Total	White	races	Total
Agriculture	112,0	1 709,3	1 821,3	98,3	1 902,3	2 000,6
Mining	62,5	550,8	613,3	60,4	539,6	600,0
Manufacturing	331,7	871,1	1 202,8	414,9	1 115,1	1 530,0
Services	715,5	1 572,1	2 287,6	850,7	1 920,6	2 771,3
Total employed	1 221,7	4 703,3	5 925,0	1 424,3	5 477,6	6 901,9
Unspecified and unemployed	16,6	268,9	285,5	–30,6	205,7	175,1
Total economically active	1 238,3	4 972,2	6 210,5	1 393,7	5 683,3	7 077,0

[19] *Economic Development Programme for the Republic of South Africa, 1965–70*,
table 3.

These figures reveal that in mining a decline was expected, and in
agriculture a moderate increase in non-white and a decline in white
workers; and that the major increase was expected in manufacturing
and services. Total employment was expected to rise by about a
million, from 5 925 000 to 6 901 900, non-white increasing by about
800 000 from 4 703 000 to 5 477 600, and white by some 200 000 from
1 221 700 to 1 424 300. This increase in white employment demanded
was, however, greater than the expected increase in the number of
economically active whites. Perhaps, the most significant figure in
this table was that of 'minus 30,6' for unemployed whites. It meant
that a 5,4 per cent growth rate would give rise to a shortage of
30 000 white workers by 1970, and the proposed target could not be
fulfilled unless (*a*) the existing white population could be made to
work harder and more efficiently, (*b*) white numbers were increased
by immigration, or (*c*) African, coloured and Asian workers were
successfully substituted for whites in skilled and supervisory jobs.

[18] For the implications of the selected rates of growth for the various sectors
of the economy see the *Economic Development Programme. . . .*

It is interesting to compare the 1970 position as forecast in 1964 with what it actually was in 1970. This is given in table 2 (p. 272). The total economically active population turned out to be nearly one million greater than expected: Whites were 1 498 000, as compared with a forecast of 1 424 000 – very close – but the other races' economic participation had been under-estimated by about 800 000. Immigration has helped to meet the scarcity of skilled labour, but it is unlikely ever to be sufficient to meet the demand. More whites have been induced to become economically active by the increased recruitment of married women and postponement of retirement age; the productivity of workers has increased;[20] and greater utilization of African, coloured and Asian workers in the higher categories has occurred. These measures enable the expansion to continue. Attention is being paid by the responsible authorities to improving the training of all categories of labour.

It is becoming increasingly clear to all industrialists that as long as traditional and legal restraints are placed upon the employment of coloured people, Asians and Africans in more skilled and responsible jobs, scarcity of workers in these categories is bound to be a major factor inhibiting growth. South Africa has been forced to face the economic reality that the maintenance of the industrial colour bar is incompatible with rapid growth, and all sections of the nation have become increasingly aware of this during the boom. Industrialists were particularly disturbed by some of the restrictive provisions of the Physical Planning Act. The Economic Advisory Council had appointed a committee to investigate labour utilization under the chairmanship of the Secretary for Labour. When reported, its findings were referred to an Inter-departmental Committee presided over by Dr. P. J. Riekert. Its report went to the Cabinet, but was not made public; but in 1971 a *White Paper on the Report of the Inter-Departmental Committee on the Decentralisation of Industires*[21] was issued by the Government in which it stated that 'to the extent indicated below the government associates itself with the recommendations made in so far as matters of policy are concerned:

(a) Sustained efforts to maintain immigration.

---

[20] So much so as to lead to a revision of the shortage of white workers estimated at 47 000 in 1969 in the first Economic Development Programme to 30 000 in 1970 in the second (see *Economic Development Programme . . . 1965–70*, pp. 86 ff).

[21] Usually referred to as the Riekert Committee.

(b) Encouragement of the utilisation of white labour in more productive occupations.

(c) Acceleration of the introduction of training schemes in terms of the Industrial Conciliation Act, and the extension of existing schemes to other sectors of industrial and commercial activity.

(d) The reclassification, in conjunction with trade unions, of artisans' work in order that the less skilled operations of the work may be undertaken by semi-skilled workers and with a resultant improvement in the status of the artisan.

(e) Upgrading of semi-skilled white workers by means of training within industry (such as the Journeyman Recognition Scheme operating in the metal and engineering industries), by the creation of special external facilities for this purpose through existing channels such as under the Training of Artisans Act, by the expansion of trade schools and technical college facilities and by the acceleration of training programmes for apprentices.

(f) Greater utilisation of white female labour in productive occupations in order to release male labour for more productive work.

(g) Training, within the framework of collective bargaining and with the co-operation of the trade unions, of coloureds and Indians, both in skilled and semi-skilled categories of work.

(h) Training of Bantu in the Homelands for employment in the Homelands and in the border areas.

(i) The continuation of the committee of the Economic Advisory Council under the chairmanship of the Secretary for Labour; the committee to report to the Advisory Council from time to time on manpower problems and steps which have been taken to alleviate the situation.'

To some this White Paper on the Riekert Committee's report may appear to be an attempt to reconcile the irreconcilable – the needs of a dynamic economy and the traditional policy of the colour bar – but others see it as introducing a greater flexibility.

It is now generally accepted that better utilization of the manpower resources of the nation has become a high priority but, as the Prime Minister has said, 'we must face economic realities but we must also face political realities', and this is a matter in which strong forces are deeply entrenched.

THE NEED TO EXPORT

Another essential for continued economic growth which the recent boom has emphasized is the need for an increasingly effective export drive. Not only must the main primary export sectors of the past – gold, other minerals and agricultural products – be protected from the adverse effects of a rising cost structure, but new export markets must be found for manufactured products. Manufacturing industry, which in the past had been oriented largely towards the protected home market, must now enter the keener competition of world markets. This necessitates greater attention to the cost structure, the elimination of all restrictive practices and the concentration upon improving the efficiency of both labour and management. Exports of manufactured goods have increased in recent years; but the prospect of a levelling off and eventual decline in gold production makes it imperative that efforts be redoubled to promote manufactured exports. Measures already adopted towards this end include strengthening of South Africa's trade representation overseas, provision of funds for medium- and long-term credit on exports of capital goods, and export credit insurance corporation, some tax concessions on exports, and the establishment by private enterprise of a national export organization, SAFTO, which has many leading manufacturers on its board.

This chapter described the relatively prosperous period of the 1960s when, except for the failure successfully to combat inflation, the country's economic progress was generally highly satisfactory. Clouds were, however, beginning to appear on both the national and international horizons. These are the subject of the next chapter.

11 Stormy Weather: 1970-75

A CHANGE IN CLIMATE

'The South African economy expanded rapidly during the past ten years and a highly satisfactory average growth rate with relative stability was attained. Thus the gross domestic product in money terms grew at an average annual rate of 8,9 per cent from 1960 to 1970. During the same period prices rose on the average by 2,9 per cent, which is low by international standards, and the gross domestic product in real terms consequently increased on the average by 5,8 per cent per year. After allowing for the population increase, this growth rate resulted in a considerable improvement in the standard of living of South Africans, as reflected in an annual average increase in the *per capita* real income of 2,7 per cent.'

Thus wrote the Governor of the South African Reserve Bank[1] about the period reviewed in the last chapter which, somewhat surprisingly in view of its inauspicious start in 1960, turned out to be a period of almost unbroken prosperity. It is true that from the middle of the decade there was a steady rise in prices which neither Government nor the monetary authorities appeared able to stem, and from time to time the balance of payments was a cause of anxiety, but apart from this the sixties were a period of steady progress.

The inflationary pressures were carried over into the new decade; but the seventies were very different from the preceding period with more deep-seated and intractable problems than there had been before. These were both of an economic and of a political character: but the two are so interwoven that it is often quite impossible to disentangle them. Where, for example, would one place the ap-

---

[1] Address by Dr. T. W. de Jongh, Governor of the South African Reserve Bank at the Annual General Meeting of Stockholders of the Bank on 24 August, 1971.

parently economic subject of the price of oil? In this chapter, therefore, the previous practice will be continued of concentrating upon
the economic aspects, but being prepared to draw attention to political events which appear to have some impact upon them. Some of
the operative forces were international and world-wide in character,
others were more specifically confined to southern Africa, although
the involvement of Russia and Cuba in Angola seems to blur even
this distinction.

Some of the rumblings of the approaching storm were heard in the
latter 1960s. The industrial nations of Western Europe, America and
Japan all seemed to be moving towards economic recession, while at
the same time the rates of inflation of their price-levels were rising,
in some cases at an alarming rate. The International Monetary Fund
resolutely refused to agree to a rise in the price of gold which, rigidly
linked to the dollar at $35 per fine ounce, provided the international
yardstick for all national currencies. In 1968, however, the two-tier
price of gold was introduced: one price for all dealings between
Central Banks in 'monetary' gold remained at the fixed parity; the
other was the price of gold on the free market which rose and fell with
supply and demand. The economic position of the United States still
continued to deteriorate and, in 1971, President Nixon announced
that the United States had suspended the payment of gold against
dollars, and had imposed a 10 per cent duty upon all imports to help
to redress the adverse balance of payments. The dollar, which since
1945 had been the recognized reserve currency of the non-communist
world, had collapsed with world-wide repercussions; and international monetary disequilibrium spread apace.

From 1972 to 1975 monetary disarray became more marked as
economic recession became increasingly pronounced in one country
after another, while unemployment figures were rising with the U.S.A.,
Britain and Japan were particularly hard hit; but the cost of living continued to rise and inflation was not effectively halted. A new term
was coined: 'stagflation' (i.e. *economic stagnation* combined with
price inflation). The economic growth of many countries declined to
zero or negative real growth rates, and *per capita* national incomes
either fell or remained static. At the same time there were signs that
the prices of many primary products were falling, ominously remini-
scent of the Great Depression of 1929/33. This had a particularly
adverse effect upon the developing countries whose economies often
depended upon a single commodity in the metals group where prices

had fallen greatly. Zambia, for example, was particularly hard hit by the fall in the price of copper.

Many of South Africa's base minerals felt the impact of low prices, but the country was fortunate that gold, for so long its staple product, did not share in the fall. The two-tier gold price, and America's abandonment of gold convertibility had a marked impact upon South Africa. The pessimists feared that these were part of the scheme supported by certain quarters in the U.S.A. for the gradual phasing out of gold as an international monetary medium and its replacement either by the dollar or by the 'special drawing rights' created by the International Monetary Fund. Optimists, on the contrary, believed that it indicated a growing general doubt about the stability of the dollar and other national currencies, and that it might herald a very much higher price for gold. In 1969 the "bulls" on the Johannesburg Stock Exchange won the day and, at the beginning of that year, there was a fantastic boom which forced even some of the best mining house shares up so high as to give a dividend yield of only 2 per cent. A leading banker is reputed to have said that he did not object to the Stock Exchange discounting future prospects to a reasonable extent, but when it discounted the whole of eternity he thought it was going too far. The crash came about the middle of the year and, thereafter, the Exchange was in a more cautious mood.

Nevertheless, the free market price of gold did rise most spectacularly. From the post-war parity of $35 per fine ounce it had about doubled by the end of 1972 and in 1973 it fluctuated around $120: by November, 1974 it reached $187, which was more than five times its original price. Then the price rise was checked by a number of new factors in the situation. First, was the decision by the I.M.F. to issue 'special drawing rights' as a substitute for gold; next, the United States Government decided to sell a portion of its gold holding in the open market; then too, Russia's need to import grain forced that country also to become a seller of gold, and finally there was the statement of intent of the I.M.F. to sell a portion of its gold reserves and to put the proceeds into a fund to assist developing countries that were in financial need. Nevertheless, although it may have seemed low to those whose expectations were based upon $180 to $200, the price remained relatively high, for it fluctuated around $130 to $140 in 1975 and early 1976, and this price was between three and four times the old parity. Gold shares fluctuated in harmony with the price of bullion, but inflation raised costs of mining, and $120 in 1976 was not nearly such an attractive proposition as it had appeared to be in 1972.

The other primary mineral product that did not follow the general downward trend was oil. When in 1960 the Organization of Petroleum Exporting Countries, (Opec), was formed, few people can have foreseen the extent of the influence that it would be able to exert on both the price of oil and upon the whole world economic order. Higher oil prices were effectively established from 1 October, 1973, but this had no sooner been done than a meeting of the six-member ministerial committee in Teheran recommended a further shattering rise in price. As a result, the price of light crude oil was raised on 1 January, 1974, from $5,00 per barrel to $11,80 – a rise of 130 per cent in three months. In all the price of oil rose from about $2,00 in 1971 to over $10,00 in 1975 or by some five times in as many years, and the excess cost to the importing countries was estimated at over $5 000 000 000 per annum. It was no wonder that the 'oil crisis' soon gave place to the 'energy crisis', and all possible economies and alternatives to oil – gas, coal, hydraulic and atomic power – were looked at with new interest and insight. The rights and wrongs of the Opec oil monopoly cannot be considered here, but it seems clear that the world had been using a scarce resource in a most extravagant manner; and that the Middle East countries saw their irreplaceable oil asset being exploited at a rate that would give it a life of only some thirty years or so. Hence their two objectives (1) to gain a larger share of oil receipts for themselves, and (2) restriction, by price or otherwise, of the rate of oil recovery so as to prolong the life of the oilfields; but the manner in which it was done without adequate warning or consultation had devastating effects upon the world economy.

There were several aspects to this. One was the direct price effect for the dependence of the industrialized nations upon oil had been becoming greater with the progressive switch from coal to oil in ships and railways, the use of oil for power and heating of both private and public buildings, in air transport, and in the internal combustion engines of motor cars, buses and lorries. Even agriculture, for so long associated with the horse, the ox and the weary ploughman, had become dependent upon oil-driven tractors, harvesters etc. Thus the five-fold rise in the price of oil fuel put up all costs and accelerated the inflationary forces. The second effect was upon the balance of payments for the industrial nations suddenly found that their new oil-import bill destroyed equilibrium and placed them in the position of having to cut down both oil and other imports, thereby starting the process of contraction of world trade. Thirdly, there was the foreign exchange and transfer problem, so well remembered from the 1920s when the huge one-way payments of war debts and reparations bedevilled the intricate system of international exchange, because the Opec countries were accumulating huge surpluses of foreign exchange which were too great for them to spend immediately or to invest abroad. Various efforts were made to recycle these immense funds to prevent the collapse of the world's monetary system but without notable success. Finally the monetary crisis, and the fact that oil was never again likely to be the world's cheapest fuel, led to recession in many countries particularly where the automobile industry played a leading role in the national economy.

All these economic forces had a direct impact upon South Africa. Moreover the Arab states placed an embargo upon all oil for South Africa because of the Republic's discriminatory racial policies. There was also an important indirect impact because foreign trade plays a large part in the national economy and takes place mainly with some half-dozen highly industrialized nations of Western Europe and Japan who were severely hit by the world recession. Therefore the demand for many South African exports declined just when additional export revenue was required to offset the increased oil bill.

Political events in Southern Africa were also a disturbing factor. These first showed themselves early in the sixties when Rhodesia declared its independence of Britain, and sanctions were imposed against that country, and when insurrection against the Portuguese Government broke out in both Mozambique and Angola.

Rhodesia was South Africa's leading trade partner in Africa and was second only to the United Kingdom in world trading relations. This was not surprising as they were adjacent to one another; much South African capital was invested there, and there were many close economic links. When the call came from the United Nations to impose economic sanctions against Rhodesia, South Africa refused to be a party to it and continued trading and transporting Rhodesian goods to and from South African ports as had formerly been the case. In spite of several abortive attempts to reach a settlement, the power struggle in Rhodesia seemed to be becoming more intense. The African National Congress, which claimed to have succeeded in uniting all African dissident groups, appeared to have split once more: one section operating within Rhodesia was attempting to reach a settlement with the Smith government; the other, operating from abroad was carrying on a guerilla war along Rhodesia's extensive frontiers. Many African countries pledged their support for the guerillas in their efforts to secure majority rule in Rhodesia. These events affecting the Republic's close neighbour and major trading partner were not without repercussions upon the South African economy.

The long wars in both Mozambique and Angola dragged on for years draining Portugal of men and resources without any decisive effect until the 1975 military coup in Portugal itself led to a change of government. The new rulers at once announced their intention to grant independence to Mozambique and Angola. In Mozambique there was a transfer to a single contender for power, Frelimo, and the take-over was relatively without incident, although many Portuguese left the country. In Angola there were three contenders for power, FNLA, UNITA and MPLA, and civil war between the factions ensued. The group with allegedly the smallest popular following, but supported by Russian equipment and Cuban troops was victorious. The MPLA assumed *de facto* government of the country, and soon obtained recognition from the majority of African states and several elsewhere, although the other two factions claimed to be carrying on guerilla warfare against the MPLA as they had done for years against the Portuguese government in Angola.

The importance of Mozambique for South Africa is great for not only is it a close neighbour with a long common frontier, but the port of Maputo (formerly Lourenço Marques) has since 1890 been the nearest and most convenient port for the Transvaal, and it has also handled a large part of the Transvaal traffic. It was estimated that three-quarters of the cargoes using the port are on South African account. Moreover, large numbers of Blacks from Mozambique have always worked on the Transvaal goldfields, and in 1976 these numbered some 100 000 who earned approximately R80 million per annum in wages. The earnings of their emigrant workers has always been a strong support to the Mozambique economy and their labour has been of great value to the mining industry. The third major link between the two countries is more recent: it is the Cabora Bassa dam and hydro-electric plant with an initial capacity of 2 000 M.W. into which very large sums of South African capital have been poured and from which South Africa expects to be able to buy a very considerable quantity of electricity to augment the Escom grid. Although Mozambique closed her frontiers with Rhodesia early in 1976, economic relations with South Africa have remained more or less normal and traffic continues to flow through Maputo; but only the future will show whether the very strong common economic interests to the two countries will be able permanently to bridge the gulf between their different political systems and ideologies.

South Africa's links with Angola are less substantial and of more recent date. The two countries have no common frontier for South West Africa, which was mandated to South Africa by the League of Nations after the First World War, lies between them. South Africa's right to administer South West Africa is rejected by the United Nations, but nevertheless South Africa has very full plans for the political evolution of the country towards independence and ambitious projects for its economic advance in which the Cunene River Scheme for irrigation and hydro-electric generation plays a major part. This was a joint project undertaken by the former Portuguese administration and the South African Government for the mutual benefit of Angola and South West Africa, and a large proportion of the capital invested in it is South African. Phase I is nearing completion and during the civil war South African troops entered Angola to protect the installations and the workers there.

Added to the disruptive economic effects of events in Rhodesia, Mozambique and Angola, is the fact that the Government's plan for eventual independence for the various African homelands is coming to fruition; and they are beginning to claim the position of independent sovereign states. The first will be the Transkei which reaches independence in October, 1976, and there are others in the pipe-line. The question being raised by some potential investors in these areas, and in South Africa itself, is whether the granting of independence will disrupt economic patterns which have developed in the past, and whether the normally centripetal forces of economics will be powerful enough to counteract the centrifugal forces of political independence. Indeed the matter is much wider: can the very real economic interests which the nations of southern Africa have in common draw them closer together to raise living standards for all their peoples and overcome differences in tribal affiliation, race, language, and political ideology?

THE PROGRESS OF THE SOUTH AFRICAN ECONOMY: 1970–75

Having drawn attention to the dangers and difficulties of the current world situation and to particular events in Southern Africa, we turn now to see how the economy stood up to the buffeting it received during the first half of the seventies. The Gross Domestic Product gives as good a general picture of the economy's progress as we can find. Below the Gross Domestic Product for the years 1970 to 1975 is given at both current prices and at constant 1970 prices.

Gross Domestic Product (R millions)

	Current Prices	Constant 1970 Prices	Percentage Change
1970	12 515	12 515	6,2
1971	13 870	13 026	4,1
1972	15 625	13 438	3,2
1973+	18 799	14 017	4,3
1974+	22 382	15 025	7,2
1975+	25 413	15 325	2,2

+ Provisional

This table is really an extension of that on page 213 except that real product is here shown at constant 1970 prices. The high level of the real growth rate of 6,2 in 1970 followed on the even higher rate of 7,6 the year before and was a fitting finale for the glorious sixties. In 1971, 1972 and 1973 the real rate of growth was much lower. These were three years of economic stagnation, but things began to improve in the fourth quarter of 1972 – the lower turning point had been reached – and in the first half of 1973 there was mild recovery. In his budget speech the Minister of Finance proposed measures aimed at a moderate acceleration of the economy without aggravating inflationary pressures,[2] and economic activity increased rapidly in the second half of that year. Of particular importance was the rise in gross domestic fixed investment. The economic expansion continued into 1974, and indeed accelerated about the middle of the year when there were signs that industrial expansion had reached the limit of its available capacity and both labour and capital markets became very tight. Gross Domestic Expenditure exceeded Gross National Product by an increasing margin; and from mid-1974 imports rose rapidly, while exports, other than gold, remained sluggish. The result was that the Balance of Payments on current account, which had shown a

[2] South African Reserve Bank *Quarterly Bulletin*, Sept., 1974, p. 5

surplus from mid-1972 to mid-1973 moved into deficit. It seemed that the upper turning point in the economy's growth occurred in the third quarter of 1974. Writing of this the South African Reserve Bank's review says[3] 'Certain external developments such as the adverse effects of the oil crisis, the general world financial and political instability, the slowing-down in the economic growth rate of South Africa's main trading partners, and a scarcity of certain important raw materials, also contributed to the levelling-off tendency in South Africa's growth rate'. Nevertheless, the year ended with a real growth rate of no less than 7,2 per cent. This was achieved at the cost of a renewed inflationary spurt, and was unlikely to be repeated because by the end of 1974 the economy had already moved into a recessive phase.

The consumer price level had risen throughout the period as the table below indicates.

Consumer Price Level: All Items
1970 = 100

1970	100,0
1971	105,7
1972	112,6
1973	123,3
1974	157,6
1975 (Sept.)	159,5

The price rise in the first two years was relatively modest but the rate was accelerating and in the last two years from September 1973 to September 1975 there was a 20 per cent rise. Various new measures to combat inflation were introduced, but prices were being forced up by the cost-push of higher oil charges affecting all sectors of the economy. Interest rates were raised and the return on long-term government stock reached the very high level of 10 per cent. A concerted drive against inflation was initiated in which the various government departments, the public corporations, and all branches of the private sector made common cause by calling for the deferment of all capital expenditure that was not essential and the exercise of the maximum restraint in price and wage increases. Meanwhile greater efforts were to be made to increase labour productivity of all races by better training facilities and motivation. The Balance of Payments had moved heavily into deficit, but the consequences were mitigated by large capital inflow.

[3] South African Reserve Bank *Quarterly Bulletin* June, 1975.

By 1975, however, the economy was really in decline and the growth rate had dropped to 2,2 per cent for the year. While many major countries could show only negative or zero rates of growth in their Gross Domestic Product, it is perhaps wrong to describe the South African situation as a *recession* because although small it was at least positive growth; but 2,2 per cent per annum was less than the rate of population growth and therefore there was a decline in the *per capita* real income. Moreover, South Africa was facing many serious problems and there was the danger that lack of confidence might cause a run on the rand and deplete the country's gold and foreign reserves. Three new factors had entered the situation: (1) it appeared that the world economic recession was more serious and long-lasting than at first thought: (2) the price of gold fell suddenly from a peak which touched more than $180 an ounce to only $135 in September, 1975: (3) it was becoming clear that the political situation in Southern Africa would necessitate heavy military expenditure by the Government.

In the light of this situation the Government decided to devalue the rand by 17,9 per cent on 22 September, 1975. In a statement accompanying the devaluation the Minister of Finance said:[4]

'In arriving at the decision to devalue the rand the Government took into account not only the need to strengthen the overall balance of payments, but also to prevent the present slowing down in domestic activity from proceeding too far. Under present circumstances, undue reliance on deflationary monetary and fiscal measures runs the risk of aggravating recessionary conditions.'

'The devaluation should have the following effects.

1. It should effectively curb speculation against the rand which has flared up again following the gold price decline.

2. It should improve the balance of payments on current account by increasing the value of the net gold output and merchandise exports, and by reducing imports below what they would otherwise have been.

3. It should have an immediate expansionary effect on export and gold mining incomes with favourable secondary effects on domestic economic activity.

[4] Statement regarding the devaluation of the rand by the Honourable O.P.F. Horwood, Minister of Finance, South African Reserve Bank *Quarterly Bulletin*, September, 1975, p. 21.

4. By raising the rand prices of imports competing with locally manufactured goods, it should stimulate industrial production and investment.

5. In the increasingly tight budgetary position which has emerged, it should raise government revenue from taxation on the additional rand income generated and thereby lessen the dependence on bank credit as a means of financing the Exchequer.'

How South Africa will weather the stormy seas around her remains to be seen. However, the brief look backwards at the country's past economic growth in the last remaining chapter of this book may perhaps provide some signposts for the future.

12 Conditions for Sustained Progress

RETROSPECT

This book is intended to be an introduction to the study of the present-day economy of the Republic of South Africa rather than a detailed investigation of how its development has come about. Nevertheless it may be in order in this concluding chapter to recall to mind some of the more important forces which have transformed it from a primitive agricultural economy into the diversified and increasingly industrialized economy of the present day. In the mid-nineteenth century South Africa was almost a textbook example of a backward country, and its slow development up to the middle of the nineteenth century can be explained by the presence of many of the inhibiting factors listed in current literature on underdeveloped countries[1] – poverty, low productivity in agriculture, which was the occupation of the vast majority of the population, lack of capital, lack of skill and technical knowledge, poor transport, limited internal markets, small volume of exports, low rate of capital formation, little to attract foreign investment, and all the rest of them.

So much is now being written about development planning and the strategy of economic growth that perhaps it should be pointed out that South Africa's initial development was not the result of any preconceived development programme, but that it grew as a result of the decisions of thousands of individuals each seeking to make personal gain. This, combined with 'a little bit of luck', was how the economy increased in size and in the variety of its activities.

The element of luck was the discovery of diamonds and gold located deep in the interior of southern Africa. Their situation was important because, had the Witwatersrand been near the coast, the

[1]The literature is vast; see bibliography compiled by A. Hazlewood in *The Economics of Under-developed Areas.*

244

effects derived from the exploitation of its mineral wealth might have been limited to a small coastal area, and would not have opened up the interior of the country as they have, in fact, done. Moreover, gold, unlike oil, required a large labour force for its recovery; and thus income from mining was widely spread and had an impact on the population generally.

Apart from South Africa's good fortune in discovering its mineral wealth, there were other factors which contributed to the rapid development of the last hundred years. Some of these had their origins in the earlier period. First in importance was the fact that South Africa had a relatively large white population derived from the economically advanced countries of Europe, and that this cultural inheritance had been maintained by continued contact. The acquisition of the Cape by Britain in 1814 was of great economic advantage to South Africa because it forged a link, albeit a colonial link, between southern Africa and the foremost industrial and commercial nation of the world at that time. When the opportunities for large-scale investment occurred in the latter part of the nineteenth century these links were of the greatest value.[2] South Africa's advantages in this respect contrast markedly with its Portuguese neighbours, where white settlement pre-dated that at the Cape by over a hundred years, but where the metropolitan power lacked the wealth and economic dynamism to export capital, industrial skill and entrepreneurship in large quantity. The British link also bestowed knowledge of a world language and made the cultural and technical literature of the British Commonwealth and the United States available to most people in the country.

In this cultural context must also be mentioned the work of many thousands of missionaries and teachers, mainly from the British Isles, who have spread not only the Christian faith, but also the elements of learning and civilization among both whites and blacks in southern Africa. Although general standards of literacy were low a hundred years ago in comparison with the present day, the fact that there were many thousands of literates, and that they included all racial groups, has been of great importance in accelerating subsequent development. The crucial importance of this will readily be recognized by all who have worked in countries where this has

---

[2] See estimate by S. H. Frankel that of the total of R700 million of foreign investment in South Africa up to 1913, R640 million was from Britain and R60 million from other countries, *Capital Investment in Africa*, p. 150.

not been the case, for it is one of the most important pre-conditions of economic development.

Law and order, communications, centralized administration, and expanding educational opportunities, were gradually extended over the whole of southern Africa. In 1910 the Act of Union created a unified political area of 1 222 000 square kilometres, and the inclusion of the British protectorates and South West Africa in a common customs policy created a common market area of some 2 800 000 square kilometres with a combined population by 1970 of about 25 million. The importance of this process of economic aggregation can hardly be overstressed, because it has enabled the main centres of industrial growth to exercise a wider influence. Indeed, even beyond this area, the impact of South Africa's economic progress has been felt through investment of capital and skills in Rhodesia, in Zambia and Mozambique; and through the earnings in the industries of the Republic of migrant workers from these territories and beyond. Indeed, were the political climate more favourable, a common market for all southern Africa would create an area with almost unlimited opportunities for achieving a high standard of living for the whole population.

From the narrower commercial point of view the growth of international and internal trade during the early nineteenth century, although it was upon a relatively small scale, played an important part in paving the way for subsequent development. The large import-export houses at the ports, shipping abroad products such as wine, ivory, hides, skins and wool, and importing manufactured products of all kinds, had by the middle of the century established connections with the major European markets, and their financial experience and associations played an important part in the development of banking institutions and in building up a commercially-minded and market-conscious section of the population.

There can be no doubt that it was the discoveries of diamonds and gold which launched the South African economy on its forward course. To this extent, therefore, economic development may be said to have been initiated by exogenous forces. But although the actual discoveries may appear to have been accidental, it should not be forgotten that there had been a long and sustained search for mineral wealth by prospectors who were aware of what they were seeking and of the economic value of any mineral deposits which they might find. A really primitive community would not have been able to make or assess the value of such discoveries. There had already developed a climate for industrial growth, which had its origin in white settlement and expanding contact with the international economy. This climate predisposed the country to accept development as a goal and aided the economic diversification once the initial push from mining had taken effect. Moreover South Africa also stood to gain from being a comparatively late arrival at the industrial stage. 'The importance of being a latecomer'[3] is that, if other conditions are favourable, the latecomer can travel forward much more rapidly than those who had to pioneer the road. In the expansion of transport, mining and industry, South Africa in the latter part of the nineteenth century could draw upon an accumulated store of technical knowledge and invention already developed and perfected in western Europe. This advantage has been enjoyed in many branches of industrial expansion where adaptation rather than invention was all that was required, so that South Africa could adopt the most up-to-date process and thus bypass the slow and often expensive path of trial and error by which this has been achieved. This goes far to explain the speed at which industrialization has been achieved in South Africa, and in other late-developing countries, once the initial difficulties had been overcome.

Without wishing to enter into the controversy about the desirability of 'balanced growth' as an objective or as a technique in economic development,[4] we should note that growth of the South African economy has exhibited few signs of balance – indeed growth through imbalance has been the general rule. Diamonds and gold were mined and exported before what might be described as the 'necessary' infrastructure had been created. In the absence of railways or rivers, ox-wagon transport was called into service on a huge scale, and it was only after the mining industries had justified themselves, and had generated sufficient income, that a modern transport system was embarked upon. For a couple of decades thousands of ox-wagons travelled the hundreds of miles from the ports to the mining areas, and many rural South Africans, white and black, made their first contact with urban life as transport riders in

---

[3] Albert O. Hirshman, *The Strategy of Economic Development*, p. 7.
[4] See Nurkse, op. cit.; and Hirshman, op. cit.

the early mining era. This direct contact between the rural community and the mining centres had important repercussions upon agriculture; for farm people, seeing the fantastic prices paid for foodstuffs in Kimberley and Johannesburg, began to plant food crops for these markets, often without any new investment other than that created by their being prepared to forgo some of the leisure they had previously enjoyed (or had been forced to enjoy) owing to the absence of a market for the product of their labours. Thus expansion of agriculture was induced by the market opportunities rather than by any preconceived intention to invest more in agriculture. It was brought about by market forces seeking to redress an imbalance, not as part of a programme of balanced growth. Instances of this sort of thing abound throughout South Africa's economic history.

As mining operations expanded, the need for a modern transport system became more imperative, and the railways were constructed. Once they had been built, they were of course available for the transport of all sorts of products other than those immediately related to mining. Thus they in turn extended the area of the modern market economy, and spread the revolution in agriculture. Similarly deep-level gold mining could not be carried out without power, and power was obtainable from coal, large deposits of which were conveniently to hand. Initially investment in coal mining was a necessary part of the investment in deep-level gold mining, but subsequently the coal-mining industry came to be an important industry in its own right, and it was in turn the basis for a whole new chemicals industry. These illustrations show clearly that 'investment is a many-sided actor on the economic scene'.[5] Hirshman lists three main roles: that of income-generator, that of capacity-creator and that of pace-setter for additional investment. All these have been apparent in the industrial expansion of South Africa. As income-generator the gold mines have raised the standards of living of large numbers of people in South Africa and thus created new demands for all types of goods, which had previously been latent. As capacity-creator the mining industry has trained hundreds of thousands of men in the basic essentials of large-scale industrial enterprise at all levels from top executives to workmen on the rock face. Many of these have subsequently provided the leadership and manpower in other

[5] Hirshman, p. 41.

developing sectors of the modern economy. As pace-setter the gold-mining industry has established standards of efficiency and of the application of modern science to industry probably unsurpassed anywhere in the world. It has undoubtedly set the pace for many other industries in the country not only in the obvious field of technical operations, but also in matters like labour management and financial and managerial organization and efficiency. Many institutions which originated from gold mining have much wider fields of application. For example, the Johannesburg Stock Exchange had its origin in the desire to trade in gold shares, but once a capital market had been developed it greatly facilitated company flotation and share-market dealings for every type of industry, and in this way helped to promote manufacturing and other modern sectors of the economy.

Investment in gold mining had a fourth effect not mentioned by Hirshman, but of major importance in South Africa. This is its effect in bringing about large concentrations of population in urban areas. When the population of a country is dispersed more or less evenly and thinly over the whole area of a country, as it tends to be in a predominantly agricultural society, the development of large-scale industry is well-nigh impossible. Urban concentrations seem, for two reasons, to be an essential prerequisite for modern factory production. On the demand side some concentration of the market is necessary to make the location of a factory at any particular place meaningful. Thus in South Africa, although the importation of consumer goods increased greatly during the nineteenth century, the demand for them was too widely spread to make local manufacturing an attractive proposition until large towns had grown up. On the supply side there must be a concentration of industries and financial and commercial institutions whose interlocking needs support one another. A modern factory requires power, light, water, housing for its workers and opportunities for their recreation, transport facilities, selling agencies, machine-maintenance shops, and other industries with which it has linkages. The basic problem in the concept of balanced growth is how all these can be started *ab initio*. Perhaps the greatest contribution of the gold-mining industry to the general advance of South Africa is that it was responsible for bringing into being large concentrations of population on the Witwatersrand, with all that this has meant to the subsequent development of modern agriculture and manufacturing.

In earlier chapters mention was made of the fact that even in 1910 the national economy was still relatively narrow-based, resting primarily upon agriculture and gold. Since then there has been the great structural change represented by the expansion and diversification of manufacturing, superimposed upon the two earlier activities. This was stimulated by World War I, and in the 1920s was assisted by a national fiscal policy designed to secure a 'more balanced economic structure'. Prior to this time the doctrine of free trade, with tariffs only as a revenue device, had been accepted as part of the British heritage almost without serious question. As South Africans came to be increasingly responsible for the formulation of national policy and as a South African national sentiment developed, the wisdom of this policy came to be questioned. Gold mining enjoyed such a comparative advantage over most other economic activities in the country that it tended to attract most of the capital and enterprise. But gold mining was by its very nature a wasting asset, and prudence seemed to dictate the need to plan for the inevitable time when there would be no more gold to mine. This fact reinforced the more general desire to develop indigenous manufacturing enterprises, a desire which was manifesting itself in many countries throughout the world. Thus for the first time in South Africa's economic development the conscious desire for a greater balance in the economic structure began to make its appearance, and the notion of planned State intervention to bring this about gained general acceptance. An additional incentive in this direction was provided by the extreme instability in the price of many agricultural products in the 1920s – the effect of this upon South Africa's terms of trade stimulated a desire for at least a somewhat larger measure of self-sufficiency.

From the 1920s onward successive governments have adopted a policy of fostering the growth of manufacturing industries. Protective duties were imposed; and although (by comparison with some other protective countries) these remained moderate, they were sufficient in conjunction with the heavy direct taxation on the gold mines to stimulate investment in a variety of manufacturing activities. Manufacturing was further advanced by a number of measures such as the placing of government contracts with local firms and direct participation by the government in the establishment of certain important manufacturing industries like iron and steel, and later through the Industrial Development Corporation in the initiation of other activities. Most of the earlier industries which came into being as a result of protective measures were established to produce consumer goods for the protected home market. This policy evoked much criticism; and its inability to achieve its specific purpose of making the country less dependent upon gold mining was clearly demonstrated by comparing the small volume of manufactured exports with the heavy import requirements of the manufacturing sector. Large though the manufacturing sector had become, it was still clearly dependent upon the foreign exchange earned by other sectors of the economy, particularly gold, for its machinery and raw materials. More recently there has been a reorientation of manufacturing policy towards emphasis upon exports. Greater discrimination is being shown in protecting manufacturing: increased attention is being given to the promotion of productive efficiency, and to the processing and increased use of South African raw materials. Economists have compiled input-output tables,[6] and a careful study of backward and forward linkages provides information on which a policy of *selective* protection is based. Import-replacement industries and those with a high export potential are being encouraged. Thus the free play of market forces which operated so largely in the initial phases of South Africa's industrial development has been modified somewhat by State intervention designed to accelerate the growth of manufacturing. Care must, however, be taken to prevent adverse effects upon the traditional exporting sectors, as agriculture and mining remain major earners of foreign exchange and an invaluable support to the whole national economy.

The rapid expansion of the economy in the sixties and its halting progress in the seventies were discussed in the last two chapters. In this recapitulation it is desirable to look further into the past. Ever since the 1860s remarkable changes had been taking place in the national economy. Some pointers to this advance are shown in figure 17 on the next page. Between 1910 and 1970 (taken because this was the most recent general census of the population) numbers had increased from 6 million to 21½ million. National income at current prices rose from R266 million to R12 000 million, and allowing both for the rise in prices and for the increase in population, this represents

---

[6] D. C. Krogh, "An Input-Output Analysis of the South African Economy, *1956–7*", *S.A.J.E.*, vol. 29 no. 4, December 1961.

SIXTY YEARS OF GROWTH 1911–70

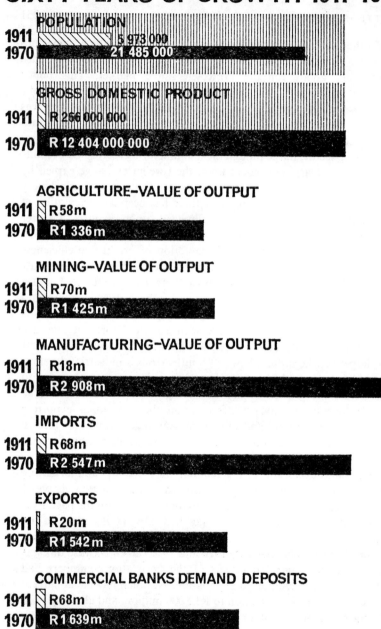

POPULATION
1911 5 973 000
1970 21 485 000

GROSS DOMESTIC PRODUCT
1911 R 256 000 000
1970 R 12 404 000 000

AGRICULTURE–VALUE OF OUTPUT
1911 R58m
1970 R1 336m

MINING–VALUE OF OUTPUT
1911 R70m
1970 R1 425m

MANUFACTURING–VALUE OF OUTPUT
1911 R18m
1970 R2 908m

IMPORTS
1911 R68m
1970 R2 547m

EXPORTS
1911 R20m
1970 R1 542m

COMMERCIAL BANKS DEMAND DEPOSITS
1911 R68m
1970 R1 639m

STATE REVENUE
1911 R28m
1970 R2 485m

FIGURE 17

more than a doubling of the real *per capita* income in the sixty years. The value of output of agriculture, mining and manufacturing at current prices increased twenty-three-fold, twenty-fold, and one hundred and sixty-fold respectively, during the same period. Foreign trade increased forty-five-fold and commercial-bank deposits twenty-four-fold.

Perhaps, however, the most fundamental change in the structure of the national economy is the way the modern industrial and commercial sector has extended its frontiers. In this process men and women from a wide variety of cultural groups have been drawn together into a common market-oriented economy. In 1921 there were only about 2 million persons occupied in the modern sector of the economy: in 1960 this number had risen to $5\frac{1}{4}$ million, of whom Africans represented 65 per cent, whites 22 per cent, coloured people 11 per cent, and Asians 2 per cent of the economically active population *in the modern sectors*. By 1970 the number was about $6\frac{1}{2}$ million. This process of economic integration has gone a long way, but is not yet complete. This is shown by the distressed state of the African areas (discussed in chapter 3), by the phenomenon of migrant labour (the subject of chapter 4), and by the impediments facing African, coloured and Asian workers and the excessive spread between skilled and unskilled wages (chapter 7). These are symptoms of maladjustment in sectors where modern economic influences have not been fully felt. Nevertheless, the greater part of the population of all races is becoming more fully committed to a modern industrial economy. This has resulted in higher standards of productive efficiency and higher *per capita* real income. There is still much poverty in South Africa, especially among the African, coloured and Asian groups; but if the past rate of growth can be maintained this can be eliminated. South Africa is indeed fortunate to have the resources and to have achieved a level of economic development which makes it possible to offer an ever-rising standard of real income to the whole of its population. S. P. Viljoen[7] has estimated that if the rate of growth can be maintained, by the end of this century South Africa would achieve an average standard of living for its whole population equal to that of Great Britain in 1960.

---

[7] S. P. Viljoen, "Higher Productivity and Higher Wages of Native Labour in South Africa", *S.A.J.E.*, vol. 29 no. 1, March 1961.

PROSPECT

When considering any country's economic prospects it is always salutary to reflect upon the old Malthusian race between the hare and the tortoise – the hare is population growth, and the tortoise is the increase in the means of subsistence. The South African hare is a strong-running animal, and the 1970 census gave further evidence of this. The 1960 census showed the population of the Republic as just under 16 million, but the 1970 census showed it to be 21½ million, giving a growth of about 34 per cent during the decade. In 1975 it was about 25 million, and every year there are well over half a million new South Africans to be fed, clothed, housed and eventually to be employed. This is the most important economic fact facing the economy of the seventies, and one which economists, business men and politicians can ignore only at their peril.

Fortunately for South Africa, the tortoise exhibited a most remarkable turn of speed during the nineteen sixties and easily out-distanced the hare. The Gross Domestic Product at current prices was R5 274 million in 1960 and this had risen to R11 339 million by 1969 – an increase of R6 065 million or 113 per cent in the ten-year period. This figure is of course inflated by rising prices and the consumer price index showed an increase of 26 per cent during the decade. Making allowance for this, however, the real progress of the tortoise was still most satisfactory, being equalled or surpassed by few other countries in the world. The real Gross Domestic Product (measured at constant 1963 prices) rose from R5 551 million to R9 325 million, or by 68 per cent in the ten-year period – almost double the rate of population growth. The difference between the speed of the tortoise and the speed of the hare represents, of course, the growth in *per capita* product; and it is this amount which is available for expanding the national capital or raising the real incomes of the people.

In the aggregate the achievement of the sixties was most satisfactory, but aggregates and averages sometimes conceal important facts. The remarkable increase in real wealth was, for example, distributed in such a way that the gap between rich South Africans and poor South Africans tended to become greater rather than less during the period. In this we were not unique and internationally a similar trend was observed between rich and poor nations. Notwithstanding this distribution, it was probably true that in South Africa, with the exception of the 40 per cent of the African population still engaged in subsistence farming in the African areas, some increase in real income was enjoyed by all sections of our people, and that the national economy certainly made very substantial progress during the decade.

The continuing growth of any economy depends upon the day-to-day decisions, both individual and collective, of the thousands of people who influence that society. If these decisions are the right decisions to maintain growth, it will be maintained. Such decisions are likely to be made and the blocks and resistances to change overcome when the forces making for economic progress have come to dominate the society. Economic expansion is then the goal, a high rate of domestic saving and expanding investment opportunities combine to assure continued rapid capital formation, production expands, and hitherto unused resources are drawn into the stream of a dynamic market-oriented economy.

South Africa reached the stage, described by Rostow as the 'take-off', in the 1930s, and since then there has been a steady drive towards economic maturity. In the normal course of events this process could be expected to continue and to yield ever-rising standards of living. But in South Africa there are certain inhibiting factors. These mostly stem from the multi-racial, multi-cultural composition of the population, and the very great difficulty of devising a political, social and economic structure in which the legitimate rights and aspirations of all groups can be satisfied. The danger is that racial attitudes and the political policies which they inspire will undermine the forces making for economic growth and destroy the momentum towards continued progress. This would be doubly disastrous, because not only would it involve the sacrifice of higher standards of living so clearly within our grasp, but the possibility of peaceful racial co-existence would be greatly reduced by economic stagnation, poverty and unemployment, which must certainly increase social tensions.

Every effort has been made to keep the presentation in this book free from racial and party-political bias: but political and racial forces impinge so greatly upon the future growth of the economy that it would be wholly false and misleading to ignore them. The whole subject has become so emotionally overcharged, both within the Republic and in the world at large, that it is difficult to disentangle fact from propaganda. Nonetheless, an attempt is made here to set down some of the basic features of the situation which South Africans of all races must take into consideration.

White settlement in South Africa dates from 1652, and the majority of the present population have regarded South Africa as their homeland for some ten to fifteen generations. They are not 'European settlers', 'colonists' or 'expatriates' any more than the white inhabitants of North America. They are white Africans, whose forebears have lived in Africa since the era of Cromwell in England, or for a hundred years before the American Declaration of Independence.

The leadership, drive, capital, skill and administrative ability, which have transformed South Africa into by far the wealthiest and most industrially advanced nation in the continent of Africa, have in the past come almost exclusively from the white group. White South Africans number some $4\frac{1}{4}$ million out of a total population of over $25\frac{1}{2}$ million. Movcrover they are conscious of the fact that the Republic is the southernmost tip of a continent of some 300 million Africans, which is at present swept by a great wave of nationalist sentiment.

The white group is not homogeneous in language or culture. Approximately 60 per cent are Afrikaans speaking and 40 per cent are English speaking, and demographic forces incline towards the increasing predominance of the former. In spite of long-standing tensions between them, both are now essentially South African in orientation and spirit. British dominance was never readily accepted by the Afrikaners, and the establishment of the republics of the Transvaal and Orange Free State was the first successful anti-colonial movement in the British Empire since the American Revolution. The Anglo-Boer War of 1899–1902 has sometimes been represented as a conflict between the forces of economic progress and the obstructionism of a conservative agricultural community, but to the Afrikaner and to practically the whole contemporary world, except the governing party in Britain, it appeared as naked imperialism motivated by the desire to acquire the political control over the gold mines. These two small republics with a total fighting force of less than 60 000 men withstood the combined might of the British Empire for two and a half years, by which time a total of 300 000 men had been mobilized against them. Lord Milner's post-war reconstruction policy included an attempt to anglicize the Boers and destroy their language and cultural identity. This attempt failed, partly because of strong resistance in the two ex-republics and partly because it did not have the backing of the majority of people in Britain; but it predisposed many Afrikaners to resist all tendencies to cultural integration.

Milner's policy was reversed when the Liberal party was returned to power in 1906 and granted responsible government to the Transvaal and the Orange Free State, and the terms settled upon for the entry of the four territories into the Union of South Africa determined the political framework for the future. The Cape retained its colour-blind, but restricted, franchise: non-white people were without representation in the other three provinces. This was not a political oversight, but a carefully calculated risk, the imperial government and the Cape believing that the more liberal tradition of the Cape would permeate the whole country. Instead, the centre of gravity of population, wealth and political power has shifted from the Cape to the Transvaal, and the political rights of Africans and coloured people have been whittled away,[8] and non-white people in the Republic have today no elected representation in the central government.

Immediately after the union it appeared that an era of co-operation between the two white groups had commenced when a party led by General Botha and General Smuts, drawing considerable support from both groups, governed the country up to 1924. A hard core of anti-British Afrikaner nationalism survived, drawing support from the fact that economic power had remained largely in the hands of the English-speaking section. Rural Afrikaners moving to town tended to be at a marked disadvantage both in the matter of language and in the acquisition of industrial skill. Afrikaner interests were furthered in the political and cultural spheres by the Broederbond and in the economic field by the Reddingsdaadbond. The election of 1948 put the National party into power, and the declaration of a republic and the withdrawal from the Commonwealth in 1961 were the fulfilment of a century-old desire. Dominance in the political field

---

[8] In 1936 Africans in the Cape were removed from the common voters' roll, and were instead given the right to elect three white representatives in the House of Assembly, voting on a separate roll, and four white senators, representing Africans throughout the whole Union, elected through rather complicated electoral colleges. In 1960 these African representatives were abolished. In 1956, after a major constitutional crisis, the coloured people in the Cape were removed from the common roll, and were given four white representatives in the Legislative Assembly, elected on a special coloured roll. These were removed in 1968.

proved easier to secure than in the economic, but an increasing number of Afrikaners have risen to commanding positions in trade, finance, banking, mining and industry, and this has tended to introduce a greater measure of economic realism into National party thinking.

The more fundamental questions for South Africa's political and economic future concern not so much the relations between the two white groups, but the relationship between the whites and the people of other groups. During the first fifty years of this century the minds of white politicians were distracted from considering the position of the unenfranchised groups by their efforts to win political support from the enfranchised white minority. Thus despite the growing urgency of racial matters, except for Milner's Native Affairs Commission of 1903, little fundamental and constructive thought was devoted by politicians to these matters until the late twenties when Hertzog first framed his comprehensive native policy. Meanwhile the economic forces described in this book had been drawing all racial groups into the modern and progressive sectors of the economy, where increased commitment to industrial society, higher incomes, greater urbanization, and fuller awareness of the principles upon which western civilization was built and of movements in the outside world, have given rise to new demands for participation in the government of the country and for fuller enjoyment of the benefits of economic progress.

Most informed and thinking white people in South Africa, regardless of their party affiliations, recognize the inequity of denying political rights in perpetuity to the vast majority of the population of the country, and the impropriety of placing legislative or other barriers in the way of the very natural desires of people for economic and cultural advancement. Action has however been inhibited by the difficulty of reconciling the just aspirations of the non-white people with the maintenance of personal security, stable government and economic opportunities for the whites. These difficulties were investigated by two commissions – the Fagan Commission (1948)[9] and the Tomlinson Commission (1955)[10] – and though they arrived at very different conclusions, their analyses of the problems were

---

[9] *Report of the Native Laws Commission*, U.G. 28/1948.

[10] *Report of the Commission for the Socio-Economic Development of the Bantu Areas within the Union of South Africa* (Summary), U.G. 61/1955.

in many respects similar. The Tomlinson Commission believed
that there was no effective middle course between complete integration, economic, political and social, on the one hand, and complete
racial separation on the other. It further believed that the whites
would never voluntarily abdicate their power and accept government
by the black majority. Moreover the past economic trends were
projected into the future to show that subsistence farming in the
reserves and agriculture on farms owned by whites could not support
any great increase in population. Therefore, all the natural increase
of the African population would have to be absorbed in modern
industry and commerce. 'If the tempo of urbanization experienced
during 1946–51 is continued to the close of the century, and the
projected figure (for the African population) of more than twenty-one
million is realized, then more than ten million will be established
in the urban areas in the non-Bantu areas. Such a numerical prepon-
derance of Africans in the industrial centres, which are the very core
of the modern economy, must necessarily represent a threat to the
maintenance of control by the whites, who were the people who
initially brought this type of industrial society to South Africa.'

Most white South Africans believe that to hand over political
control to the African majority, as must occur if the principle of
one-man-one-vote were to be applied, would be to place the whole of
their modern society in jeopardy. Similar views have also been
expressed elsewhere. An American authority on economic development has recently stated:[11]

'My main concern is the source of economic development in these
parts in the past, together with what needs to be done in the future
if a high rate of economic progress is to be maintained . . . Relating
as it does to southern Africa, and particularly to parts where relatively many whites live, my argument is to the effect that most of this
area will continue to develop markedly only if it remains under white
hegemony. For economic development requires a combination of
hard-to-realize conditions and these conditions are far more likely
to be realized under white hegemony than under any hegemony as
is likely to arise in the event of white abdication.'

It is for reasons such as these that the present government of the
Republic evolved its policy of separate development for the various

---

[11] J. J. Spengler, *The Economic Future of "White" Southern Africa* (a paper
delivered to the African Studies Association in Washington, October 1962).

Bantu-speaking ethnic groups, in areas of their own where they would be free to develop to the full limit of their capacities. It was clearly recognized by the Tomlinson Commission that, from agricultural pursuits alone, these areas would never be able to provide an adequate living for the future African population, nor even support those at present domiciled there. The whole programme of separate development must rest upon the recognition that the future sphere of employment of the great mass of the African population must be found in industry. Therefore rapid industrialization of the African areas, together with a modernization of agricultural methods, and the development of tertiary activities and all the other manifestations of a modern industrial economy, are absolutely essential to the success of the scheme of separate development. Recognizing this the Tomlinson Commission recommended the establishment of towns and industrial cities in the Bantu areas; and that the government, assisted by private white capital and entrepreneurship, should accelerate industrialization of these areas. The government, however, rejected white participation in industrial development within the African areas on the ground that this would tend to defeat the whole objective of separate development, and that Africans must be free to develop without being subject to competition from whites in African areas.[12] Government assistance, financial and technical, would, however, be available for the industrial development of the African areas, and a Bantu Investment Corporation was established with this end in mind. Realizing that this process of industrialization must necessarily be slow, the government has come forward with the scheme of encouraging white capital and enterprise to establish industries on the periphery of the African areas. Some aspects of these 'border industries' were discussed in chapter 6 and it was seen that, compared with industries within the African areas, they possess definite locational advantages; but how far Africans will be permitted to rise to skilled and managerial posts in these industries is not yet clear. Speaking of these 'border industries', the Minister of Bantu Administration and Development said:[13]

[12] Government White Paper on the Recommendations of the Tomlinson Report, May 1956.
[13] Speech delivered by the Hon. Dr. M. D. C. de Wet Nel, Minister of Bantu Administration and Development, at the 42nd annual convention of the Federated Chambers of Industries, 5 November 1959 (issued by the Information Service of the Department of Bantu Administration and Development, Pretoria, 1960).

'It is usually maintained that one of the main limiting conditions to
the rapid industrial development of this country consists in the
limited purchasing power of its population. It is my sincere con-
viction that the most important way of increasing this purchasing
power is to increase the productivity, and hence the purchasing
power, of our large Bantu population. This can best be achieved by
absorbing the surplus Bantu population in secondary industries in
areas near their own territories, where industrial development will be
associated with far lower social costs and less disruption to the
traditional social and family standards than has been the case with the
industrialization of our large urban centres.'

The political aspect of the programmes was that the denial of
political rights to Africans in the 'white' areas should be offset by
granting them political rights and an increasing measure of self-
government in their own areas. All Africans in the Republic, whether
domiciled in an African area or not, were deemed to be citizens of the
appropriate African area for their ethnic group, and to have citizen-
ship rights there. The first African area to receive a constitution was
the Transkei; in 1962 it received a draft constitution, which came into
operation in 1963. This provided for a parliament of 109 members,
comprising 4 paramount chiefs, 60 chiefs and 45 elected members.
The electorate consists of all Transkei citizens over 21 years of age.
Xhosa living outside the Transkei are allowed to vote by post.
The town of Umtata is the capital, and the national anthem is
Nkosi Sikelel' i-Afrika (God Bless Africa).[14] Power to legislate on
certain matters in the fields of finance, justice, interior, land, agriculture, forestry, education, welfare and labour were conferred
upon the Transkeian government, subject to the assent to all measures by the government of the Republic. Control over defence,
foreign affairs, internal security and some other matters are retained
wholly by the government of the Republic, but these restraints will
fall away when the Transkei reaches full independence as a sovereign
state in October, 1976.

The Transkei is the area where separate development has the
greatest chance of success because it is a large tract of land (nearly
38 557 square kilometres), inhabited by 2 million people speaking
the same language (Xhosa), and having a tradition of common local
administration through the evolution of the Transkeian Territories

[14] This hymn has long been regarded by the Xhosa as their national anthem.

General Council from the Glen Grey Act of 1894. Financially the Transkei is not at present economically viable and in 1975 the Transkeian government was supported by a grant of R60 million from the Republic; and continued subvention will obviously be necessary for some time to come, in addition to whatever sums the Transkeian government may raise through taxation of its people. Lying as it does in the high-rainfall area of South Africa, it has considerable potential for agricultural development. It has several excellent rivers, which could supply water and some hydro-electric power for industrial development, railway links with both the Natal system and the Cape Eastern system already exist, and in certain areas it has exploitable mineral deposits. Government spokesmen have made it clear that the Transkei is only the first of the areas selected for separate development, and areas are being developed on similar lines for the six or seven other major ethnic groups. Hence the importance of what is happening in the Transkei.

While the idea of development of the Bantu areas is widely accepted as a desirable end in itself, because of their general backwardness, the basic concept of separate development has been strenuously opposed on several grounds. In the first place the economic integration of the races in South Africa in agriculture, mining, industry and commerce has already gone so far that total racial separation appears to many people to be wholly impracticable. In the 'white' areas in 1960, Africans constituted 65 per cent of the economically active population, while the African areas were largely dependent upon the earnings of the 500 000 migrant workers who at any one time were away working in the large industrial areas. Grave doubt is expressed about the economic viability of either the 'white' areas or the Bantu areas apart from one another. Advocates of separate development admit the great economic integration that has already taken place, but they declare that racial separation is an *ultimate* objective and that it may take a long time before it can be fully implemented.[15] The Tomlinson Commission estimated that even with the maximum foreseeable development of the Bantu areas, the African population in the 'white' areas would have increased from 4 902 000 in 1951 to 5 922 000 in 1981. In spite of the Commission's belief that there could be no just middle course between total

---

[15] Perhaps they give less than due weight to the causal relationship between this integrative process and the great forward movement of the national economy.

separation and total integration, it seems to be tacitly assumed that for a long time to come there must be a very considerable number of Africans employed within the 'white areas.'

This raises the problem of how the political aspirations of this most westernized and progressive section of the African people are to be met under the scheme of separate development. The proposal that they should all be regarded as domiciled in one or other of the African areas and exercise their political rights there is unlikely to be acceptable to them, nor is it very realistic. After all, a person does not only want political powers to make his wants felt in some theoretical homeland, but also and more urgently in the place where he works and earns his living, where public policy on wages, housing and social conditions affect his daily life.[16]

Another line of criticism relates to the ultimate status of these African areas, and the meaning to be attached to 'self-government'. The vital importance of the common market area and the free movement of goods and factors of production has repeatedly been referred to in these pages. Fears have been expressed that separate development may jeopardize this. The Minister of Bantu Administration and Development categorically denied this intention in 1957.

'In effecting this development, there can be no question of bringing about the dismemberment of our economy. The Union will remain an economically integrated entity, but this unity will be associated with the increased activity and differentiation of its constituent parts. This is the way in which social development has always taken place.'[17]

However, the Prime Minister, speaking on separate development in parliament[18] in 1959 and again in 1962, stated categorically that ultimately separate states must be created for the African areas. In reply to a no-confidence motion in 1964, after referring to the imminent creation of independent states in Basutoland, Swaziland and Bechuanaland and other territories to the north, he said:

'Let us then accept as a fact something similar as far as the Transkei and Zulu territory are concerned . . . as well as other

[16] There is also the matter of political representation for the 2,7 million coloured people and Asians.
[17] From the same speech as that quoted earlier in this chapter: see footnote 13, p. 260.
[18] House of Assembly, *Debates*, 20 May 1959, col. 6221; — 23 January 1962, col. 60; — 23 April 1964, col. 4817.

territories. Let the Republic, in accordance with that concept of separation, try to build a basis of good-neighbourliness and co-operation by which it tries to avoid the possibility of conflict. After all, all these territories are near enough to each other to have common interests. These common interests must be promoted on the basis of political independence from one another, and not on political conflicts in one area . . . Therefore I and my party adopt the standpoint that separate states are better, and in addition, by applying our policy correctly, we will try to obtain co-operation and friendship and good-neighbourliness in the international political sphere, in the economic sphere and in every other possible sphere.'

In general terms the objection to separate development is that it appears to run counter to history. The steps by which the Union of South Africa was formed indicate the faith of the leaders of that time in the benefits to flow from 'closer union' (as it was then referred to) – *ex unitate vires* – a faith that has been abundantly vindicated by the subsequent expansion of the national economy. Whether they advocated union or federation those architects of South Africa's future sought *aggregation* not *separation*, some even hoping to include Rhodesia and the High Commission Territories in the greater South Africa. Future economic progress would seem to demand the continuance of the process of integration upon which South Africa's past growth and prosperity have rested, and even an acceleration of the rate at which Africans are being drawn into a common and expanding market-orientated economy. These views were clearly enunciated in the report of the Fagan Commission. If this be the case, it is inevitable that political rights in a common society will increasingly be demanded by Africans and other non-white peoples, and they will become more and more difficult to resist. A relatively small section of the whites, recognizing a common society as desirable and political rights for Africans as a reasonable demand, are prepared to countenance the gradual extension of political rights to non-white people as members of a single polity, such franchise rights to be based on the attainment of some degree of civilization, education or economic status (as for the old Cape franchise), rather than merely upon colour.

The difficulty of winning mass support from the white electorate for such a policy has been greatly increased by recent events outside South Africa. The disappearance of the colonial empires and the rise of national states in Africa is part of a world movement. In

1952 there were only four independent states in the whole African continent – Egypt, Ethiopia, Liberia and South Africa. Ten years later thirty additional independent African states had appeared, and some twenty of these achieved independence between 1960 and 1962. Moreover this vast African revolutionary movement with its ideas of Pan-Africanism has generated a bitter hatred of South Africa, combined with expressions of determination to intervene in the affairs of South Africa,[19] and in some cases this had been carried to the length of training saboteurs and guerilla fighters. To many in South Africa this looked more like the declaration of a race war against all whites in Africa than like the normal process of attaining political independence. Moreover the first fruits of independence in the new African states do not inspire confidence in the abilities of some of these new governments to maintain a free and stable political society and achieve economic growth and development. Too frequently there have been one-party governments, military dictatorship, and violent revolution, and the conditions for economic progress have been lacking.

In New York the voting strength of the Afro-Asian group in the United Nations is being used to bring international pressures upon the Republic. As early as November 1962 a motion asking the Security Council to consider expelling South Africa from the United Nations and calling upon member nations to break off diplomatic relations with South Africa and impose complete economic sanctions against the country because of its race policies, was passed in the General Assembly by 67 votes to 16, twenty-three countries abstaining. Although the United States, some countries of Europe and the Commonwealth, and others, voted against the resolution, many of them have made it very clear that they do not condone the Republic's racial policies. Further resolutions against South Africa

---

[19] John R. Marcum, writing of the *Joint Declaration and Communiqué by the Government of Liberia, Ghana and Guinea, July 19, 1959*, recommending a charter for the Community of Independent African States, says that while respecting the principle of non-interference in the affairs of member states, the Community should take collective action to 'finish the job' by dislodging hardcore colonial control in Portuguese, French (i.e. Algerian), Spanish and Boer areas. Quoted from *Pan-Africanism Reconsidered*, edited by the American Society for African Culture, 1962, p. 60. Also in 1960 Mr. Tom Mboya stated, 'We shall strive by every means within our power to help our brothers in South Africa and Portuguese territories to achieve freedom.' Quoted in *New Forces in Africa*, ed. William H. Lewis, 1962, p. 40. In 1963 the heads of African states meeting in Addis Ababa affirmed their intention of taking all possible measures to 'liberate' South Africa.

were repeatedly passed in the United Nations, and in 1971 the application of sanctions was raised in the Security Council.

Criticism of South Africa is often ill-informed or lacking in appreciation of the difficulties of the situation. Sometimes too it may be influenced by the grand strategy of the 'cold war'. Nevertheless there has been built up a deep hatred of these policies, so that apartheid[20] throughout much of the world has become a synonym for *evil*, and South Africa has come to be regarded as the anti-Christ.[21] In the face of these attitudes it is futile to point out that in the Republic the African is materially better off than in most other parts of Africa or to refer to the progress in South Africa in education, housing, and health services, or to speak of rising standards of living. It seems that apartheid has come to represent for many a racial arrogance which denies the common humanity between man and man, and wounds every African and Asian in his very soul.

Be this as it may, the widespread antipathy towards South Africa's racial policies is a fact: and a fact which has direct bearing upon the future economic and political progress of the country. Resolutions such as those recently taken in the United Nations are unlikely to promote confidence, attract capital or expand foreign trade. Meanwhile disaffection at home necessitates the adoption of more restrictive measures, all of which receive the maximum publicity abroad and increase the anger against South Africa. Nevertheless the South African economy still remains relatively bouyant in an economically depressed world and its inherent strength was nowhere better illustrated than by its recovery after the huge flight of capital in 1961.

The South African dilemma is that most whites believe that the future progress of the country depends upon the maintenance of white hegemony. Yet in attempting to maintain this white hegemony they find themselves forced to adopt measures which conflict with the very requirements of economic growth. These operate both in the economic and the political spheres. In the economic, white voters

---

[20] The word 'apartheid' has recently been abandoned in favour of 'separate development' by government spokesmen, but more than a change in nomenclature is necessary to persuade the world to revise its judgement.

[21] This term is actually used, see William H. Lewis, ed. *New Forces in Africa*, 1962, p. 40, 'Should Lisbon and Pretoria league up in a military defence of enforced European supremacy, they must automatically become the anti-Christ symbols of the African revolution.'

have used their monopoly of political power to entrench their economic position by restrictions on the movement and advancement of African workers by maintaining differentials in educational opportunities and by legislative methods to give the whites a monopoly of certain kinds of jobs. These contrived scarcities and imperfections in the labour market have a corrosive effect upon economic growth, and prevent optimum resource allocation. Moreover the existence of these barriers discourages initiative and enterprise in both those thus protected and those against whom the discrimination is applied. In the political field, the denial on the ground of colour of what Africans consider their just rights builds up frustration and disaffection towards the government, which tends to weaken confidence in the stability of the whole social order, both at home and abroad, and thus to check investment and retard economic progress.

Realizing these things, the Government of the Republic has adopted in the last few years a much more enlightened approach in both external relations and domestic policies. Under the vigorous leadership of the Prime Minister, The Honourable John Vorster, South Africa has made strenuous efforts to establish better relations with neighbouring African states based upon fuller understanding of each other's problems and mutual respect for the right of each to manage its own affairs – the so-called policy of *détente*. In domestic matters, the coming to fruition of the 'homelands policy' with the forthcoming independence of the Transkei, has established the Government's *bona fides* in promising independence. Increasingly a call for a new deal for Black workers by leading industrialists, the Federated Chamber of Industries and the Handelsinstituut is heard. The need to improve labour relations and productivity by better training facilities and greater employment opportunities is receiving more sympathetic responses from the Trade Unions and the Government and many restraints are gradually being relaxed.

If the economic progress and political stability of South Africa are to be maintained there are certain imperatives which must be recognized. Briefly these would seem to be:

I. The maintenance of the government in the hands of those sections of the population who are fully committed to a modern industrial economy, and who have the wisdom and experience to recognize the essential prerequisites of this type of society. This is not the same thing as an exclusively white electorate, but it would exclude Africans still oriented towards the tribal way of life and those migrant workers who are only partially committed to the modern economy. On the other hand, it would specifically require the extension of political rights to those urban Africans and the coloured people who have become fully committed to the modern economy, if for no other reason than to prevent a monopoly of political power in white hands from being used restrictively for sectional interests which conflict with the real requirements of growth for the society as a whole.

II. Society must be organized so that all racial groups share in the increasing prosperity of the common society. This is not to advocate a policy of 'bread and circuses', but an equitable distribution of the national income in terms of effort and ability, unhampered by differential restrictive devices. Economic opportunities for all individuals, irrespective of race, must be enlarged; so that men can become more productive and be assured that they can enjoy the increased output from their labours. In this way they themselves may come to realize that they stand to gain more from the existing order than they could hope for from any alternative order of society. This implies the belief that if people are free to choose and are fully aware of the implications of their choice, they will tend to choose greater material wealth above most other things. There may be some who would prefer 'white dominance' or 'African dominance' to a rising standard of living, but these should also count the probable costs not only in material terms, but in terms of the possibility of bloodshed and civil war, and in the necessity of debasing their own moral standards.

III. The promises of independence to African territories like the Transkei and other "homelands" have advanced the position too far for this to be reversed, and these lands will in due course take their place as independent political entities; but separation does not necessarily eliminate conflict as the history of India, Palestine and Ireland unfortunately demonstrates. Whatever their political status, they will remain, like the Republic itself, inter-dependent in the economic sphere, and the urgent task ahead is to devise a structure of association which will preserve and strengthen their economic links in fields such as currency, trade, transport, investment and labour mobility, so as to advance the common cause of the welfare of all peoples in the sub-continent.

IV. Once the various racial groups have devised some method of living together in their common homeland of southern Africa, every effort can be directed to increasing the rate of economic growth, so that the admittedly great resources of the country, both natural and human, can be fully deployed in the conquest of poverty and in raising the standards of living of all its peoples. This in no way precludes schemes for developing the black areas nor for extending to them some measure of political self-government provided that there is no fragmentation of the general economy. Indeed, as an interim measure for reducing racial tensions and as a means of combating poverty at its source in the low productivity of traditional agriculture, there is much to commend them: for independence may release new sources of social energy, drive and initiative; provided always that the underlying unity of interest of all in South Africa is not forgotten.

Some form of Confederation or a Council for the Common Market of Southern Africa would seem to be desirable at an early stage.

South Africa has great difficulties to face; but it also has great opportunities – greater perhaps than any other part of the continent. It is the task of our political leaders of all racial groups to devise a social and political structure which will guarantee to each group and to every individual the safety of his person and family, freedom to work at the calling of his choice, the right to enjoy the fruit of his labours, the opportunity to contribute to the wealth of his nation to the limit of his powers, and the right of each individual to his inner integrity and of each group to maintain its own identity, if it so wishes, without any imputation of inferiority towards any other group or person, so that all South Africans, whatever their race, colour, language, culture or creed, can feel a common loyalty to a common homeland, and be drawn both by self-interest and by patriotism to work for the common good.

Statistical Appendix

TABLE 1

The Population of the Republic of South Africa at date of Census

A. NUMBERS (IN THOUSANDS)

Census Year	1911	1921	1936	1946	1951	1960	1970	1975*
Whites	1 276	1 521	2 003	2 372	2 642	3 088	3 773	4 240
Africans	4 019	4 697	6 596	7 831	8 560	10 928	15 340	18 136
Coloured people	525	545	769	928	1 103	1 509	2 050	2 368
Asians	152	164	220	285	367	477	630	727
All races	5 973	6 927	9 588	11 416	12 671	16 003	21 794	25 471

B. PERCENTAGE OF TOTAL

Census Year	1911	1921	1936	1946	1951	1960	1970
Whites	21,4	22,0	20,9	20,8	20,9	19,3	17,4
Africans	67,2	67,8	68,8	68,6	67,6	68,3	70,3
Coloured people	8,8	7,9	8,0	8,1	8,7	9,4	9,4
Asians	2,6	2,4	2,3	2,5	2,9	3,0	2,9
All races	100,0	100,0	100,0	100,0	100,0	100,0	100,0

C. PERCENTAGE URBAN

Whites	53,0	59,7	68,2	75,6	79,1	83,6	86,7
Africans	13,0	14,0	19,0	24,3	27,9	31,8	33,0
Coloured people	50,4	52,4	58,0	62,5	66,2	68,3	74,3
Asians	52,8	60,4	69,5	72,8	77,6	83,2	86,2
All races	25,9	28,2	28,2	39,3	43,4	46,7	48,8

D. AVERAGE ANNUAL PERCENTAGE INCREASE FROM ONE CENSUS YEAR TO THE NEXT CENSUS YEAR

	1911–21 (10 years)	1921–36 (15 years)	1936–46 (10 years)	1946–51 (5 years)	1951–60 (9⅜ years)	1960–70 (10 years)
Whites	1,76	1,86	1,70	2,18	1,69	2,00
Africans	1,57	2,29	1,73	1,79	1,90	2,80
Coloured people	0,37	2,32	1,89	3,51	3,43	3,07
Asians	0,86	1,90	2,65	5,15	2,87	2,72
All races	1,49	2,19	1,76	2,10	2,54	2,75

*Estimates – no census.

Sources: *Bulletin of Statistics*, June 1975 p 1.1
South African Statistics, 1974 pp. 1.8, 1.15

TABLE 2

Occupations by Main Sectors, Race and Sex: Census 1970

	Total Population			Whites		Coloured Persons		Asians		Africans	
	T	M	F	M	F	M	F	M	F	M	F
Agriculture, hunting, forestry and fishing	2 239 190	1 567 930	671 260	94 320	4 630	107 940	11 260	6 330	330	1 359 340	655 040
Mining and quarrying	676 140	670 230	5 910	58 540	4 250	7 350	140	600	20	603 740	1 500
Manufacturing	1 023 720	810 190	213 530	221 550	58 260	97 260	71 660	49 920	13 530	441 460	70 080
Electricity, gas and water	48 690	48 140	1 550	12 920	1 320	3 000	10	180	—	32 040	220
Construction	446 360	437 260	9 100	89 260	6 400	76 120	710	9 520	110	262 360	1 880
Commerce, catering and accommodation	716 070	519 180	196 890	156 270	116 770	53 240	24 350	45 470	5 510	264 200	50 260
Transport, storage and communication	338 320	310 850	27 470	138 360	25 230	26 950	620	7 340	200	138 200	1 420
Financing, insurance and real estate	190 380	115 160	75 220	76 160	69 700	5 410	1 480	2 430	400	31 160	3 640
Community, social and personal services	1 573 990	590 380	983 610	183 120	142 270	50 190	110 960	16 890	6340	340 180	724 040
Unemployed	303 070	130 630	172 440	3 140	1 490	6 460	5 370	2 150	560	118 880	165 020
Unspecified	429 290	171 450	257 840	18 110	15 390	22 640	20 500	5 720	6 450	124 980	215 500
Total economically active	7 986 220	5 371 400	2 614 820	1 051 750	445 710	456 560	247 060	146 550	33 450	3 716 540	1 888 600
Not economically active	13 416 250	5 174 700	8 241 550	804 430	1 424 650	537 890	779 920	161 580	276 560	3 670 800	5 760 420
Total Population	21 402 470	10 546 100	10 856 370	1 856 180	1 870 360	994 450	1 026 980	308 130	310 010	7 387 340	7 649 020

Source: *South African Statistics*, 1974 p. 1.33

TABLE 2 (cont.)

Occupations by Main Sectors and Race

TOTAL PERSONS (THOUSANDS)

	CENSUS 1960						CENSUS 1951					
	All races	Per-centage	Whites	Africans	Coloured people	Asians	All races	Per-centage	Whites	Africans	Coloured peoples	Asians
Agriculture, forestry and fishing	1 698	30	118	1 451*	119	10	1 509	33	145	1 252†	98	13
Mining	605	11	62	539	4	–	510	11	57	449	4	1
Manufacturing	679	12	229	320	97	33	502	11	183	228	70	22
Construction	279	5	72	165	40	2	240	5	67	132	39	2
Electricity, gas and water	38	1	10	25	3	–	25	–	7	17	2	–
Commerce and finance	458	8	234	158	39	27	328	7	179	101	25	23
Transport	215	4	122	72	17	4	203	4	113	73	14	2
Services	1 228	21	252	813	141	22	1 073	24	204	741	111	17
Unemployed	493	9	41	335	90	27	202‡	4	28‡	118‡	42‡	14‡
Total economically active (a)	5 691§	100	1 140	3 877	548	126	4 592§	100	984§	3 111§	404§	94§
Total population (b)	15 981		3 088	10 908	1 509	477	12 671		2 641	8 560	1 103	367
(a) as percentage of (b)	(36%)		(37%)	(35%)	(36%)	(26%)	(36%)		(37%)	(36%)	(39%)	(26%)

N.B. Columns do not always add correctly due to rounding.
* Including approximately 500 thousand peasant farmers in the reserves.
† Including approximately 438 peasant farmers in the reserves.
‡ Including industry unspecified.
§ Including only those 15 years of age and over.

Sources: Population Census 1960, Sample Tabulation no. 1. Industrial Divisions, Age Groups and Home Languages, Whites, p. 2. Population Census 1960, Sample Tabulation no. 2, Industrial Divisions, Age Groups and Home Languages, Coloureds and Asiatics, pp. 2 and 40. Population Census 1960, Sample Tabulation no. 5, Industrial Divisions, Age Groups and Home Languages, Bantu, p. 2. The total population 15 981 000 does not exactly tally with the figure of 16 033 000 given in table 1 as the occupational analysis is based on the sample tabulations

TABLE 3

Gross Domestic Product by Kind of Economic Activity 1912–74

(R millions)

Year ending	Farming¹	%	Mining²	%	Manu-facturing³	%	Trade	%	Transport	%	Government	%	Other	%	G.D.P. at factor cost
June 1912	46	(17)	72	(27)	18	(7)	36	(14)	—		—		94	(35)	266
,, 1920	102	(21)	104	(21)	52	(11)	82	(17)	—		—		147	(30)	487
,, 1925	102	(22)	80	(17)	56	(12)	73	(15)	—		—		161	(34)	470
,, 1930	70	(14)	88	(17)	78	(15)	73	(15)	—		—		197	(39)	506
,, 1935	81	(14)	126	(21)	91	(15)	82	(14)	—		—		220	(37)	602
,, 1940	101	(12)	196	(23)	151	(18)	123	(14)	—		—		290	(34)	863
,, 1945	164	(12)	192	(14)	265	(20)	188	(14)	—		—		524	(39)	1 408
Dec. 1950	454	(18)	338	(13)	594	(23)	375	(16)	236	(9)	195	(7)	357	(14)	2 549
,, 1955	578	(15)	470	(12)	972	(25)	583	(15)	373	(10)	301	(8)	542	(14)	3 819
,, 1960	601	(12)	684	(14)	1 298	(26)	696	(14)	566	(10)	421	(8)	747	(15)	4 953
,, 1965	760	(10)	947	(13)	2 225	(30)	1 055	(14)	710	(10)	624	(8)	1 109	(15)	7 430
,, 1970	973	(8)	1 207	(10)	3 644	(31)	1 762	(15)	1 074	(9)	1 123	(10)	1 908	(16)	11 691
,, 1974	1 894	(9)	3 193	(15)	6 191	(29)	2 868	(13)	1 799	(8)	2 064	(10)	3 240	(15)	21 249

¹ Farming includes Agriculture, Forestry and Fishing. ² Mining includes Quarrying. ³ Manufacturing from 1950 includes Construction, Electricity, Water and Gas.

Sources: Union Statistics for Fifty Years, Table S-3 up to 1945, thereafter S.A.R.B., A Statistical Presentation of South Africa's National Accounts for the Period 1946 to 1970, p. 20 N.B. The two series are not strictly comparable. Also S.A.R.B. Quarterly Bulletin: March, 1976, p. S-71.

TABLE 4

Gross Domestic Product 1946–75

	G.D.P. at market price (R millions)	Real G.D.P. at 1963 prices (R millions)	% Increase on previous year	Real G.D.P. at 1970 prices (R millions)	% Increase on previous year
1946	1 751	2 905	—	—	—
1947	1 932	3 059	5,4	—	—
1948	2 136	3 321	8,6	—	—
1949	2 290	3 401	2,4	—	—
1950	2 662	3 594	5,7	—	—
1951	2 909	3 801	8,5	—	—
1952	3 116	3 904	2,7	—	—
1953	3 537	4 107	5,2	—	—
1954	3 808	4 381	6,7	—	—
1955	4 025	4 620	5,5	—	—
1956	4 339	4 861	5,2	—	—
1957	4 583	5 076	4,4	—	—
1958	4 711	5 189	2,2	—	—
1959	4 993	5 369	3,5	—	—
1960	5 274	5 551	3,4	—	—
1961	5 546	5 735	3,3	—	—
1962	5 912	6 054	5,6	—	—
1963	6 555	6 555	8,1	—	—
1964	7 209	6 986	6,7	—	—
1965	7 879	7 448	6,6	—	—
1966	8 555	7 799	4,7	—	—
1967	9 511	8 391	7,6	10 618	—
1968	10 255	—	—	11 097	4,5
1969	11 535	—	—	11 988	8,0
1970	12 576	—	—	12 576	4,9
1971	13 951	—	—	13 179	4,8
1972	15 612	—	—	13 575	3,0
1973	19 010	—	—	14 115	4,3
1974*	22 612	—	—	15 106	6,7
1975*	25 771	—	—	15 440	2,2

*Provisional figures.
Source: S.A.R.B., *A Statistical Presentation of South Africa's National Accounts for the Period 1946 to 1970*, p. 12 and S.A.R.B. *Quarterly Bulletin*, March, 1976

TABLE 5

Consumption and Investment as a Percentage of Gross Domestic Expenditure 1960–75
(R millions)

	Private consumption expenditure		Government consumption expenditure		Gross domestic fixed investment		Change in inventories	Residual item	Gross domestic expenditure	
	%			%		%				%
1960	67,8	3 381	485	9,7	1 061	21,3	+ 89	— 33	4 983	100
1961	69,2	3 493	525	10,4	1 068	21,1	+ 79	—116	5 049	100
1962	68,7	3 680	619	11,6	1 072	20,0	+ 46	— 59	5 358	100
1963	63,0	3 874	690	11,2	1 302	21,2	+211	— 25	6 152	100
1964	63,7	4 463	779	11,1	1 611	23,0	+147	— 2	7 002	100
1965	61,5	4 857	868	10,9	1 977	25,0	+221	— 28	7 895	100
1966	63,7	5 267	978	11,8	2 084	25,0	+ 20	— 85	8 264	100
1967	60,9	5 685	1 041	11,2	2 219	23,8	+472	— 85	9 332	100
1968	64,1	6 252	1 146	11,7	2 316	23,7	+ 23	+ 18	9 755	100
1969	61,5	6 889	1 301	11,6	2 620	23,4	+325	+ 65	11 200	100
1970	59,6	7 698	1 552	12,0	3 221	24,9	+396	+ 39	12 906	100
*1971	59,2	8 546	1 862	12,9	3 780	26,1	+407	—162	14 433	100
*1972	62,9	9 520	1 969	13,0	4 249	28,0	—373	—221	15 144	100
*1973	60,8	11 001	2 238	12,4	4 782	26,4	+ 89	— 22	18 088	100
*1974	57,8	12 962	2 816	12,5	5 865	26,1	+961	—161	22 443	100
*1975	56,5	14 902	3 709	14,1	7 400	28,1	+355	+ 12	26 378	100

Source: Adapted from S.A.R.B., *A Statistical Presentation of South Africa's National Accounts for the Period 1946 to 1970*, p. 13. and S.A.R.B. *Quarterly Bulletin*, December, 1975, p. S-69

* Provisional.

TABLE 6

Private Consumption Expenditure 1960-75
(R millions)

	Food, beverages and tobacco	Clothing and footwear	Rent fuel and power	Furniture	Medical	Transport	Recreation and education	Miscellaneous	Total private consumption
1960	1 183	342	376	469	107	411	178	315	3 381
1961	1 249	341	394	479	113	402	183	332	3 493
1962	1 299	357	415	502	119	439	194	355	3 680
1963	1 380	390	436	553	127	494	209	385	3 974
1964	1 521	438	467	634	136	594	231	442	4 463
1965	1 675	478	505	684	147	631	250	487	4 857
1966	1 806	511	553	732	163	699	274	529	5 267
1967	1 942	547	606	778	172	771	294	575	5 685
1868	2 089	601	682	855	186	862	335	642	6 252
1969	2 231	671	760	956	206	994	379	692	6 889
1970	2 480	763	854	1 013	235	1 142	420	791	7 698
1971	2 703	857	977	1 115	279	1 285	461	869	8 546
*1972	3 051	911	1 104	1 259	301	1 430	516	949	9 520
*1973	3 567	1 065	1 272	1 415	328	1 685	598	1 071	11 001
*1974	4 393	1 259	1 445	1 659	363	1 926	680	1 237	12 962
*1975	5 017	1 507	1 883	1 761	413	2 259	968	1 094	14 902

Source: S.A.R.B., *A Statistical Presentation of South Africa's National Accounts for the Period 1946 to 1970*, p. 21. and **S.A.R.B.** *Quarterly Bulletin*, December, 1975, and March, 1976.

* Provisional

TABLE 7

Gross Value of Arable Farming and Livestock Products 1911–75
(R millions)

Season ending in:	Total	Arable	Livestock	Season ending in:	Total	Arable	Livestock
1911	58	25	33	1936	112	61	51
1912	62	28	34	1937	130	66	64
1913	74	34	40	1938	125	62	63
1914	66	29	38	1939	136	75	61
1915	66	33	33	1940	146	76	69
1916	73	35	38	1941	157	85	72
1917	80	39	41	1942	183	94	89
1918	94	44	50	1943	234	123	111
1919	111	48	63	1944	240	121	119
1920	153	64	89	1945	246	129	117
1921	96	45	51	1946	263	138	124
1922	82	43	40	1947	307	168	139
1923	104	51	52	1948	374	208	166
1924	104	44	60	1949	368	183	186
1925	121	59	62	1950	426	222	204
1926	104	47	58	1951	590	266	324
1927	117	56	61	1952	516	243	273
1928	129	58	71	1953	642	315	327
1929	124	55	69	1954	681	340	342
1930	102	50	53	1955	670	340	330
1931	85	43	42	1956	696	364	332
1932	76	44	33	1957	768	382	386
1933	75	40	35	1958	719	364	355
1934	110	56	54	1959	729	397	332
1935	101	53	48	1960	786	410	376

	Total	Field crops	Horticulture	Livestock
1961	854	360	127	367
1962	882	373	130	379
1963	927	391	138	399
1964	959	362	157	439
1965	1 031	403	176	452
1966	1 082	403	184	495
1967	1 332	627	194	510
1968	1 203	478	200	525
1969	1 293	517	228	549
1970	1 336	570	216	550
1971	1 527	701	265	562
1972	1 677	771	284	622
1973	1 739	587	330	821
1974	2 403	1 105	349	949
1975	2 524	1 168	373	984

Sources: *Union Statistics for Fifty Years*, pp. I–23–25 for years to 1958; thereafter *Statistical Year Book, 1964*, pp. J–17, 18, to 1960; thereafter *Annual Report of the Secretary for Agricultural Economics and Marketing, 1969/70*, R.P. 23/1971, p. 110 and R.P. 51/1975 p. 101 and *Abstract of Agricultural Statistics, 1975*.

TABLE 8

Gross Value of Main Farming Products 1970 and 1960
(R Millions)

	1969–70	1959–60
Field crops		
Maize	246	146
Wheat	90	43
Sugar cane	82	38
Hay	42	22
Tobacco	26	13
Groundnuts	25	16
Kaffircorn	17	9
Other	42	33
Sub-total	570	320
Horticulture		
Deciduous fruit (fresh and dried)	65	30
Vegetables (ex potatoes) ...	45	25
Citrus fruit	32	18
Viticulture	29	16
Potatoes	26	11
Tropical fruit	12	7
Other	7	6
Sub-total	216	113
Livestock		
Cattle slaughtered	147	78
Fresh milk	83	56
Wool	82	93
Sheep and goats slaughtered ...	77	42
Dairy products	47	36
Eggs	36	23
Poultry slaughtered	34	15
Pigs slaughtered	24	15
Other	20	15
	550	373
Grand total	1 336	806

Source: *Abstract of Agricultural Statistics, 1971*, p. 85.

TABLE 9

Production, Consumption, Imports and Exports of Maize in 1924/25 to 1974/75 Marketing Seasons

Average			('000 t)	
Marketing season	*Total production*	*Net domestic consumption*	*Imports*	*Exports*
Average 1924/25–1928/29	1 522	1 077	25	470
Average 1929/30–1933/34	1 533	1 236	54	365
Average 1934/35–1938/39	1 907	1 358	5	515
Average 1939/40–1943/44	2 082	1 730	—	320
Average 1944/45–1948/49	2 098	2 015	110	110
Average 1949/50–1953/54	2 693	2 581	46	132
Average 1954/55–1958/59	3 896	2 888	—	1 067
Average 1959/60–1963/64	5 128	3 338	—	1 708
Average 1964/65–1968/69	5 781	4 243	53	1 626
Average 1969/70–1973/74	6 743	5 061	118	1 922
1959/60	3 975	3 094	—	621
1960/61	4 288	3 285	—	952
1961/62	5 275	3 200	—	1 617
1962/63	6 002	3 453	—	2 586
1963/64	6 099	3 657	—	2 765
1964/65	4 279	3 871	—	1 101
1965/66	4 490	4 182	112	480
1966/67	5 056	4 237	153	482
1967/68	9 762	4 233	—	3 111
1968/69	5 316	4 691	—	2 956
1969/70	5 340	4 884	503	947
1970/71	6 133	5 150	73	1 302
1971/72	8 600	4 868	16	2 835
1972/73	9 483	5 206	—	3 917
1973/74	4 160	5 199	—	607
1974/75	11 105	5 776	—	3 698

Source: *Report on Maize 1975*, Report of Maize Board for year ended 30 April, 1975, p. 21.

TABLE 10

Sales of Maize and Maize Products to Lesotho, Botswana, Swaziland and South West Africa in 1965/66 to 1974/75 Marketing Seasons
(tons)

Marketing season	Lesotho	Botswana	Swaziland	South West Africa	Total
1965/66	39 013	39 577	15 876	38 498	132 964
1966/67	28 947	14 976	9 736	21 204	74 863
1967/68	14 043	8 767	6 450	16 073	45 333
1968/69	32 848	17 255	26 031	24 725	100 859
1969/70	29 010	10 037	25 113	39 515	103 675
1970/71	34 545	18 137	23 422	125 693	201 797
1971/72	13 205	11 273	14 960	30 166	69 604
1972/73	22 253	8 781	18 487	33 463	82 984
1973/74	52 112	27 868	24 129	35 165	139 274
1974/75	16 791	6 284	19 991	17 083	60 149

Source: Maize Board, *Report on Maize* for financial year ending April 1975, p. 43

TABLE 11

Average Yield – Wheat and Maize 1946–71
(kilograms per hectare)

Year	White farmers		African peasants in Bantu areas
	Wheat	Maize	Maize
1945–6	477	551	—
1946–7	508	647	—
1947–8	615	880	—
1948–9	541	615	—
1949–50	519	742	—
1950–1	668	806	—
1951–2	678	647	—
1952–3	572	848	—
1953–4	647	922	—
1954–5	657	880	220
1955–6	753	922	146
1956–7	720	1 018	299
1957–8	551	848	212
1958–9	551	879	254
1959–60	614	911	212
1960–1	625	1 112	254
1961–2	625	1 229	187
1962–3	561	1 250	204
1963–4	614	847	180
1964–5	674	964	143
1965–6	411	1 085	194
1966–7	419	1 855	293
1967–8	688	954	159
1968–9	600	976	230
1969–70	560	1 186	230
1970–1	563	1 587	—

Source: Figures kindly supplied by the Department of Agricultural Economics and Marketing and the Department of Bantu Administration and Development.

TABLE 12

Price Movements of Wool, Maize, Beef and Mutton
1950–70

	Maize[1]	Wool[2]	Beef[3]	Mutton[4]
1950–51	2,50	195,06	13,62	21,98
1951–52	2,85	98,52	17,44	32,39
1952–53	3,00	115,28	18,70	36,00
1953–54	3,20	117,04	18,56	38,78
1954–55	3,10	97,40	19,33	42,48
1955–56	3,00	84,86	21,30	40,39
1956–57	2,95	114,04	23,41	38,87
1957–58	2,87½	87,94	25,00	40,94
1958–59	2,82½	65,61	24,12	38,07
1959–60	2,92	80,89	24,07	36,88
1960–61	3,12½	72,88	24,27	39,04
1961–62	3,07½	74,96	23,94	35,52
1962–63	2,80	83,49	25,60	41,23
1963–64	2,87	98,74	25,73	44,05
1964–65	3,00	80,40	33,49	45,50
1965–66	3,15	83,80	34,46	43,14
1966–67	3,57½	78,29	37,63	48,41
1967–68	3,35	75,42	42,92	46,94
1968–69	3,30	80,62	42,73	43,89
1969–70	3,55	n.a.	40,43	46,91

[1] Producers' price of white maize in rands per bag (90,7 kg).
[2] Merino wool, average auction prices in cents per kg.
[3] Average price at auction on the hook in cents per kg.
[4] Average price at auction on the hook in cents per kg.

Source: *Abstract of Agricultural Statistics, 1971*, pp. 65, 77, 79.

TABLE 13

Sales of Mining Output: Gold and Other Mining 1911–74
(R millions)

Year	Gold	Other	Total	Year	Gold	Other	Total
1911	70	25	95	1943	215	29	244
1912	77	28	105	1944	206	39	245
1913	75	31	106	1945	211	44	254
1914	71	19	91	1946	206	52	257
1915	77	10	97	1947	193	58	251
1916	79	22	101	1948	200	62	262
1917	77	28	105	1949	230	79	308
1918	72	24	95	1950	290	104	393
1919	71	32	103	1951	286	124	411
1920	69	41	111	1952	294	137	431
1921	69	18	87	1953	295	144	439
1922	60	12	72	1954	329	168	498
1923	78	22	100	1955	365	217	582
1924	81	27	109	1956	397	252	649
1925	82	27	109	1957	425	281	706
1926	86	33	117	1958	440	288	728
1927	86	36	122	1959	500	289	789
1928	88	45	133	1960	536	321	857
1929	88	33	122	1961	575	318	893
1930	91	28	119	1962	637	314	951
1931	92	17	110	1963	686	326	1 012
1932	98	11	109	1964	730	355	1 085
1933	94	12	105	1965	767	386	1 153
1934*	145	12	157	1966	776	474	1 249
1935	153	15	168	1967	763	516	1 279
1936	159	18	177	1968	777	578	1 355
1937	165	23	189	1969	779	646	1 425
1938	173	24	197	1970	830	733	1 563
1939	198	23	221	1971	893	677	1 570
1940	236	23	259	1972	1 160	782	1 942
1941	242	25	267	1973	1 789	1 055	2 844
1942	237	27	264	1974	2 619	1 309	3 928

*1934 onwards – Gold taken at average price realized; pre-1934 – Gold taken at value R8,496 per oz.

Sources: *Annual Report of Government Mining Engineer* . . . R.P. 18/1962 to year 1960; thereafter *Statistical Year Book, 1966* p. L-5 to 1965; later figures from *Bulletin of Statistics*, March 1975, p. 5,2.

TABLE 14

Principal Minerals: 1973 and 1960

	Production (1 000 metric tons unless otherwise stated)	Value (R millions)	
	1973	1973	1960
Precious minerals			
Gold (kg)	855 179	1 789	536,0
Silver (kg)	113 591	7	1,5
Diamonds (metric carats)	7 198	90	33,8
Prescribed atomic materials	n.a.	n.a.	98,5
Metallic minerals			
Chrome	1 650	17	6,0
Copper	176	171	21,4
Iron Ore	10 955	35	7,2
Manganese	4 243	53	14,1
Tin (ore and concentrates)	—	—	1,9
Non-metallic minerals			
Asbestos	333	47	21,6
Coal	58 440	127	55,1
Limestone	16 825	26	8,5
Phosphates	2 063	14	1,8
Salt	391	5	2,1
Other minerals	—	364	44,9
Total all mineral production		2 844	856,7

Sources: *Bulletin of Statistics*, March 1975, p. 52 for 1973.
Statistical Year Book, 1964, pp. L–5, 6, 7, 8, 9 for 1960.

TABLE 15

Coal: Quantity and Value 1911–74

Year	Metric tons*	Sales (R millions)
1911	6,9	3,9
1915	7,7	4,3
1920	10,9	9,0
1925	12,4	7,7
1930	12,3	7,0
1935	13,6	7,1
1940	17,5	10,6
1945	23,6	17,0
1950	26,5	29,6
1955	32,2	34,7
1960	38,2	55,1
1965	48,4	81,3
1970	53,0	109,3
1971	57,0	119,4
1972	57,1	126,8
1973	61,5	152,1
1974	66,1	200,0

*1 metric ton = 1,10231 tons (2 000 lb).

Sources: *Union Statistics for Fifty Years*, p. K–15 (converted to metric tons) up to 1955; *Statistical Year Book, 1965*, p. L–8 for 1960 and 1965; *Bulletin of Statistics*, March, 1975, p. 5.3.

TABLE 16

Growth of Private Manufacturing Industry 1925–74

Year ending June	Number of establishments	Total employment (thousands)	Value of gross output (R millions)	Value of net output (R millions)
1925	6 009	115	115	49
1939	8 614	236	281	128
1945	9 316	361	608	276
1946	9 642	379	669	305
1947	9 999	397	780	347
1948	11 376	434	922	401
1949	12 060	473	1 062	457
1950	12 517	498	1 217	512
1951	12 983	543	1 583	622
1952	12 887	576	1 809	700
1953	13 260	596	1 908	775
1954	13 881	622	2 013	860
1955*	13 725	652	2 221	964
1955*	9 685	616	2 154	852
1956	10 378	640	2 334	907
1957	10 291	661	2 465	980
1958	10 640	676	2 603	1 033
1959	10 967	677	2 650	1 058
1960	11 411	668	2 792	1 129
1961	11 885	689	3 024	1 228
1962	12 514	709	3 220	1 329
1963	11 985	767	3 518	1 442
1964	11 944	832	4 045	1 641
1966	12 727	942	5 104	2 038
1968	13 142	994	5 983	2 419
1970	13 121	1 095	7 502	3 102
1971	—	1 202	7 546	—
1972	—	1 228	8 356	—
1973	—	1 268	10 347	—
1974	—	1 316	12 646	—

* Figures are comparable to 1955 when some repair units and workshops were removed. The second set of figures for 1955 is comparable with latter years.

Sources: *Union Statistics for Fifty Years* to 1955; after 1955, *Statistical Year Book, 1965*, p. M–12; from 1964. *Bulletin of Statistics* December, 1975.

TABLE 17

Manufacturing Industries 1968 and Totals for 1970

	Number of establishments	Employees	Salaries and wages (R millions)	Gross output (R millions)	Net output (R millions)	Value of physical assets (R millions)	
						Land and buildings	Plant and machinery
1. Food	1 462	122 712	102,8	1 036	263	132	171
2. Beverages	288	18 641	21,2	180	63	39	42
3. Tobacco	23	3 704	4,9	57	27	3	3
4. Textiles	301	76 243	59,2	347	135	44	79
5. Clothing	2 034	113 680	95,9	389	171	18	26
6. Wood products	571	39 629	21,9	96	42	16	20
7. Furniture	635	26 123	28,3	98	50	6	9
8. Paper and paper products	164	29 865	36,8	212	95	33	74
9. Printing and publishing	718	29 924	56,7	157	100	22	36
10. Leather and leather products	96	6 168	5,9	29	10	2	2
11. Rubber products	274	18 004	23,0	116	58	13	21
12. Chemical products	531	58 113	81,2	525	228	79	185
13. Non-metallic mineral products	693	68 972	56,4	239	133	57	101
14. Basic metal products	196	63 859	103,6	499	206	133	292
15. Metal products	1 711	104 912	131,6	508	227	43	88
16. Machinery	963	66 736	115,2	414	191	36	55
17. Electrical machinery	498	37 170	55,6	260	99	21	28
18. Transport equipment	1 034	65 178	92,4	486	154	37	75
19. Miscellaneous	950	39 313	57,5	337	142	30	196
TOTAL 1968	13 142	988 946	1 150,0	5 983	2 398	762	1 504
TOTAL 1970	13 121	1 095 570	1 422	7 502	3 102	—	—

N.B. Numbers do not always add to totals given due to rounding.
Source: South African Statistics 1974.

TABLE 18

Growth in Selected Branches of Manufacturing Industry 1925–70

Year ended June	Metal products and machinery (Groups 14, 15, 16, 17, 18)		Food, beverages and tobacco (Groups 1, 2, 3)		Textiles and wearing apparel (Groups 4 & 5)		Chemicals (Group 12)		All manufactures (Groups 1–19)	
	Employment (thousands)	Net output (R millions)	Employment (thousands)	Net output (R millions)	Employment (thousands)	Net output (R millions)	Employment (thousands)	Net output (R millions)	Employment (thousands)	Net output (R millions)
1925	21	8	32	15	12	4	9	1	115	49
1939	58	33	47	32	39	14	13	5	236	128
1945	97	55	73	61	56	40	23	11	361	275
1955*	202	344	110	154	109	122	33	36	653	964
1955*	168	273	110	145	109	117	33	34	616	852
1960	193	371	115	197	113	146	42	95	668	1 128
1962	205	431	121	244	126	173	45	120	709	1 328
1964	268	564	126	273	154	207	47	152	826	1 641
1966	313	760	139	307	176	257	53	182	936	2 038
1968	338	891	145	352	189	305	58	228	988	2 393
1970	387	1 150	155	438	213	382	60	306	1 096	3 102

*Owing to a change in industrial classification, figures before and after 1955 are not comparable. Both sets of figures are given for 1955.

Sources: Up to 1955 annual *Census of Industrial Establishments*, after 1955 *Statistical Year Book, 1964*, pp. M-16 to M-25 *South African Statistics* 1974 pp. 12–10 to 12–19.

TABLE 19

Employment and Earnings 1950, 1960, 1970

		Mining	Manu-facturing	Con-struc-tion	Trans-port	Public autho-rities
Number of workers (all races) (thousands)	1950	503,3	486,3	77,8	187,9	—
,, ,, ,, ,,	1960	620,1	615,7	114,5	218,0	510,3
,, ,, ,, ,,	1970	675,8	1 171,3	367,8	232,3	645,1
Earnings (all races) (R millions)	1950	125,4	240,8	34,2	129,0	—
,, ,, ,,	1960	249,0	496,1	77,6	217,2	445,7
,, ,, ,,	1970	410,9	1 636,6	450,8	474,7	1 028,0
Average earnings per worker (R p.a.)	1950	249,2	514,2	439,6	686,5	—
,, ,, ,, ,,	1960	401,5	805,7	677,7	996,3	873,4
,, ,, ,, ,,	1970	608,0	1 397,3	1 225,7	2 043,5	1 593,6
Number of white workers (thousands)	1950	55,9	155,1	19,1	103,3	—
,, ,, ,, ,,	1960	67,7	162,8	22,9	110,0	205,7
,, ,, ,, ,,	1970	62,5	275,4	60,5	110,7	238,0
Earnings of white workers (R millions)	1950	79,8	151,1	20,2	105,9	—
,, ,, ,,	1960	156,5	313,7	42,8	185,3	334,0
,, ,, ,,	1970	273,1	1 003,4	231,9	402,4	769,6
Average earnings of white workers (R p.a.)	1950	1 427,5	974,2	1 057,6	1 025,2	—
,, ,, ,, ,,	1960	2 311,7	1 926,9	1 870,0	1 684,5	1 623,7
,, ,, ,, ,,	1970	4 369,6	3 643,4	3 833,1	3 635,1	3 233,6
Number of coloured workers (thousands)	1950	2,5	69,7	7,9	9,7	—
,, ,, ,, ,,	1960	3,9	87,3	15,8	9,7	38,7
,, ,, ,, ,,	1970	6,5	196,1	45,5	14,3	60,8
Earnings of coloured workers (R millions)	1950	—	26,1	3,7	—	—
,, ,, ,,	1960	—	49,2	10,5	—	28,6
,, ,, ,,	1970	5,6	172,2	59,2	—	69,6
Average earnings of coloured workers (R p.a.)	1950	—	374,4	468,4	—	—
,, ,, ,, ,,	1960	—	563,6	664,6	—	739,0
,, ,, ,, ,,	1970	875,0	878,1	1 301,1	—	1 144,7
Number of Asian workers (thousands)	1950	0,6	19,6	0,2	0,6	—
,, ,, ,,	1960	0,5	29,2	0,6	0,6	7,5
,, ,, ,,	1970	0,6	75,1	4,4	1,2	13,7
Earnings of Asian workers (R millions)	1950	—	7,5	0,1	—	—
,, ,, ,,	1960	—	17,3	0,6	—	6,0
,, ,, ,,	1970	0,7	70,3	8,1	—	18,0
Average earnings of Asian workers (R p.a.)	1950	—	382,7	500,0	—	—
,, ,, ,, ,,	1960	—	592,5	1 000,0	—	800,0
,, ,, ,, ,,	1970	1 166,7	936,1	1 840,9	—	1 313,8
Number of African workers (thousands)	1950	444,2	241,8	50,5	74,2	—
,, ,, ,, ,,	1960	547,9	336,3	75,0	96,6	258,1
,, ,, ,, ,,	1970	606,2	624,6	257,4	97,1	332,5
Earnings of African workers (R millions)	1950	—	56,1	10,3	—	—
,, ,, ,, ,,	1960	—	115,9	23,6	—	77,1
,, ,, ,, ,,	1970	131,5	391,2	151,6	—	170,8
Average earnings of African workers (R p.a.)	1950	—	232,0	204,0	—	—
,, ,, ,, ,,	1960	—	344,6	314,7	—	298,7
,, ,, ,, ,,	1970	216,9	626,3	589,0	—	513,7
Number of non-white workers (thousands)	1950	447,4	—	—	84,6	—
,, ,, ,, ,,	1960	552,4	—	—	108,0	—
,, ,, ,, .	1970	613,3	—	—	121,6	—
Earnings of non-white workers (R millions)	1950	45,6	—	—	23,1	—
,, ,, ,, ,,	1960	92,5	—	—	31,9	—
,, ,, ,, ,,	1970	137,8	—	—	72,3	—
Average earnings of non-white workers (R p.a.)	1950	98,1	—	—	273,0	—
,, ,, ,, ,,	1960	167,5	—	—	295,4	—
,, ,, ,, ,,	1970	224,7	—	—	594,6	—

Sources: 1950 and 1960 *Statistical Year Book*, 1964 pp. H–23, 25, 32, 46, 47, 54; 1970 from *Statistical Press Release* 19/3/1971 and ~ 18/6/1971 for public authorities. Annual earnings = earnings for September × 12.

TABLE 20

South African Imports and Exports 1950–75
(*including South West Africa, Botswana, Lesotho and Swaziland*)

	Imports (*R millions*)	Exports (*excluding gold*) S.A. Produce	Re-exports	Total
1950	613,7	390,0	47,0	437,0
1955	962,0	663,7	74,9	738,5
1960	1 111,1	799,5	84,5	884,0
1965	1 752,5	964,5	93,5	1 805,0
1970	2 547,1	1 425,9	116,9	1 542,8
1972	2 622	—	—	1 967
1973	3 275	—	—	2 364
1974	4 905	—	—	3 006
1975	2 727	—	—	1 611

Sources: *Statistical Year Book* to 1964; thereafter *Monthly Abstract of Trade Statistics*, January–December 1969 and 1970, and *Statistics in Brief*, 1976.

TABLE 21

South African Imports and Exports by Area and Main Countries
1970 and 1973
(*including South West Africa, Botswana, Lesotho and Swaziland*)
(*R millions*)

	Imports from 1970	1973	Exports to 1970	1973
Africa	*131,2*	*191*	*263,9*	*342*
Europe	*1 392,0*	*1 839*	*793,5*	*1 389*
U.K.	560,6	632	466,4	700
W. Germany	372,4	607	109,1	189
France	89,0	125	40,2	69
Netherlands	58,6	69	34,9	60
Switzerland	49,6	69	5,1	31
Sweden	45,0	56	7,7	11
Belgium	34,0	55	55,7	120
America	*516,2*	*609*	*176,5*	*269*
U.S.	423,8	528	129,3	164
Canada	70,5	41	28,2	57
Asia	*409,8*	*515*	*219,3*	*371*
Japan	221,1	381	180,6	246
Hong Kong	19,3	25	24,0	48
Oceania	*65,2*	*97*	*15,2*	*28*
Australia	60,5	91	12,6	24
Unallocated	*25,7*	*22*	*2,3*	*3*
Ships Stores	—	—	*67,2*	*19*
Emigrants and immigrants	*7,0*	*7*	*4,9*	*6*
Grand Total	2 547,1	3 283	1 542,8	2 427

Source: *Monthly Abstract of Trade Statistics*, January–December 1970. *Foreign Trade Statistics, 1973* pp. 140–147.

TABLE 22

South African Imports and Exports by Major Categories 1973

Categories according to Brussels nomenclature		Imports (R millions)	Exports (R millions)
1, 2	animals and animal and vege-table products	113	313
3, 4	processed animal and vegetable products, beverages and tobacco	83	289
5	mineral products	39	218
6, 7	chemical products, resins, rubber etc.	396	103
8	hides, skins, leather	20	70
9, 10	wood and paper making material	170	71
11, 12	textiles and clothing	345	207
13, 14	asbestos, ceramics, glass, pre-cious stones and precious metals	78	490
15	base metals and articles of base metal	244	362
16	machinery	978	106
17	vehicles, aircraft, ships	601	33
18	optical photographic and preci-sion instruments	129	10
19, 20, 21	other	68	156
	Totals	3 283	2 425

Source: *Monthly Abstract of Trade Statistics*, January–December 1973

TABLE 23

Balance of Payments 1955–75
(R millions)

Item	1955	1956	1957	1958	1959	1960	1961	1962	1963	1964
CURRENT ACCOUNT										
Merchandise exports	737	819	888	776	879	881	923	948	1 024	1 074
Net gold output	366	395	429	440	503	530	576	632	688	736
Service receipts	178	199	215	205	217	229	236	253	262	305
Merchandise imports	−972	−997	−1 109	−1 126	−995	−1 124	−1 017	−1 041	−1 283	−1 578
Service payments	−423	−449	−458	−457	−454	−472	−490	−484	−538	−603
Transfers (net receipts +)	21	22	19	20	18	−7	−13	9	13	18
Balance on current account	−93	−11	−16	−142	168	37	215	317	166	−48
CAPITAL MOVEMENTS										
Private	27	36	−69	73	−55	−183	−100	−69	−95	−56
Government	24	−1	22	61	−6	3	−29	−19	15	15
Total capital movement (net inflow +)	51	35	−47	134	−61	−180	−129	−88	−80	−41
Balance of payment										
S.D.R. allocations and adjustments										
Total change in gold and foreign exchange	−42	24	−63	−8	107	−143	86	229	86	−89

TABLE 23 (cont'd)

Item	1965	1966	1967	1968	1969	1970	1971	1972	1973	1974	1975
CURRENT ACCOUNT											
Merchandise exports	1 067	1 216	1 323	1 513	1 484	1 413	1 556	2 218	2 550	3 218	3 618
Net gold output	775	769	775	769	847	837	922	1 161	1 769	2 565	2 540
Service receipts	319	350	433	486	501	534	640	730	918	1 085	1 306
Merchandise imports	−1 799	−1 645	−1 942	−1 885	−2 149	−2 578	−2 937	−2 852	−3 548	−5 723	−6 681
Service payments	−681	−723	−811	−880	−1 003	−1 055	−1 224	−1 330	−1 608	−2 091	−2 530
Transfers (net receipts +)	23	32	41	72	58	61	40	62	13	76	131
Balance on current account	−296	−1	−181	75	−262	−788	−1 003	−11	94	−870	−1 616
CAPITAL MOVEMENTS											
Private	170	160	241	389	203	403	568	351	79	632	1 316
Government	85	−19	−79	70	−6	98	196	64	−189	143	458
Total capital movement (net inflow +)	255	141	162	459	197	501	764	415	−110	775	1 774
Balance of payment	−41	140	−19	534	−65	−287	−239	404	−16	−95	158
S.D.R. allocations and adjustments	−3		−8		7	−24	83	33	−96	−28	33
Total change in gold and foreign exchange	−38	140	−27	534	−58	−263	−156	437	−112	−67	191

Source: S.A.R.B., *A Statistical Presentation of South Africa's Balance of Payments for the Period 1946 to 1970*, March 1971, pp. 9, 10.
S.A.R.B., *Quarterly Bulletin*, December 1975, p. s–57.
S.A.R.B., *Quarterly Bulletin*, March 1976, p. s–56, for 1975.

TABLE 24

Indices of Prices 1938 to 1975
(Base: 1953 = 100)

Year	Agricultural* Field crops and animal products	Wholesale† S.A. goods	Imported goods	All goods	Retail† Food	Clothing	Other items	All items
1938	—	43,6	32,6	38,3	43,3	34,7	—	52,0
1941	—	47,0	44,9	45,6	48,7	44,2	—	56,2
1942	—	53,3	49,7	51,2	53,7	48,2	—	61,0
1943	—	58,3	53,5	55,6	58,3	52,3	—	64,7
1944	—	60,7	55,0	57,6	60,9	55,5	—	66,9
1945	—	62,6	54,5	58,4	62,3	57,8	—	68,7
1946	—	65,7	53,9	59,8	63,8	59,4	—	69,7
1947	—	67,8	57,8	62,7	67,3	63,0	—	72,6
1948	66,8	69,9	64,8	67,0	69,5	78,6	83,1	76,8
1949	64,2	71,8	70,9	70,7	71,4	88,2	84,2	79,6
1950	79,4	74,8	78,3	75,7	75,5	89,8	87,0	82,8
1951	97,0	81,7	94,1	86,5	80,9	97,4	93,4	88,9
1952	87,2	96,1	104,0	99,2	94,9	101,2	96,5	96,6
1953	100,0	100,0	100,0	100,0	100,0	100,0	100,0	100,0
1954	95,0	100,8	100,6	100,8	100,8	100,7	103,2	101,8
1955	93,5	105,7	101,7	103,9	104,1	101,3	107,3	105,0
1956	94,0	108,0	102,0	105,4	106,1	101,6	109,9	107,0
1957	102,2	110,3	102,5	107,0	109,9	101,9	113,6	110,2
1958	90,7	111,0	102,0	107,2	114,1	102,2	118,4	114,0
1959	93,9	110,4	102,6	107,1	114,3	101,2	121,5	115,4
1960	96,2	112,3	103,4	108,5	116,2	101,1	123,3	117,0
1961	96,7	114,8	104,3	110,3	118,7	101,1	126,0	119,2
1962	94,9	115,0	106,0	111,1	118,0	100,7	129,7	121,0
1963	99,6	116,6	107,7	112,4	119,3	99,7	130,9	122,5
1964	106,0	120,1	110,4	115,1	124,8	100,2	134,3	125,5

* Department of Agriculture – producers' prices.
† Office of Census and Statistics/Bureau of Statistics.

(Base: 1963 = 100)

	Consumer Prices Services	Goods	Wholesale Prices
1963	100,0	100,0	100,0
1964	103,0	102,5	102,4
1965	108,0	106,1	105,6
1966	113,6	109,1	109,6
1967	118,7	112,2	112,2
1968	123,2	113,6	113,6
1969	129,8	115,9	116,2
1970	137,1	119,5	119,9

Source: S.A.R.B., *Quarterly Bulletin*, June 1971, pp. S–82, S–83.

(Base: 1970 = 100)

	Consumer Prices (All Items)	Wholesale Prices
1970	100,0	100,0
1971	105,7	105,2
1972	112,6	113,9
1973	123,3	125,2
1974	137,6	150,8
1975	156,2	182,6

Source: S.A.R.B. *Quarterly Bulletin*: March, 1976, pp. S–88, 89

TABLE 25

Government Revenue and Expenditure on Current Account* 1946–70

	Indirect taxes	Direct taxes	Other†	Total current revenue	Current expenditure	Current surplus
1946	139	145	7	291	268	23
1947	145	178	8	331	327	4
1948	152	160	4	316	269	47
1949	139	181	–2	318	285	33
1950	144	202	23	369	328	41
1951	175	234	31	440	352	88
1952	185	291	13	489	420	69
1953	211	336	18	565	457	108
1954	227	330	57	614	476	138
1955	247	330	70	647	501	146
1956	257	379	40	676	540	136
1957	278	396	44	718	557	161
1958	306	384	33	723	590	133
1959	343	408	45	796	623	173
1960	361	424	92	877	655	222
1961	352	447	80	879	702	177
1962	383	449	91	923	815	108
1963	428	659	117	1 204	898	306
1964	496	682	142	1 320	1 007	313
1965	518	780	123	1 421	1 125	296
1966	562	873	79	1 514	1 256	258
1967	644	1 017	168	1 829	1 355	474
1968	714	1 113	127	1 954	1 479	475
1969	916	1 229	84	2 229	1 692	537
1970	1 017	1 361	107	2 485	1 931	554

*This includes all current revenue and expenditure of the central government, the provinces, and local authorities, the administration of South West Africa, the S.A. Bantu Trust, and the Transkeian government; but excludes the business enterprises of any of these.
†'other' includes income from property and other minor items less interest on public debt.

Source: S.A.R.B., *A Statistical Presentation of South Africa's National Accounts for the Period 1946 to 1970*, p. 38.

Select
Reading List

CONTENTS

ABBREVIATIONS

B.E.R.	Bureau for Economic Research, University of Stellenbosch.
O.U.P.	Oxford University Press.
S.A.I.R.R.	South African Institute of Race Relations.
S.A.J.E.	*South African Journal of Economics.*
S.A.R.B.	South African Reserve Bank.
S.E.P.C.	Social and Economic Planning Council.
U.G. ⎫	Official 'blue books' of the South African government; number
R.P. ⎬	and date follow.
W.P. ⎭	White Paper.

A. GENERAL

DE KIEWIET, C. W.: *A History of South Africa: Social and Economic* (O.U.P., London, 1968).

DE KOCK, M. H.: *Selected Subjects in the Economic History of South Africa* (Juta, Cape Town, 1924).

FRANKEL, S. H.: 'The Tyranny of Economic Paternalism in Africa . . .', supplement to *Optima*, vol. 10, December 1960.

FRANZSEN, D. G. and REYNDERS, H. J. J. (ed.): *Die Ekonomiese Lewe van Suid-Afrika* (Van Schaik, Pretoria, 1960).

GOODFELLOW, D. M.: *A Modern Economic History of South Africa* (Routledge & Kegan Paul, London, 1931).

HAILEY, LORD: *An African Survey – a Study of Problems Arising in Africa South of the Sahara*, revised ed. (O.U.P., London, 1968).

HORWITZ, RALPH: *The Political Economy of South Africa* (Weidenfeld & Nicholson, London, 1967).

HOUGHTON, D. HOBART and DAGUT, JENIFER (ed.): *Source Material on the South African Economy 1860–1970*, 3 vols. (O.U.P., Cape Town, 1972 and 1973).

KNOWLES, L. C. A.: *The Economic Development of the British Overseas Empire*, vol. 3: *South Africa* (Routledge & Kegan Paul, London, 1936).

ROBERTSON, H. M.: *South Africa – Economic and Political Aspects* (Duke University Press, Durham N.C., 1957).

VAN DER HORST, SHEILA T.: 'The Economic Implications of Political Democracy: The Road to Economic Progress', supplement to *Optima*, vol. 10, June 1960.

WILSON, MONICA and THOMPSON, LEONARD (ed.): *The Oxford History of South Africa*, 2 vols. (Clarendon Press, Oxford, 1969 and 1971).

B. THE DEVELOPMENT OF THE SOUTH AFRICAN ECONOMY

B.E.R.: *A Survey of Contemporary Economic Conditions and Prospects . . .* (annual since 1959).

DU PLESSIS, J. C.: *Economic Fluctuations in South Africa 1910–1949* (B.E.R., Stellenbosch, 1950).

ENKE, STEPHEN: 'South African Growth: A Macro-Economic Analysis', *S.A.J.E.*, vol. 30 no. 1, March 1962.

FRANKEL, S. H.: *Capital Investment in Africa: Its Course and Effects* (O.U.P., London, 1938).

FRANKEL, S. H.: 'Whither South Africa? An Economic Approach', *S.A.J.E.*, vol. 15 no. 1, March 1947.

FRANKEL, S. H. and Herzfeld, H.: 'An Analysis of the Growth of the National Income of the Union in the Period of Prosperity before the War', *S.A.J.E.*, vol. 12 no. 2, June 1944.

FRANZSEN, D. G.: *Economic Growth and Stability in a Developing Economy* (Van Schaik, Pretoria, 1960).

GRAAFF, J. de V.: 'Alternative Models of South African Growth', *S.A.J.E.*, vol. 30 no. 1, March 1962.

HOUGHTON, D. HOBART: 'Economic Development 1865–1965', being chapter 1 of the *Oxford History of South Africa*, vol. 2 (Clarendon Press, Oxford, 1971).

KROGH, D. C.: 'An Input-Output Analysis of the South African Economy 1956-7', *S.A.J.E.*, vol. 29 no. 4, December 1961.

LOMBARD, J. A., STADLER, J. J., VAN DER MERWE, P. J.: *The Concept of Economic Co-operation in Southern Africa:* Econburo, Pretoria, 1968.

PALMER, G. F. D.: 'The South African Economy: Policies and Prospects', *Optima*, vol. 11, December 1961.

RICHARDS, C. S.: 'Problems of Economic Development in the Republic of South Africa', *S.A.J.E.*, vol. 30 no. 1 March 1962.

RICHARDS, C. S.: 'Some Thoughts on the Union's Economic Outlook', *S.A.J.E.*, vol. 17 no. 2, June 1949.

RICHARDS, C. S. and PIERCY, MARY V.: 'Economic Budgeting in South Africa: A Comment', *S.A.J.E.*, vol. 30 no. 4, December 1962.

RIEKERT, P. J.: 'Economic Budgeting in South Africa: A Reply', *S.A.J.E.*, vol 31 no. 1, March 1963.

SADIE, J. L.: 'An Evaluation of Demographic Data Pertaining to the Non-White Population of South Africa': Parts I (Asian) and II (Coloured), *S.A.J.E.*, vol. 38 no. 1, March 1970; Part III (Bantu), *S.A.J.E.*, vol. 38 no. 2, June 1970.

SADIE, J. L.: 'Population and Economic Development in South Africa', *S.A.J.E.*, vol. 39 no. 3, September 1971.

SCHUMANN, C. G. W.: *Structural Changes and Business Cycles in South Africa, 1806–1936* (Staples Press, London, 1938).

SCHUMANN, C. G. W. (festschrift) – see University of Stellenbosch: *Ekonomiese Opstelle . . .*

S.A.R.B.: *Annual Economic Report.*

S.A.R.B.: *Quarterly Bulletin.* Contains reviews of the state of the national economy.

UNIVERSITY OF STELLENBOSCH: *Ekonomiese Opstelle Opgedra aan Professor C. G. W. Schumann . . .* (Van Schaik, Pretoria, 1960).

Official

Economic and Wage Commission, Report of the (Clay), U.G. 14/1926.

Economic Commission, Report of the (Chapman), U.G. 12/1914.

Fundamentals of Economic Policy in the Union, being the Third Interim Report of the Industrial and Agricultural Requirements Commission (Van Eck), U.G. 40/1941.

Protection of Industries, Report of the Commission of Enquiry into Policy Relating to the (Viljoen), U.G. 36/1958.

Planning, Department of: *Economic Development Programme for the Republic of South Africa, 1964–9* (and subsequent years).

Statistics

BUREAU OF MARKET RESERCH, UNIVERSITY OF SOUTH AFRICA: *A Guide to Statistical Sources in the Republic of South Africa* (Pretoria, 1972).

S.A.R.B.: *Quarterly Bulletin.*

S.A.R.B.: *A Statistical Presentation of Selected Economic Indicators of South Africa for the Period 1946* to *1970* (1971).

S.A.R.B.: *A Statistical Presentation of South Africa's Balance of Payments for the Period 1946 to 1970* (1971).

S.A.R.B.: *A Statistical Presentation of South Africa's National Accounts for the Period 1946 to 1970* (1971).

S.A.R.B.: *A Statistical Presentation of South Africa's quarterly national accounts for the period 1960 to 1974* (1976).

STATISTICS, BUREAU of: *Union Statistics for Fifty Years – Jubilee Issue 1910–1960* (1960).

STATISTICS, DEPARTMENT [formerly Bureau] OF: *Bulletin of Statistics* (monthly until 1967, thereafter quarterly).

STATISTICS, DEPARTMENT [formerly Bureau] OF: *South African Statistics,* called *Statistical Year Book* until 1968 (every second year).

C. FARMING (EXCLUDING AFRICAN PEASANTS)

KELLY, THOMAS H. *et al.*: 'Economists Protest: The Dairy Produce and Maize Marketing Schemes: Memorandum of Objections', *S.A.J.E.*, vol. 6 no. 1, March 1938.

KELLY, THOMAS H. *et al.*: 'Economists Protest: Marketing Act, 1937, Scheme Relating to Marketing of Wheat: Memorandum of Objections', *S.A.J.E.*, vol. 6 no. June 1938.

KELLY, THOMAS H. *et al.*: 'Economists Protest: The Operation of the Wheat Marketing Scheme, 1938–9: Memorandum of Objections', *S.A.J.E.*, vol. 8 no. 1, March 1940.

McLoughlin, J. R.: 'A Defence of Control in the Marketing of Agricultural Products', *S.A.J.E.*, vol. 6 no. 3, September 1938.

Richards, C. S.: 'The 'New Despotism' in Agriculture: Some Reflections on the Marketing Bill', *S.A.J.E.*, vol. 4 no. 4, December 1936.

Richards, C. S.: 'Subsidies, Quotas, Tariffs and the Excess Cost of Agriculture in South Africa', *S.A.J.E.*, vol. 3 no. 3, September 1935.

Robertson, H. M.: 'The Cabinet Committee and the Control Boards', *S.A.J.E.*, vol. 6 no. 1, March 1938.

Tinley, J. M.: 'Control of Agriculture in South Africa', *S.A.J.E.*, vol. 8 no. 3, September 1940.

Van der Horst, J. G.: 'Two Conferences', *S.A.J.E.*, vol. 1 no. 1, March 1933.

Van Waasdijk, T.: 'Agricultural Prices and Price Policy', *S.A.J.E.*, vol. 22 no. 1, March 1954.

Viljoen, P. R.: 'Planned Agriculture in South Africa', *S.A.J.E.*, vol. 6 no. 3, September 1938.

Wilson, Francis: 'Farming 1866–1966', being chapter 3 of the *Oxford History of South Africa*, vol. 2, edited by Monica Wilson and Leonard Thompson (Clarendon Press, Oxford, 1971).

Official

Agriculture, Report of the Commission of Enquiry into (M. D. Marais). *Interim Report*, R.P. 61/1968; *Second Report*, R.P. 84/1970. *Third Report* R.P. 19/1972.

Co-operation and Agricultural Credit Commission, Report of the, U.G. 16/1934. *System of Distribution Prevailing in the Union with Particular Reference to Essential Foodstuffs and the Principles of State Controlled Marketing, The*, being the Second Report of the Distribution Costs Commission, U.G. 28/1947.

Water Matters, Report of the Commission of Enquiry into, R.P. 34/1970.

Agriculture, Department of: Reports of the Division of Agricultural Marketing Research. These include many valuable studies of particular aspects of farming and marketing.

Agriculture, Department of: *Agro-Economic Survey of the Union* (1948).

Agriculture, Department of: *Annual Reports of . . .*

Agriculture, Department of: *(Annual) Progress and Programme Reports of the Union (Republic) of South Africa to the Food and Agriculture Organization of the United Nations* (annual since 1948).

Agriculture, Department of: *White Paper on Agricultural Policy*, W.P. 10/1946.

Agriculture, Department of, Reconstruction Committee: *The Reconstruction of Agriculture, 1944–5*.

National Marketing Council: *Annual Reports*.

National Marketing Council: *Marketing Boards 1938–1946, Report on the*, U.G. 27/1947.

S.E.P.C.: Report no. 4, *The Future of Farming in South Africa*, U.G. 10/1945.

Statistics

Agriculture, Department of: *Abstract of Agricultural Statistics* (irregular until 1968, annual thereafter).

Agriculture, Department of: *Crops and Markets* (monthly).

Statistics, Department (formerly Bureau) of: *Agricultural Census*.

D. AFRICAN AREAS AND THE ROLE OF THE AFRICAN IN THE NATIONAL ECONOMY

Benbo: *Transkei Revue:* Pretoria, 1975.

Benbo: *Ciskei Revue:* Pretoria, 1975.

Benbo: *Black Development* (The economic development of the Black nations of the R.S.A.), Pretoria, 1975.

BROOKES, E. H.: *The History of Native Policy in South Africa from 1830 to the Present Day* (Nasionale Pers, Cape Town, 1924).
BROOKES, E. H. and Hurwitz, N.: *The Native Reserves of Natal*, being vol. 7 of *Natal Regional Survey* (O.U.P., Cape Town, 1957).
EISELEN, W. W. M.: 'Harmonious Multi-Community Development', *Optima*, vol. 9, March 1959.
FAIR, T. J. D. and GREEN, L. P.: 'Development of the "Bantu Homelands",' *Optima*, vol. 12, March 1962.
HORRELL, MURIEL: *A Survey of Race Relations in South Africa* (S.A.I.R.R., Johannesburg, annual).
HOUGHTON, D. HOBART: 'Economic Dangers of Separate Bantu Development', *Optima*, vol. 9, December 1959.
HOUGHTON, D. HOBART and WALTON, EDITH M.: *The Economy of a Native Reserve*, being vol. 2 of *Keiskammahoek Rural Survey* (Shuter & Shooter, Pietermaritzburg, 1952).
PATTEN, J. W.: 'Separate Development: A Look at the Facts', *Optima*, vol. 13, March 1963.
ROBERTSON, H. M.: '150 Years of Economic Contact between Black and White', *S.A.J.E.*, vol. 2 no. 4, December 1934 and vol. 3 no. 1, March 1965.
VAN DER HORST, SHEILA T.: 'A Plan for the Union's Backward Areas: Some Economic Aspects of the Tomlinson Commission's Report', *S.A.J.E.*, vol. 24 no. 2, June 1956.
VAN HEERDEN, W.: 'The Road to Separate Racial Development in South Africa', *Optima*, vol. 10, December 1960.
VAN HEERDEN, W.: 'Why Bantu States?', *Optima*, vol. 12, June 1962.
WILSON, FRANCIS: *Migrant Labour in South Africa* (Spro-Cas, Johannesburg, 1973).

Official

Government Decisions on the Recommendations of the Commission for the Socio-Economic Development of the Bantu Areas within the Union of South Africa (White Paper), W.P. F/1956.
Native Economic Commission, 1930–2, Report of the, U.G. 22/1932.
Native Laws Commission, 1946–8, Report of the (Fagan), U.G. 28/1948.
Socio-Economic Development of the Bantu Areas within the Union of South Africa, Summary of the Report of the Commission for the (Tomlinson). This full report of 18 volumes is available only in certain libraries. The official *Summary of the Report* . . . has been published as U.G. 61/1955.
BANTU ADMINISTRATION AND DEVELOPMENT (formerly Native Affairs), DEPARTMENT OF: *Annual Report*.
S.E.P.C.: Report no 9, *The Native Reserves and Their Place in the Economy of the Union of South Africa*, U.G. 32/1946.

E. MINING

BLACK, R. A. L.: 'Development of South African Mining Methods', *Optima*, vol. 10, June 1960.
CARTWRIGHT, A. P.: *The Gold Miners* (Purnell, Cape Town, 1962).
DE KOCK, W. P.: 'Die Rol van die Minerale Hulpbronne in die Ekonomiese Ontwikkeling van Suid-Afrika', *Tydskrif vir Wetenskap en Kuns*, October 1953.
EWING, J. M. M.: 'Analysis of Mine Operating and Capital Expenditure', *S.A.J.E.*, vol. 31 no. 1 March 1963.
FARNIE, D. A.: 'The Mineral Revolution in South Africa', *S.A.J.E.*, vol. 24 no. 2, June 1956.
GREGORY, SIR THEODORE: *Ernest Oppenheimer and the Economic Development of Southern Africa* (O.U.P., Cape Town, 1962).
HALL, P. E.: 'The Coal Industry in the Union of South Africa', *S.A.J.E.*, vol. 16 no. 3, September 1948.

JEPPE, C. B.: *Gold Mining on the Witwatersrand*, 2 vols. (Transvaal Chamber of Mines, Johannesburg, 1946).
LEEPER, SIR R.: 'The Development of the Diamond Industry', *Optima*, vol. 7, September 1957.
MARTIN, J.: "Group Administration of the Gold Mining Industry of the Witwatersrand", *Economic Journal*, vol. 39, December 1929 (London).
OPPENHEIMER, H.: 'The Orange Free State Gold Fields', *S.A.J.E.*, vol. 18 no. 2 June 1950.

Official

Deep Level Mining, Report of the Committee on, U.G. 18/1945.
Low Grade Ore Commission, Report of the, U.G. 16/1932.
Low Grade Mines Commission, Report of the, U.G. 34/1920.
State Mining Commission, Report of the, U.G. 19/1917.
MINES, DEPARTMENT OF: *Annual Report, Including Report of the Government Mining Engineer and Geological Survey.*
S.E.P.C.: Report no. 11, *Economic Aspects of the Gold Mining Industry*, U.G. 32/1948.

Statistics

Minerals (quarterly).
MINES, DEPARTMENT OF: *Annual Report, Including Reports of the Government Mining Engineer and the Geological Survey.*
TRANSVAAL AND ORANGE FREE STATE CHAMBER OF MINES: *Annual Report.*
TRANSVAAL AND ORANGE FREE STATE CHAMBER OF MINES: *Mining Survey* (quarterly).

F. MANUFACTURING

BAK, C.: 'The Structure of the Cotton Textile Industry in South Africa', *S.A.J.E.*, vol. 26 no. 2, June 1958.
BARKER, H. A. F.: 'The Clothing Industry in South Africa', *S.A.J.E.*, vol. 29 no. 4, December 1961.
BELL, TREVOR: *Industrial Decentrali ation in South Africa* (O.U.P., Cape Town, 1973).
INDUSTRIAL DEVELOPMENT CORPORATION OF SOUTH AFRICA: *Annual Report.*
MEYER, F.: 'The Development of the Iron and Steel Industry in South Africa', *S A J.E.*, vol. 20 no. 2, June 1952.
PALMER, G. F. D.: 'Some Aspects of the Development of Secondary Industry in South Africa since the Depression of 1929–32', *S.A.J.E.*, vol. 22 no. 1, March 1954.
VAN DER HORST, SHEILA T.: 'The Effects of Industrialization on Race Relations in South Africa', in Guy Hunter (ed.) *Industrialization and Race Relations: A Symposium* (O.U.P., London, 1965).
VAN ECK, H. J.: *Some Aspects of the South African Industrial Revolution* (S.A.I.R.R., Johannesburg, 1951).

Official

Railway Rating Policy and Industrial Location in South Africa, Report of the Committee on (Schumann) (1964).
EOARD OF TRADE AND INDUSTRIES: *Annual Report.*
EOARD OF TRADE AND INDUSTRIES: INDUSTRIAL DEVELOPMENT SERIES: 1. *The Industrial Potential of the Textile Industry in the Union of South Africa* (1961); 2. *The Industrial Potential of the Chemical and Allied Industries of the Republic of South Africa* (1963); 3. *Textile and Clothing Industries* (1964); 4. *Timber and Allied Industries* (1967); 5. *Supplementary Survey of Chemical and Allied Industries* (1968); 6. *Iron, Steel, Metallurgical and Engineering Industries*, 5 vols. (1968/69).

The Board of Trade and Industries also issues a series of general reports, of which over 1 300 had been published by 1971. The following are some of the more important:

No.   282, *Investigation into Manufacturing Industries* (21/5/45).
No.   286, *Investigation into Iron, Steel, Engineering and Metallurgical industries* (15/2/46).
No.   294, *The Tanning and Footwear Industry* (21/1/47).
No.   295, *Investigation into the Cement Industry* (3/2/47).
No.   296, *The Fruit and Vegetable Canning Industry* (2/4 47).
No.   298, *The South African Sugar Industry* (28/2/47).
No.   303, *The Clothing Industry* (2/3/48).
No.   311, *The Iron, Steel, Engineering and Metallurgical Industries in the Union* (in 5 parts) (30/6/48).
No.   313, *The Motor Industry* (21/1/49).
No.   323, *The Textile Manufacturing Industry* (29/12/50 .
No.   332, *The ElectricalGoods Manufacturing Industry* (18/6/52).
No.   613, *Investigation into the Motor Industry of South Africa* (13/5/60).
No.   676, *Investigation into the Fruit and Vegetable Canning Industry* (20/1/61)
No.   745, *Investigation into the Refining of Sugar* (15/12/60).
No. 1 220, *Investigation into Resale Price Maintenance* (December 1967).
No. 1 347, *The Basic Chemicals Industry* (January 1971).
INDUSTRIES, DEPARTMENT OF: *Decentralisation of Industries, White Paper on the Report by the Inter-Departmental Committee on the* (Riekert).

Statistics

STATISTICS, DEPARTMENT (formerly Bureau) OF: *Census of Industrial Establishments* (annual).

G. LABOUR, WAGES AND STANDARDS OF LIVING

BERG, ELLIOT, J.: 'Backward-Sloping Labour Supply Functions in Dual Economies – the Africa Case', *Quarterly Journal of Economics*, vol. 75 no. 3, August, 1961.
BUREAU OF MARKET RESEARCH, UNIVERSITY OF SOUTH AFRICA: *Income and Expenditure Patterns of Urban Bantu*, several reports since 1961.
CLARK, G.: 'Industrial Peace in South Africa,' *British Journal of Industrial Relations*, vol. 1.
DE GRUCHY, JOY: *The Cost of Living for Urban Africans in Johannesburg 1959* (S.A.I.R.R., Johannesburg, 1960).
DOXEY, G. V.: *The Industrial Colour Bar in South Africa* (O.U.P. Cape Town, 1961).
HORRELL, MURIEL: *South African Trade Unionism: A Study of a Divided Working Class* (S.A.I.R.R., Johannesburg, 1961).
HORRELL, MURIEL: *South Africa's Non-White Workers* (S.A.I.R.R., Johannesburg, 1956).
HORWOOD, O. P. F.: 'Is Minimum Wage Legislation the Answer for South Africa?', *S.A.J.E.*, vol. 30 no. 2, June 1962.
KATZEN, L. B.: 'The Case for Minimum Wage Legislation in South Africa', with a comment by Steenkamp, W.F.J., *S.A.J.E.*, vol. 29 no. 3, September 1961.
MARQUARD, D.: *Farm Labour in the Orange Free State* (S.A.I.R.R., Johannesburg, 1939).
NATAL UNIVERSITY, DEPARTMENT OF ECONOMICS: *The African Factory Worker* (O.U.P., Cape Town, 1950).
NEL, P. A., LOUBSER, M., STEENKAMP, J. J. A.: *The Minimum Subsistence Level and the Minimum Humane Standard of Living of Non-Whites living in the Main Urban Areas of the Republic of South Africa*: Bureau of Market Research, University of South Africa, Pretoria, 1973.
PIERCY, MARY V.: 'Statutory Work Reservation – Requirement of a Static or of an Expanding Economy?' *S.A.J.E.*, vol. 28 no. 2, June 1960; [continued

in] 'Statutory Work Reservation in the Union of South Africa', *S.A.J.E.*, vol. 28 no. 3, September 1960.

PURSELL, D. E.: 'Bantu Real Wages and Employment Opportunities in South Africa', *S.A.J.E.*, vol. 36 no. 2, June 1968.

ROBERTS, MARGARET: *Labour in the Farm Economy*, 2nd ed. (S.A.I.R.R., Johannesburg, 1959).

ROUTH, GUY: 'Industrial Relations in South Africa', *S.A.J.E.*, vol. 20 no. 1, March 1952.

ROUX, EDWARD RUDOLF: *Time Longer than Rope: A History of the Black Man's Struggle for Freedom in South Africa* (Gollancz, London, 1948).

SACHS, E. S.: *Rebel's Daughters* (Macgibbon & Kee, London, 1957).

SADIE, J. L.: 'The White Labour Force of South Africa', *S.A.J.E.*, vol. 28 no. 2, June 1960.

SPANDAU, A. M. K. M.: 'Income Distribution and Economic Growth in South Africa 1971', 2 vols. (unpublished thesis, University of South Africa, Pretoria).

STEENKAMP, W. F. J.: 'Bantu Wages in South Africa', *S.A.J.E.*, vol. 30 no. 2, June 1962.

STEENKAMP, W. F. J.: 'Labour Policies for Growth during the Seventies in the Established Industrial Areas', *S.A.J.E.*, vol. 39 no. 2, June 1971.

VAN DER HORST, SHEILA T.: *Native Labour in South Africa* (O.U.P., London, 1942).

VAN DER HORST, SHEILA T.: 'A Note on Native Labour Turnover and the Structure of the Labour Force in the Cape Peninsula', *S.A.J.E.*, vol. 25 no. 4, December 1957.

VAN DER HORST, SHEILA T.: 'Some Effects of Industrial Legislation on the Market for Native labour in South Africa', *S.A.J.E.*, vol. 3 no. 4, December 1935.

VILJOEN, S. P.: 'Higher Productivity and Higher Wages of Native Labour in South Africa', with a comment by Steenkamp, W. F. J., *S.A.J.E.*, vol. 29 no. 1, March 1961.

WALKER, I. L. and WEINBREN, B.: *2 000 Casualties: A History of the Trade Unions and the Labour Movement in the Union of South Africa* (S.A. Trade Union Council, Johannesburg, 1960).

WILSON, FRANCIS: *Labour in the South African Gold Mines 1911–1969* (Cambridge University Press, Cambridge, 1972).

WILSON, FRANCIS: *Migrant Labour in South Africa* (Sprocas, Johannesburg, 1973).

Official

Industrial Legislation Commission, 1934, Report of the (Van Reenen), U.G. 37/1935.

Industrial Legislation Commission, Report of the, U.G. 62/1951.

Native Farm Labour Committee 1937–9, Report of the (1939).

Witwatersrand Mine Native's Wages Commission, Report of the (Lansdowne), U.G. 21/1944.

LABOUR, DEPARTMENT OF: *Annual Report*.

S.E.P.C.: Report no. 13, *The Economic and Social Conditions of the Racial Groups in South Africa*, U.G. 53/1948.

STATISTICS, DEPARTMENT OF: periodic reports on labour statistics.

H. FOREIGN TRADE

KELLY, T. H.: 'South Africa's Foreign Trade 1933–53', *S.A.J.E.*, vol. 22 no. 1, March 1954.

KELLY, T. H.: 'The Transition to Customs Union in Southern Africa', *S.A.J.E.*, vol. 22 no. 3, September 1954.

VAN WAASDIJK, T.: 'Changes in South Africa's Terms of Trade, 1950–8', *S.A.J.E.*, vol. 27 no. 2, June 1959.

VAN WAASDIJK, T.: *The Technique and Policy of Import Control in the Union of South Africa, 1948–52* (University of the Witwatersrand, Department of Commerce, Johannesburg, 1952).

WOODS, I. R.: 'Some Aspects of South Africa's Foreign Trade in Relation to Her Aggregate Income 1910–54', *S.A.J.E.*, vol. 26 no. 2, June 1958.

Official

Customs Tariff Commission, 1934–5, Report of the, U.G. 5/1936.
Export Trade of the Republic of South Africa, Report of the Commission of Inquiry into (Reynders) R.P. 69/72.
Protection of Industries, Report of the Commission of Enquiry into Policy Relating to the (Viljoen), U.G. 36/1958.

Statistics

Customs and Excise, Department of: *Foreign Trade Statistics* (annual).
S.A.R.B.: *A Statistical Presentation of South Africa's Balance of Payments for the Period 1946 to 1970* (March 1971).

I. MONEY AND BANKING

ARNDT, E. H. D.: *Banking and Currency Development in South Africa (1652–1927* (Juta, Cape Town, 1928).
DE JONGH, T. W.: *An Analysis of Banking Statistics in the Union of South Africa 1910–45)* (Van Schaik, Pretoria, 1947).
DE KOCK, G.: *A History of the South African Reserve Bank (1920–52)* (Van Schaik, Pretoria, 1954).
DE KOCK, H. M.: *Central Banking*, 3rd ed. (Staples Press, London, 1954).
KANTOR, BRIAN: 'The Evolution of Monetary Policy in South Africa', *S.A.J.E.*, vol. 39 no. 1, March 1971.
PALMER, G. F. D.: 'The Development of a South African Money Market', *S.A.J.E.*, vol. 26 no. 4, December 1958.
PALMER, G. F. D. and DICKMAN, A. B.: 'The South African Money Market – Some Further Developments', *S.A.J.E.*, vol. 28 no. 4, December 1960.
RICHARDS, C. S.: 'Central Banking in South Africa: A Study in Adaptation', *S.A.J.E.*, vol. 23 no. 4, December 1955.
RISSIK, GERARD: 'Review of Monetary and Banking Changes in the Union since 1932', *S.A.J.E.*, vol. 22 no. 1, March 1954.

Bank Reviews

BARCLAYS NATIONAL BANK: *Barclays Trade Review* (monthly).
NETHERLANDS BANK OF SOUTH AFRICA: *Economic Bulletin* (monthly).
S.A.R.B.: *Quarterly Bulletin*.
STANDARD BANK: *Review* (monthly).
UNION ACCEPTANCES LIMITED, *UAL Economic and Financial Review* (monthly).
VOLKSKAS: *Finance and Trade Review* (quarterly).

Official

Fiscal and Monetary Policy in South Africa, Reports of the Commission of Enquiry into (Franzsen). First Report, *Taxation*, R.P. 24/1969; Second Report, *Taxation*, R.P. 86/1970; Third Report, *Fiscal and Monetary Policy in South Africa*, R.P. 87/1970.
REGISTRAR OF BANKS: *Annual Report*.
S.E.P.C.: Report no. 12, *Central and Commercial Banking in South Africa*, U.G. 42/1948.

J. TRANSPORT

HORWITZ, R.: 'The Restriction of Competition between Road Motor Transport and Railways in the Union of South Africa', *S.A.J.E.*, vol. 5 no. 2, June 1937.

LAIGHT, J. C.: 'Railway Expansion during the Post-War Period', *S.A.J.E.*, vol. 25 no. 2, June 1957.

LAIGHT, J. C.: 'Railway Finances during the Post-War Period', *S.A.J.E.*, vol. 25 no. 3, September 1957.

SMITH, H. H.: 'The Control of Motor Transport in South Africa' and 'Principles and Practice of Railway Rating in South Africa', being appendices E and F in Houghton, D. Hobart (ed.), *Economic Development in a Plural Society* (O.U.P., Cape Town, 1960).

THRELFELL, R. L.: 'Notes and Memoranda on Railway Rating Policy', *S.A.J.E.*, vol. 14 no. 4, December 1946.

VERBURGH, C.: *Road Transport of Goods in South Africa* (B.E.R., Stellenbosch, 1958).

Official

Co-ordination of Transport in South Africa, Report of the Commission of Inquiry into the (Marais), R.P. 32/1969.

Railway Rating Policy and Industrial Location in South Africa, Report of the Committee on (Schumann) (1964).

Railway Rating Policy in South Africa, Report of the Committee Appointed to Enquire into (Newton), U.G. 32/1950.

Road Motor Transportation, Report of the Commission of Inquiry into (Page), U.G. 46/1947.

BOARD OF TRADE AND INDUSTRIES: Report no. 285, *Analysis of Railway Rating Principles and the Effect of Transport Costs on Industrial Development in the Union* (1946).

NATIONAL TRANSPORT COMMISSION: *Annual Report*.

SOUTH AFRICAN RAILWAYS AND HARBOURS: *Annual Report of the General Manager*.

Index